West Po.
the United States Air Force

West Point Graduates and the United States Air Force

Shaping American Aerospace Power

Charles F.G. Kuyk, Jr.,
with Charles F.G. Kuyk III

Foreword by RICHARD P. HALLION

McFarland & Company, Inc., Publishers
Jefferson, North Carolina

Library of Congress Cataloguing-in-Publication Data

Names: Kuyk, Charles F.G., Jr., 1926– author. | Kuyk, Charles F.G., III, 1951– author. | Hallion, Richard, 1948– writer of foreword.
Title: West Point graduates and the United States Air Force : shaping American aerospace power / Charles F.G. Kuyk, Jr., with Charles F.G. Kuyk III ; foreword by Richard P. Hallion.
Other titles: Shaping American aerospace power
Description: Jefferson, North Carolina : McFarland & Company, Inc., Publishers, 2020 | Includes bibliographical references and index.
Identifiers: LCCN 2020020593 | ISBN 9781476680941 (paperback) | ISBN 9781476639383 (ebook)
Subjects: LCSH: United States. Air Force—History. | Aeronautics, Military—United States—History. | United States Military Academy—Biography. | Astronautics—United States—History.
Classification: LCC UG633 .K89 2020 | DDC 358.40092/273—dc23
LC record available at https://lccn.loc.gov/2020020593

British Library cataloguing data are available

ISBN 978-1-4766-8094-1 (softcover : acid free paper) ∞
ISBN 978-1-4766-3938-3 (ebook)

Front cover: Cadets marching in the 1992 homecoming parade at the United States Military Academy in West Point, New York (Joseph Sohm/Shutterstock); (top) the Air Demonstration Squadron Thunderbirds in delta formation (Technical Sergeant Manuel J. Martinez/United States Air Force)

Printed in the United States of America

McFarland & Company, Inc., Publishers
  Box 611, Jefferson, North Carolina 28640
  www.mcfarlandpub.com

To the 1950 class of the U.S. Military Academy at West Point and the wives and families who supported them.

Contents

Acknowledgments

We first wish to acknowledge and thank the many graduates of the U.S. Military Academy at West Point who served their country bravely, sometimes at the cost of their lives, and without whom this book would not have been possible. Those graduates who chose to enter the new and sometimes dangerous realm of flight in the Army Air Forces or later in the U.S. Air Force provided the inspiration for this account of their contributions.

We benefited greatly from the thoughtful reviews and comments on early drafts of the manuscript from several individuals to whom we are greatly indebted.

In particular, Richard P. Hallion, former USAF historian, one of the founding curators of the Air and Space Museum, prolific author and all-round authority on the history of the Air Force provided many insightful suggestions as well as ongoing encouragement to tell this important story.

Similarly, Phil Meilinger, Air Force Academy graduate, retired Air Force colonel and C-130 pilot, author and former dean of the School of Advanced Airpower Studies (SAAS) at the Air Force's Air University provided extremely knowledgeable feedback both as an historian and biographer that was of tremendous value.

Ron Fogleman, Air Force Academy graduate and retired Air Force chief of staff, contributed his unique perspectives on a variety of Air Force topics, particularly concerning military airlift. We also are very grateful for feedback or materials received from West Point classmates from the Class of 1950, each of whom brought their unique experiences to our story: Frank Borman, Skip Scott, Bill DeGraf, Phil Bardos, Dick Newton, Carol Guthrie, wife of graduate Joe Guthrie and an accomplished author, and Joe Buccolo, who made available the Class of 1950 *Memories* notebooks.

We also are grateful for input received from Clarence Elebash (USMA 1948) and West Point historian Sherman Fleek.

Lastly and most importantly, we wish to extend our thanks to our family support team of Merri Ellen Kuyk and Connie McCauley for their patience and understanding during the writing of this story, to Kathy Oswald for her timely computer assistance and to the loving memory of Joyce Kuyk, the best possible example of an Air Force wife and mother.

Charlie Jr. and Joyce Kuyk at West Point graduation, 1950.

Foreword

by Richard P. Hallion

In 1918, faced with air attacks on British cities and ports by German bombers and airships, the British government directed the formation of the Royal Air Force (RAF), the world's first independent air force. On April 1, 1918, airmen of the Royal Naval Air Service and the Royal Flying Corps—both appendages of the Royal Navy and British Army, respectively—awoke to find themselves members of a new service of a type unknown in the previous history of the world's militaries.

The wisdom of that decision became evident over southeastern England in the late summer and fall of 1940 when the Royal Air Force battled the Luftwaffe in a remorseless struggle upon which the fate of their nation rested—and won. Arguably, had Britain not established an independent RAF and maintained its Royal Flying Corps and Royal Naval Air Service, it would have lost. The British Army—like the French—showed little appreciation for any air mission other than artillery observation and reconnaissance, and the Royal Navy seemed at times puzzled why it even had airmen in its midst. Instead of Spitfires and Hurricanes meeting the Messerschmitts, Dorniers, Heinkels, and Junkers of Goering's air force, the RAF would have had, at best, aging biplanes and ineffectual general purpose airplanes. The victory of the Royal Air Force was thus not merely a victory for air power, it was a victory for the notion of an independent air force and the centrality of air power well-employed.

The United States, having invented the airplane in 1903, let its lead erode so that, in the First World War, its airmen were, in the words of General John "Black Jack" Pershing, "entirely dependent upon the Allies" for their aircraft and equipment. Air-minded officers, like then–Colonel William "Billy" Mitchell, struggled to convince superiors of the significance of what was happening in the sky over the Western Front. In the early postwar years, various individuals repeatedly sought an independent status for American airmen. Unfortunately, such calls became caught up in the interservice politics of the time, and so nothing happened.

The tremendous advances in aviation during the interwar years, and the dramatic example of what air attack could do in the hands of ruthless aggressors, became all to evident in the skies over Ethiopia, Spain, China, and, after September 1939, over Western Europe itself. In May 1941 came restructuring of the U.S. Army into the Army Air Forces (under Hap Arnold) and Army Ground Forces (under Leslie McNair). With the Japanese assault on Pearl Harbor, America's Army and Naval airmen were plunged into the full fury of a global war.

The accomplishments, sacrifices, and heroism displayed by American airmen from 1941 through 1945 ennobled the quest for an independent Air Force. At Normandy, in 1944, Dwight Eisenhower—who was a pilot himself, though of light aircraft—recognized not only the centrality of air power to the success of the land invasion, but also that without air supremacy—not simply air superiority—he would have been unable to put his forces ashore with any assurance of success. Not surprisingly, in Congressional testimony after the war, Dwight Eisenhower became the strongest champion of an independent United States Air Force, established in September 1947.

The subsequent history of the United States Air Force—from the days of the Berlin Airlift to the War on Terror in the present day—has confirmed, as with the Battle of Britain and creation of the RAF, the wisdom of its formation.

But where did its leaders come from? Today there is an Air Force Academy, perched high in the mountains of Colorado, with its own tradition of excellence, courage, and sacrifice. But it did not exist in 1947, and indeed did not for many years. To professionally guide, shape, and man the Air Force of the Cold War, the service depended largely on graduates of the two existing service academies: West Point and Annapolis. It was their graduates who had led the nation's airmen to victory in the great air battles of the past, from the skies of the Western Front in the "Great War" to the naval war in the Pacific, the combined bomber offensive in the Second World War, the breakout across France, the strategic air offensive against Imperial Japan, and all that went with those and myriad other actions. Consequently, well into the late 1980s, the general officers commanding the Air Force came from West Point or Annapolis.

As well, a separate independent Air Force could best employ, shape, and exploit the new technologies of aeronautics—flight within the atmosphere—and astronautics—flight into space. As readers will discover, technology is a key theme throughout this book. Until the twentieth century, warfare had been two-dimensional, fought on the surface of land and sea. The submarine and the airplane introduced the era of three-dimensional warfare, and the advent of rocket propulsion took flight into space as well, making possible the ballistic missiles and orbiting satellites upon which the United States depended to ensure international stability over the Cold War. Only an independent service, one hundred percent devoted to flight, could best oversee and manage the application of these technologies. This challenge and the appeal of flight was why many of those West Point graduates elected to join the Air Force rather than the Army—it was a new service based on entirely new, exciting, and vitally important world-altering technologies.

This remarkable book, by a father-and-son team distinguished both by their accomplishments and by their love of country and flight, looks at the history of the Air Force through the workings of the graduates of the U.S. Military Academy at West Point. The roster of distinguished graduates who chose the Air Force over the Army is a long one, and for many, having done so represented a decision that marked them out as separate from their fellow cadets. Having chosen to serve in the Air Force, they did so with a fierce drive that matched the fury innate in the bombers and fighters and missiles that they flew and mastered. In the early years of the service, West Point graduates shot down MiGs over the Yalu; commanded globe-girdling intercontinental bombers; flew into space and to the moon; and in many other ways shaped America's aerospace future.

It is important that their story, their contributions, not be lost. Institutions reflect those who form and shape them, and the graduates of West Point, so well paid tribute by this book, were, collectively and individually, figures of seminal importance both to the growth and expansion of American air— and space—power and to the fight for freedom that witnessed, in 1989, the end to tyranny in Eastern Europe and the disestablishment of the Soviet Empire. West Point has a rich and treasured history. So do its airmen, God bless them all.

Richard P. Hallion served as the Historian of the U.S. Air Force; as a Senior Issues and Policy Analyst for the Secretary of the Air Force; as the H.K. Johnson Visiting Professor at the Army War College Military History Institute; and as a founding Curator of the National Air and Space Museum, Smithsonian Institution.

Preface

by Charles F.G. Kuyk, Jr.

As a retired Air Force officer and member of the West Point Class of 1950, I often have reflected on the influence that many West Point graduates have had upon U.S. Army air services and later the U.S. Air Force (USAF). Through this book, we hope to tell the story of their many contributions that helped shape the Air Force as we've come to know it today. Much of this book is based on my personal experience and observations of other West Point graduates serving with me in the Air Force. Unfortunately, due to the passage of time, most of those with whom I served are no longer with us to tell their personal story, so their writings and my memory of events must suffice. My son, a 1973 Air Force Academy graduate and former Air Force captain, has been my co-author in this effort and adds the perspective of a former ICBM launch officer and satellite project control officer. However, in most instances, first-person narratives reflect my personal experiences and observations.

In writing this book we sought to recognize the significant contributions made by West Point graduates who worked together with many other military and civilian leaders in shaping the U.S. Air Force. For example, aviation pioneers such as Billy Mitchell, Benjamin Foulois, Jimmy Doolittle and others were not West Point grads, yet played a huge role in the development of the Air Force and we certainly highlight their contributions in this story. But our emphasis is upon the history of the U.S. Air Force and how West Point grads strongly influenced its development and growth. These contributions were made over a roughly 40-year period during which momentous changes were taking place not only in the military but in our entire society. Among the transformations were the integration of scientific advancements and weapon system development with the resulting explosion of new technologies and weapon systems; the establishment of an entirely new branch of the military—

the U.S. Air Force; and the adaptations required from the cultural shifts taking place in America leading to the integration of minorities and women into the military. Though our focus is upon West Point grads, this story encompasses a far broader context because these grads built not only upon what had come before in the U.S. Army, but what they continued to advance in collaboration with many other organizations and individuals, both civilian and military. Indeed, it is this collaboration and adaptation—be it scientific, organizational, or cultural—that makes this story so unique. For this reason, our narrative rests upon both historical research as well as the personal experiences of West Point grads who played such a significant role in making the U.S. Air Force what it is today.

I served in several distinguished organizations during my military career—early training while enlisted in the U.S. Marine Corps taught discipline and the importance of putting unit before self. Then, in 1946, and armed with a basic military foundation, I joined the U.S. Military Academy (USMA or West Point) Class of 1950. While at West Point, we were imbued with the long-respected tradition of "Duty, Honor, Country." Many of our tactical officers (Tacs) were heroes from World War II who brought their hard-earned experiences from the battlefield to West Point cadets.

On the football field, Coach Earl Blaik taught us, as he said in his book, *You Have to Pay the Price*, that hard work is necessary to develop consistently winning teams and success in life. To accomplish his goals, he recruited and led an exceptional group of coaches that included the legendary Vince Lombardi; he trained All-American players such as Doc Blanchard and Glenn Davis. Coach Blaik's efforts and dedication led to winning teams during his tenure, including West Point's national championship team in 1946. It is noteworthy that 78 percent of the football letterman from the Class of 1950 became career officers, with six becoming general officers.

After West Point, my next opportunity to work with champions was in the mid–1950s at the USAF Test Pilot School followed by assignment as a test pilot at the Air Force Flight Test Center at Edwards Air Force Base (AFB) in California's Mojave Desert. These experiences provided the launching pad for 30 years of service in the Air Force where I had the privilege to serve with some outstanding individuals. Our story spans the years from the early 1900s at the dawn of aviation through the early 1990s when most of these grads had retired and passed the mantle of Air Force leadership to graduates of the U.S. Air Force Academy, which graduated its first class in 1959.

My Air Force career, like many new West Point grads of that era, initially was near "the tip of the spear" where actions taken, or not taken, could result in life or death. Like many in our Air Force group, I stood Cold War nuclear alert in bombers and flew combat tours in the Korean and Vietnam wars. These were exciting, informative years and, in many ways, fortunate years for me as many of my classmates and others made the ultimate sacrifice for their country. Later, after much schooling at the Navy and Air Force War Colleges on the theory and philosophy of war and politics, I went to the Pentagon as a USAF deputy chief of staff (DCS) R&D requirements staff officer and later as director of requirements. This is where I had the opportunity to provide data, information and years of flight experience in support of Air Force ideas and positions. Decisions affecting U.S. defense policy on weapons systems acquisitions and billions of taxpayer dollars were the everyday issues. Importantly, as a squadron, wing, and then numbered Air Force commander, I was proud to take part in directing military operations and integrating a racially diverse population of men and women into the Air Force.

As we were writing this book, I often reflected on the mind-boggling advances in technology that took place during my career. For example, when I was training as a World War II Marine, my weapon was an M-1 rifle. As a cadet at West Point, training on horseback as a cavalry officer was still an elective class. When I was a crew member in a Cold War strategic bomber standing alert in the 1950s, we carried one 15-kiloton nuclear bomb. In the 1970s, my son and co-author, a USAF lieutenant at the time, stood alert in an underground launch control center with another officer ready to launch 10 Minuteman III intercontinental ballistic missiles (ICBMs), each armed with three independently targetable 170-kiloton thermonuclear warheads. In another example, the old long-range reconnaissance Boeing RB-29 Superfortress, a World War II and Korean War–vintage aircraft, was replaced by the Lockheed SR-71 Blackbird. This aircraft, which served from 1964 to 1998, routinely flew above 80,000 feet at speeds as high as Mach 3.2. These two aircraft were just a quarter-century apart and illustrate the incredible advances in technology that are an important part of this story.

The origins of the Air Force go back only to a few years after the invention of the airplane in 1903, in marked contrast to the centuries-old histories of the U.S. Army and Navy. The invention of the airplane was followed by rapid and steady technological advancements and recognition by a few visionaries that the airplane could be an effective reconnaissance vehicle and, later, a weapon of war. Since some West Point graduates—like Henry H. "Hap" Arnold (USMA 1907), taught to fly by the Wright brothers and who later commanded the Army Air Forces (AAF)—set the stage for the new U.S. Air Force; we open the book with a brief history of these early pioneers.

During the period of just over 40 years from 1903 to 1947, the U.S. Army gained responsibility for land-based aerial warfare. In 1942, recognizing the need for educated and trained pilots, the War Department authorized the U.S. Military Academy to commission up to 60 percent of its graduates in the Army Air Forces.[1] Then, in the years shortly after the establishment of the of the U.S. Air Force in 1947, many West Point graduates elected to enter the Air Force rather than the Army. The U.S. Air Force Academy had barely been conceived when the Air Force was founded in 1947 and this new military service needed trained and motivated young military officers. So, what better place to look than West Point and the U.S. Naval Academy (USNA or Annapolis)? In fact, 36 percent of the West Point Class of 1948 and 42 percent of the Class of 1949 elected to enter the Air Force upon graduation.[2] Commencing with the Class of 1950 through the Class of 1958, approximately 25 percent of West Point and Annapolis graduating classes entered the Air Force.[3] Over the 10-year period, 1948 to 1958, 1,604 West Point graduates entered the Air Force, representing about 28 percent of those graduating classes.[4] These graduates became a significant component of the Air Force officer corps since the Air Force Academy would not graduate its first class until 1959.

Early Army aviation pioneers rapidly advanced aerial warfare during World War II. Shortly thereafter, jet engines were developed, providing greater power and faster speeds. In 1945, air power and war in general dramatically changed with the introduction of nuclear warfare. Nuclear weapons were, and still are, a game changer. The science of rocket engines rapidly expanded and opened up entirely new ICBM long-range weapon delivery systems along with new capabilities in space. Because of these advancements, high-level philosophical debate was waged concerning the use of nuclear weapons and how they fit into national defense strategy. Then, in 1949, successful testing of a nuclear bomb by the USSR opened the floodgates and the "Cold War" race between these two world powers began in earnest for nuclear weapon superiority.

By World War II, West Point graduates—led by General Arnold, commander of the Army Air Corps (AAC) after 1938, and then, after 1941 and until 1946, the Army Air Forces (AAF)—were prominently represented in the highest ranks of the Army's air units. From 1947 through 1990, 10 of the first 13 chiefs of staff of the Air Force (CSAF) were West Point graduates; it wasn't until 1994 that a graduate of the U.S. Air Force Academy (USAFA) became CSAF. The West Point Association of Graduates (AOG) named 10 distinguished graduates for their service in the Air Force during this period. More recently, West Point named its newest cadet barracks in honor of USAF Lt. General Benjamin O. Davis (USMA 1936).

These early beginnings, spanning a period of just over 40 years from 1903 to 1947 when the U.S. Army was responsible for aerial warfare, provide the foundation of our story of the contributions made by West Point graduates to the Air Force. In the early 1950s, the Cold War was accelerating and the Air Force, as well as all U.S. armed services, faced a unique military challenge not only to fight a war in Korea (1950 to 1953) but to maintain national and technological military leadership. It was a high-stakes, high-tech struggle to stay ahead of the Soviet Union. Better aircraft and more capable weapon systems such as ICBMs with payloads measured in megatons rather than kilotons were needed. Winning the race into space with its new opportunities for surveillance, intelligence gathering, communications, and precise navigation became vital. Dramatic advances in technology were changing modern warfare and the Air Force was at the forefront of these developments. Some of these advanced systems have had an equally dramatic impact on society when applied to the civilian sector, one example being the NAVSTAR Global Positioning System (GPS) developed and operated by the Air Force and used today by anyone with a cell phone.

The story of these West Point graduates is best told by describing some of the graduates who played a significant role in shaping the early days of the Air Force. Many who had graduated from West Point in the early decades of the twentieth century became generals in the AAF. As noted earlier, after the establishment of the U.S. Air Force in 1947, many West Point graduates from the 1948–58 era elected to receive their commissions as lieutenants in the Air Force upon graduation. This book addresses both eras of West Point grads serving the country's armed air forces: those who preceded the formation of the U.S. Air Force and those who came after.

The book is organized in terms of broad categories of weapon systems and operations within the Air Force. It tells the story of the careers and experiences of those officers who served in the early years of the AAF and USAF up through the early 1990s with emphasis on the graduates from the classes of 1948 through 1958. Memorable events, perspectives and anecdotes are interwoven into the story whenever possible.

The aircraft, missiles, satellites, sensors, communications systems and missions into space that West Point graduates helped to develop and operate have provided a legacy of technological advancement that has served the Air Force and our country well. Four aircraft, including the B-52 *Stratofortress*, have been in operation for more than 60 years while variations of the Minuteman missile have been in service for more than 50 years. Many satellite space systems are still in active service today. A number of these weapon systems are being employed by the next generation of Air Force officers, some of whom are our children and even grandchildren!

These technological advancements, together with the creation of a separate and equal military service and the establishment of the Air Force Academy represent key elements of our legacy. All West Pointers should stand tall and be proud of these major achievements.

We must note that many Naval Academy, ROTC and graduates from other universities during this same period also entered the Air Force and faced the same challenges and worked side-by-side with the West Point grads addressed in the book. Perhaps another book heralding their contributions is in the works. While this is a book about a slice of history telling the story about contributions made by West Point graduates to the U.S. Air Force, NASA and other government agencies, in no way does it seek to diminish the magnificent contributions made by so many others to the success of these organizations.

Finally, this is first and foremost a story about people and of the systems and organizations they helped to build. In the interest of brevity, as characters are introduced in the narrative, we provide only brief summaries of their backgrounds and relevant accomplishments drawn from both personal experience as well as from the more expansive resumes of these individuals on the Air Force's website at www.af.mil/about-us/biographies.

Abbreviations

AAC	Army Air Corps
AAF	Army Air Forces
ADCOM	Aerospace Defense Command
AFB	Air Force Base
AFGSC	Air Force Global Strike Command
AFIT	Air Force Institute of Technology
AFLC	Air Force Logistics Command
AFSC	Air Force Systems Command
ALCM	Air-Launched Cruise Missile
AMC	Air Mobility Command
ANG	Air National Guard
AOC	Air Officer Commanding
AOG	Association of Graduates
ARDC	Air Research and Development Command
ARPA	Advanced Research Projects Agency
ARPS	Aerospace Research Pilots School
ASC	Aeronautical Systems Center
ASD	Aeronautical Systems Division
A/TA	Airlift/Tanker Association
ATC	Air Training Command, previously Air Transport Command
ATO	Air Training Officer
AWACS	Airborne Warning and Control System
BMD	Ballistic Missile Division

BMEWS	Ballistic Missile Early Warning System
BSD	Ballistic Systems Division
CAPCOM	Capsule Communicator
CEP	Circular Error Probability
CIA	Central Intelligence Agency
CINC	Commander-in-Chief
CINCSAC	Commander-in-Chief, Strategic Air Command
CM	Command Module
CONUS	Continental United States
CSAF	Chief of Staff of the Air Force
CSM	Command/Service Module
CSO	Chief Signal Officer
CSOC	Consolidated Space Operation Center
DARPA	Defense Advanced Research Projects Agency
DCS	Deputy Chief of Staff
DG	Distinguished Graduate
DOD	Department of Defense
ECM	Electronic Counter Measure
ESD	Electronic Systems Division
EVA	Extravehicular Activity
FOC	Full Operational Capability
GHQ Air Force	General Headquarters Air Force
GPS	Global Positioning System
HQ	Headquarters
ICBM	Intercontinental Ballistic Missile
IOC	Initial Operational Capability
IRBM	Intermediate Range Ballistic Missile
JCS	Joint Chiefs of Staff
JPL	Jet Propulsion Laboratory
JSTARS	Joint Surveillance Target Attack Radar System
LABS	Low Altitude Bombing System
LM	Lunar Module
MAC	Military Airlift Command
MAD	Mutual Assured Destruction
MAJCOM	Major Command
MASH	Mobile Army Surgical Hospital

MATS	Military Air Transport Service
MIA	Missing in Action
MIRV	Multiple Independently Targetable Reentry Vehicle
MIT	Massachusetts Institute of Technology
MOL	Manned Orbital Laboratory
MS	Master of Science degree
MX	Missile Experimental
NASA	National Aeronautics and Space Administration
NATO	North Atlantic Treaty Organization
NAVSTAR	Navigation System Using Timing and Ranging
NORAD	North American Aerospace Command
NRO	National Reconnaissance Office
OCS	Officer Candidate School
OSAF	Office of the Secretary of the Air Force
OSD	Office of Secretary of Defense
Plebes	First year cadets at West Point
POW	Prisoner of War
R&D	Research and Development
RAF	Royal Air Force (United Kingdom)
RAND	The RAND Corporation, a nonprofit research organization founded in 1948 (abbreviation of Research and Development)
ROTC	Reserve Officer Training Corps
RPV	Remotely Piloted Vehicle
SAB	Scientific Advisory Board
SAC	Strategic Air Command
SAFSP	Secretary of the Air Force Special Projects
SAG	Scientific Advisory Group
SAGE	Semi-Automatic Ground Environment
SAIC	Science Applications International Corporation
SAMOS	Satellite Missile Observation System
SAMSO	Space and Missile Systems Organization
Sc.D.	Doctor of Science
SecAF	Secretary of the Air Force
SecDef	Secretary of Defense
SIOP	Single Integrated Operational Plan

SLBM	Submarine-Launched Ballistic Missile
SPO	System Program Office
SSA	Source Selection Authority
SSB	Source Selection Board
SSD	Space Systems Division
STEM	Scientific, Technology, Engineering and Math
STS	Space Transportation System (Space Shuttle)
TAC	Tactical Air Command
Tacs	Tactical Officers (at West Point)
TLI	Trans-Lunar Injection
TPP	Total Package Procurement
TPS	Test Pilot School
UAV	Unmanned Aerial Vehicle
UN	United Nations
USAF	United States Air Force
USAFA	United States Air Force Academy
USAFE	United States Air Forces in Europe
USMA	United States Military Academy (West Point)
USNA	United States Naval Academy (Annapolis)
USSR	Union of Soviet Socialist Republics (Soviet Union)
VMI	Virginia Military Institute
WAF	Women in the Air Force
WDD	Western Development Division

Chapter 1

The Early Years of U.S. Army Aviation (1903–47)

To understand the role West Point graduates played in shaping the early Air Force, it is useful to understand the state of U.S. military aviation before the Air Force was officially established in 1947. It is a story about the vision, ingenuity, creativity and daring of a few individuals and the urgent needs of war. It is best told through the lives of early pioneers of military flight, many of whom were West Point graduates. Today's Air Force is a product of the steady advances in technology led by these innovative and bold leaders. The early beginnings span a period of 44 years from the inception of flight in 1903 by the Wright brothers through the founding of the Air Force in 1947, shortly after World War II. Over this relatively short period of time and under the leadership of many West Point grads serving in the U.S. Army, the airplane evolved from a spindly invention of fabric, wood and wire into the most potent weapon of war the world had ever seen.

Following the Wright brothers' momentous invention, military figures had a far-reaching impact on the early development of the airplane and military airpower. Benjamin Foulois and William "Billy" Mitchell, both strong airpower advocates, used entirely different methods to advance their visions of the aircraft's role in combat. Though visionaries, each suffered setbacks. One left the Air Service as a result of intimidating congressional pressure, the other by court martial. Foulois, whom Orville Wright taught to fly by correspondence and who later became chief of the Air Service, is now known as the "Father of Military Flight." Mitchell, by virtue of his ferocious advocacy of airpower, is known by many as the "Father of the U.S. Air Force."

The Wright brothers, Orville and Wilbur, made the first powered, controlled, and sustained flight of a heavier-than-air vehicle at Kitty Hawk, North Carolina, on December 17, 1903. It was the start of an era that would not only revolutionize transportation but would put the U.S. on a course to become the greatest military power in the world. Some early Air Force pioneers learned to fly side by side with the Wright brothers such that the beginnings of U.S. military aviation parallel that of the earliest aviators.

George Squier (USMA 1887 and PhD from Johns Hopkins University), as executive officer to the chief signal officer of the U.S. Signal Corps in 1907, was instrumental in establishing the Aeronautical Division of the U.S. Signal Corps. This was the first organizational ancestor of the U.S. Air Force. He also was the first military passenger in an airplane on September 12, 1908, and, working with the Wright brothers, was responsible for the purchase of the first airplanes by the U.S. Army in 1909, the Wright Military Flyer.

General Henry Harley "Hap" Arnold (USMA 1907) was taught to fly by Wilbur Wright and he was the only officer to become a five-star commander in both the Army and the Air Force. General James "Jimmy" H. Doolittle was a scholar of aeronautics with advanced degrees from MIT, and, as a very active military leader, became the commander of the 8th Air Force in World War II. General Carl A. Spaatz (USMA 1914) demonstrated a strong mix of command and staff performance leading to command of all Air Forces in Europe and then in the Pacific during World War II. He later became the first chief of staff of the new Air Force.

Of course, in addition to these notable visionaries, there were many, many other dedicated, hard-working airmen who contributed their efforts, and sometimes their lives to the successful development of the U.S. Air Force.

The Wright Brothers

Any discussion of flight—whether applied to civilian or military pursuits—of necessity must begin with the Wright brothers. Orville and Wilbur first conceived of mechanical flight based on their observations of birds in flight and experiments with kites. Step by step they solved the challenges of designing an adequate structure, wings that could produce sufficient lift, a control system to enable steering and directing the airplane, and propulsion. Although they studied the work of many, their accomplishment was entirely their own and that of their innovative bicycle mechanic, Charles Edward Taylor, who designed and built the first aircraft engine based on crude sketches from the Wright brothers. The aluminum, water-cooled engine produced 12 horsepower and weighed only 152 pounds.[1] The Wright's first flight on December 17, 1903, lasted 12 seconds and spanned 120 feet. Orville and Wilbur each flew twice that day, making successfully longer flights, with Wilbur's 59-second flight covering 852 feet. Rising winds rolled up the Flyer, bringing an

The first successful flight of the Wright Flyer by the Wright brothers on December 17, 1903, at Kitty Hawk, North Carolina (Library of Congress Prints and Photographs Division).

end to what had been an incredible day. Their momentous accomplishments ushered in a new era in transportation and, soon to be seen, warfare.

The Wright brothers and Charlie Taylor steadily improved their fragile airplane and soon sought to sell their machine to the American and European governments. On September 17, 1908, during flight tests of the aircraft with an Army lieutenant on board (Thomas E. Selfridge, USMA 1903), Orville circled the field at Fort Myer, Virginia, several times at about 150 feet and then crashed as a result of mechanical failure. Regrettably, at the young age of 26, Lt. Selfridge was killed in the accident, making him the first person to die in a crash of a powered airplane.[2] The head of the accident board, Major George O. Squier (USMA 1887) said of the accident (and as would be said of airplane accidents for years to come), "it is very unfortunate, but only a temporary setback." However, these flights clearly demonstrated the feasibility of the new heavier-than-air-vehicle.

General Benjamin Delahauf Foulois

The U.S. Army recognized and adopted the advantages of the new fixed wing airplane relatively quickly. Balloons provided eyes in the sky and initially it was not obvious what benefits greater airborne mobility could provide. In 1907, while attending the Army Signal School, then Lieutenant Benjamin Foulois, wrote a thesis titled "The Tactical and Strategic Value of Dirigible Balloons and Aerodynamic Flying Machines."[3] He saw both a future for aerial reconnaissance and, possibly, even aerial engagement with the enemy. He also observed that France and Germany were moving ahead of the U.S. in this new field. As he said in his memoirs, he "felt sure that flying machines would revolutionize the conduct of war."

Foulois was commissioned as a 1st lieutenant in the Signal Corps in 1908 with assignment to the office of the Army's chief signal officer (CSO). Among the many observations he made, one that proved particularly prescient regarding air power was that "in all future warfare, we can expect to see engagements in the air between hostile aerial fleets. The struggle for supremacy in the air will undoubtedly take place while the opposing armies are maneuvering for position."[4]

Foulois's first experiences aloft came from flying dirigibles at Fort Myer, Virginia. While he was at Fort Myer, he had the opportunity to watch Orville Wright demonstrate his Military Flyer. From that point onwards, he recognized the value of the airplane as a critical instrument of war.

On July 3, 1909, the Army selected Foulois to accompany Orville as an observer on the final qualifying flight of the Wright Model A flying machine before an Army selection committee at Fort Myer. In his memoirs, Foulois jokingly stated that he liked to think he was chosen on the basis of intellectual and technical ability, but he realized later that it was his 5-foot-6-inch stature and light 126-pound weight that contributed to his selection by the Wrights. The Wrights would earn a 10 percent bonus for every mile per hour in excess of the required 40 miles per hour speed that had been specified, so the lighter the observer, the better! On July 30, 1909, climbing to a record-breaking altitude of 400 feet, Orville Wright and Benjamin Foulois flew the course at an average 42.583 mph, gaining a bonus of $5,000 over the $25,000 purchase price.[5] This aircraft became the Signal Corps' Aeroplane No. 1.

A final requirement of the Wright brothers' contract was to train two pilots. In October 1909, Lieutenant Frank Lahm (USMA 1901) and Lieutenant Frederic E. Humphreys each soloed in the new Army airplane. Interestingly, four West Point graduates flew with the Wright brothers in these early beginnings of Army aviation: Thomas Selfridge (USMA 1903), Frank Lahm (USMA 1901), George Squier (USMA 1887), and Henry H. Arnold (USMA 1907).

Over the ensuing years before World War I, Foulois continued to promote the advantages of air power. By 1917, having been promoted to the rank of major general, Foulois had responsibility for the production, maintenance, organization and operations of all aeronautical material and personnel in the United States. He worked closely with Major General George Squier, then the

Wright Military Flyer arrives at Fort Myer in 1908 (Dept. of Defense photo).

chief signal officer, and the National Advisory Committee for Aeronautics to detail plans for appropriations of $54 million to support 16 aero squadrons, 16 balloon companies, and nine aviation schools.[6] After the war, he served as air attaché in Germany, witnessing the already formidable advances being made in aerodynamics, structures, and all-metal monoplane design. Foulois eventually became chief of the Air Corps in 1931. Foulois was well known as a "flier's flier" who often logged more flying time each year than most junior pilots. In 1935, he retired as a major general at the end of his four-year term as chief of the Air Corps and after 36 years of service.

Even General Douglas MacArthur (USMA 1903) had an early experience with these new aerial machines. When Lt. Foulois attempted to land the Army's only airplane (at the time) next to a row of Army tents at Fort Sam Houston in Texas, he overshot his intended touchdown spot and found himself headed for one of two options: the officers' tents or a passing horse and buggy. He wisely chose to avoid the tents, but the collision with the buggy caused the horse to wildly gallop away and left behind a very angry buggy driver. In the commotion that followed, who appeared from one of the officers' tents but then Captain Douglas MacArthur. Recognizing his classmate and former baseball teammate at the helm of the flying machine, MacArthur was quoted as saying that Foulois "made the right decision!"[7] Clearly, aviation was in its infancy but a few West Point grads, including MacArthur, had witnessed the value—and danger—of this new aerial machine.

As an interesting aside drawn from his memoirs, Foulois recognized that in promoting his vision of airpower he would likely antagonize his cavalry brethren when he suggested that the Army's horses might be used only for ceremonial purposes someday after aircraft had been perfected. In hindsight, Foulois's vision proved to be accurate. However, up through the graduating class of 1950, West Point continued instruction in horsemanship.[8] Interestingly, that same graduating class produced its first astronaut, Frank Borman (USMA 1950).

In 1960, as a young captain test pilot at Edwards Air Force Base (AFB), I was assigned to give General Foulois, then 81 years old, a walking tour of the flight line and aircraft facilities. He was intensely interested in all aspects of the latest military aircraft, the flight line facilities and base operations. As a living example of the brief passage of time from the invention of the airplane to modern air warfare, here was a man who had taught himself to fly in 1910 (by correspondence nonetheless with the Wright brothers) who now, more than 50 years later, was walking the flight line to view the latest supersonic Air Force aircraft.

Another anecdote regarding General Foulois comes from a former F-84, B-57, U-2, and SR-71 pilot, retired USAF Major General Patrick Halloran. General Halloran was having dinner at the Andrews Air Force Base officers' club one night when he saw an elderly gentleman sitting by himself, finishing his dinner. Recognizing General Foulois, he introduced himself and explained that he was a pilot in the very squadron that General Foulois formerly commanded (the 1st Provisional Aero Squadron). General Foulois, 87 years old at the time, was apparently delighted that he had been recognized and was quite interested in the historical connection the two shared. Though Halloran attempted to steer the conversation toward the early days flying Jennies (Curtiss JN series), apparently Foulois wanted only to talk about the SR-71![9]

One of Foulois's final comments in his memoirs provide a good summary of just how far flight had come in such a short time: "My lifetime has spanned the entire history of powered flight. I have seen the airplane grow from a primitive bundle of wire, fabric and wood to an instrument of national power. I am proud to have been a part of the organization that has done more to bring it to its present state of development than any other—the United States Air Force."[10]

George O. Squier

The Signal Corps staff became increasingly interested in dirigibles and the Wright Brothers' new aerial invention. Major George O. Squier (USMA

1887), while acting as executive officer to the chief signal officer, recommended the establishment of an aeronautical division. The division was eventually approved and as Major General Foulois later would say, an embryonic air force was born. In part due to Squier's efforts and as described earlier regarding Foulois, on August 2, 1909, the Army awarded the Wrights $30,000 for delivering Aeroplane No. 1.

As noted in Squier's biographical memoirs from the National Academy of Science:

> From the earliest days of the Wright Brothers' flying machine, Squier recognized the immense military importance of the airplane. A large part of his work as Chief Signal Officer was directed toward improving the range, power and effectiveness of this arm of the service as a separate branch of the military art. He succeeded in bringing the American military airplane into the front line of effectiveness during the World War. He foresaw that the bombing airplane would become a mighty engine of destruction in future wars.[11]

However, it wasn't until 1911 that Congress appropriated funds ($125,000) to expand what, at the time, was a one plane, one pilot (Foulois) military air force. And this after one member of Congress objected stating, "Why all this fuss about airplanes for the Army? I thought we already had one."[12]

In 1926, Congress established the Army Air Corps (AAC) as the aviation arm of the Army. In 1934 during the Great Depression, President Franklin D. Roosevelt canceled all airmail contracts and assigned that duty to the AAC. Foulois, now a major general and chief of the Air Corps, named Hap Arnold to command one of the three military zones of the controversial Army Air Corps Mail Operations. After numerous fatalities due to weather and inadequate equipment and training, the Post Office returned to using private contractors for air delivery, demonstrating the sad state of affairs for the military's aviation services at that time.

In 1935, General Headquarters Air Force (GHQ Air Force) was created for all operational aviation activities. Thus, prior to World War II, there were two organizational units involved in air operations: the Air Corps managing material and training and GHQ Air Force managing air operations. Recognizing the need for a larger role for air power, the Army Air Forces (AAF) came into existence on June 20, 1941, six months prior to Pearl Harbor. It was led by General Hap Arnold.

General William Lendrum "Billy" Mitchell

William "Billy" Mitchell was one of the early visionaries who recognized the dawning era of military aviation. In 1906, he wrote a magazine article forecasting the future of military aviation and long-range bombers. Although the U.S. government initially showed little interest in the Wright brothers' 1903 flight and their continued improvements to the aircraft, the French, with considerable experimental flight activity were themselves quite interested. Accordingly, in 1907, Wilbur went to Europe to visit the French and spent almost two years demonstrating his airplane. He set new records in every phase of flight. Mitchell was intrigued and convinced that the airplane was for real and pushed even harder for U.S. acceptance and advancement. As General Arnold would later say, Mitchell was instrumental in bringing to the forefront the need for air superiority.

General Mitchell was so respected by his colleagues, including General Arnold, that many airmen in the Air Service named their sons "Billy" after him. Because of his continued strong airpower advocacy and interviews with the press, the public considered him the key military spokesman even though he was only second in command of the Air Services. In 1921, he told Congress that bombers could sink any ships afloat. He went on to prove his point, much to the irritation of the Navy, when his Air Service bombers sank several captured German armored ships in Chesapeake Bay, culminating in the sinking of the battleship *Ostfriesland,* a veteran of the Battle of Jutland. But the success and national publicity from this event was way ahead of the Army's official position (including that of the secretary of the Army) that bombers were not an effective means of destroying enemy ships.

Since neither General John Joseph "Black Jack" Pershing (USMA 1886) nor Pershing's classmates, Major General Charles Thomas Menoher (USMA 1886) nor Major General Mason Patrick (USMA 1886) could control Mitchell's extremely outspoken advocacy of air power, he was transferred to the outpost at Fort Sam Houston in Texas.[13] But General Mitchell would not relent, and as he told his longtime friend General Arnold, "when senior officers won't see facts or something unorthodox, perhaps an explosion is necessary. I'm doing this for the future of the Air Force."[14] In 1925 Mitchell wrote a book, *Winged Defense,* emphasizing that now both the land and sea of any opponent were exposed to attack from the air. That same year, after the Navy dirigible airship USS *Shenandoah* broke up in bad weather over Ohio, killing many of its crew and its skipper (and Mitchell's close personal friend) Commander Zachary Lansdowne, he publicly accused the Navy and War Department of "incompetence and criminal negligence." That was it. General Mitchell was court-martialed for "conduct prejudicial to good order and military discipline."[15] He was convicted and rather than serve a five-year sentence resigned his commission.

General Arnold wrote in his memoirs that Mitchell "was a hard man to make peace with. He was a fighter and the public was on his side. He was righter than hell and he knew it. And whoever wasn't with him 100% was against him."[16]

General Douglas MacArthur said later that, as a member of the court martial board, he had voted to acquit Mitchell because as he wrote in his memoirs, "a senior officer should not be silenced for being at variance with his superiors in rank and accepted doctrine." (A sign of things to come from General MacArthur.)

Finally, in 1942, many years after his court-martial, President Franklin Roosevelt, in recognizing Mitchell's contributions to air power, elevated him to the rank of major general (two stars) on the AAC retired list and petitioned Congress to posthumously award Mitchell the Congressional Gold Medal "in recognition of his outstanding pioneer service and foresight in the field of American military aviation." It was awarded in 1946.

General William L. "Billy" Mitchell. An early advocate of military aviation, he was known as the "Father of the U.S. Air Force" (Library of Congress, Prints and Photographs Division).

General Henry Harley "Hap" Arnold

In 1911, 2nd Lt. Henry J. "Hap" Arnold (USMA 1907) was transferred to the Aeronautical Division of the Army Signal Corps where he began flight training with the Wright brothers. After 10 days of dual flight instruction, he soloed and became a qualified pilot on July 6. The training philosophy at the time was to maximize hands-on experience as expressed by the often-used phrase, "You could never learn to ride a horse or fly an airplane without getting on and taking control." Arnold, his fellow trainee Lt. Thomas DeWitt Milling (USMA 1909) and Foulois thus became the first Army pilots on flight duty.

These three became instructors at the country's first military airfield at College Park, Maryland, through which most of the new aviators received their flight training. From his experience as an early aviator, Arnold recognized and promoted the airplane primarily as a reconnaissance vehicle and became the first flier to win the coveted Mackay Trophy for outstanding aerial accomplishments.

In those early years, airplanes were a work in progress and flying was a very dangerous business. How to use these machines was still not clear, nor was the airplane embraced by the Army. Records for altitude, speed, passengers carried, and distance flown were established on practically every flight as pilots pushed the boundaries of these new machines. On one flight, General Arnold narrowly escaped a fatal crash—but many of his friends and classmates were not so lucky. After surviving a near-death accident and on the verge of getting married, General Arnold assessed the odds of survival and accepted a "ground job" and didn't come back to flying for several years. He returned in no small measure because Billy Mitchell, who he knew and respected, suggested that Arnold get back into aviation.[17]

Despite his initial hesitancy of flying resulting from his early experiences in flight, General Arnold went on to promote and supervise the expansion of the Air Service during World War I. Rather than focusing solely on the life of a pilot, he applied himself to all aspects of flight, including aircraft production and procurement, the construction and operation of training facilities and airfields, and the recruitment and training of large numbers of pilots and support personnel. He also was a staunch supporter of research and development efforts and the use of civilian expertise in furthering military objectives. For example, he directed Air Corps funding to the California Institute of Technology and to Dr. Theodore von Kármán (a brilliant Hungarian-born aerodynamicist and director of its Guggenheim Aeronautical Laboratory) to head a committee of scientists to establish a plan of research to assess how inventions such as the jet engine, radar and rockets could be best used for national defense. As historian C. V. Glines has written, "Arnold told von Kármán that he did not want the Army Air Forces ever again to be caught unprepared, as it had been in 1939."[18]

General of the Air Force, Henry Harley "Hap" Arnold (USMA 1907). Taught to fly by Orville Wright, he led Army Air Forces through World War II (National Museum of the U.S. Air Force).

As an ardent believer in airpower, General Arnold and colleague Ira C. Eaker (later to become a lieutenant general and the Eighth Air Force commander during World War II) collaborated on three books on the subject: *This Flying Game* (1936, reprinted 1943), *Winged Defense* (1941), and *Army Flyer* (1942). As a lieutenant colonel assigned to March Field in California in 1931, Arnold helped formulate strategy, tactical air and air defense doctrines and continued to promote the development of advances in aircraft, including both long-range bombers and fighters. Throughout the 1930s, Arnold advocated the need to upgrade the country's military aviation capabilities to counter the growth of German air power that was threatening Europe. This included the development of improved aircraft such as the P-38, P-47, P-51, B-17, B-24 and the B-29 that were so heavily relied upon in World War II. As noted by one author, "Unique among the Army's top brass, General Arnold understood aircraft production, especially the nuances of logistics chains, lead times, and financing issues, and he was a trusted friend of the industry's leaders, including Don Douglas, whose company was one of the nation's leading aircraft manufacturers."[19]

Another West Point graduate, Major General Oscar Westover (USMA 1906), was chief of the Air Corps from December 1935 until September 1938, and was, in part, responsible for the beginning of a period of expansion that ended with the emergence of the U.S. Air Force as a separate service. As was too often the case in early aviation, Westover died in an aircraft crash in 1938

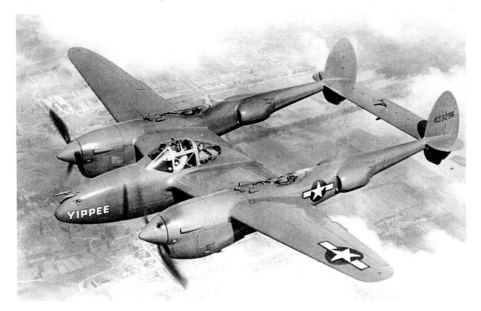

Lockheed P-38J Lightning. First flight, 1939. A key fighter aircraft used by top U.S. aces; 10,037 were produced (U.S. Air Force photo).

Top: P-51 Mustang in flight during an air show at Langley Air Force Base (later identified as F-51). More than 15,000 were produced. A long-range fighter-bomber used in World War II and (as F-51) in Korea (U.S. Air Force photo). *Above:* Boeing B-17G Flying Fortress. There were 12,731 produced between 1937 and 1945. Dropped more bombs in World War II than any other airplane (Air Force Historical Research Agency photo).

Boeing B-29 Flying Superfortress. There were 3,970 produced. Strategic bomber in World War II; dropped the two atomic bombs on Japan and served as conventional bomber in Korea (U.S. Air Force photo).

and was replaced by his vice commander, Hap Arnold. By this sad and unfortunate circumstance, Arnold rose to command the Allies' most powerful global air force during the cataclysm of the Second World War.

During the Depression years, funding for the development of combat aircraft was not a priority. It wasn't until 1938 that President Roosevelt authorized the production of greater numbers of aircraft, from 10,000 planes in 1940, 20,000 the year after, and later to 50,000. Only 300 pilots per year were trained prior to 1939 but once World War II began, pilot training increased to 3,000 per year in early 1941 and then grew to 33,000 after the Japanese attack on Pearl Harbor on December 7, 1941. After being promoted to lieutenant general, Arnold was thereafter included in all military meetings at the White House and other high-level strategic meetings.[20]

During World War II, under General Arnold's leadership, military air power began to grow exponentially, from 22,000 officers and 3,900 planes to 2,500,000 men and women and 75,000 aircraft. In addition, there were many new organizations created within the AAF to manage this dramatic expansion in air power.

In 1938 President Franklin D. Roosevelt appointed General Arnold chief of the Air Corps with the rank of major general. Soon after the U.S. entered World War II, he was promoted to lieutenant general. On March 9, 1942, the Army adopted the reorganization that Arnold had previously advocated, leading the War Department to grant Army Air Corps full autonomy, equal to and separate from the Army Ground Forces and Services of Supply. In 1941, Arnold became commanding general of the Army Air Forces (AAF) and an ex officio member of both the Joint Chiefs of Staff and the Combined Chiefs of Staff. In 1943, Arnold was promoted to full general, and in 1944 was appointed a five-star general of the Army. Consistent with his advocacy of applying advanced research and development to military requirements, in 1945, Arnold directed the founding of Project RAND (later becoming the RAND Corporation, one of the country's foremost "think tanks"). In a report to the Secretary of War that illustrates Arnold's view of the importance of close collaboration between the scientific community and the Air Force, he wrote: "During this war the Army, Army Air Forces, and the Navy have made unprecedented use of scientific and industrial resources. The conclusion is inescapable that we have not yet established the balance necessary to insure the continuance of teamwork among the military, other government agencies, industry, and the universities. Scientific planning must be years in advance of the actual research and development work."[21]

Later in 1949, the designation of Arnold's final rank was changed to that of general of the Air Force. He remains the only officer to have held the five-star rank in two military services.

General James H. "Jimmy" Doolittle

After Pearl Harbor, President Roosevelt wanted to take the war to Japan in such a way that it would have a profound psychological impact not only on Japan but on the United States. General Arnold and his naval counterpart, Admiral Ernest J. King, and their respective staffs developed a plan for the launch of bombers from the deck of the Navy's latest aircraft carrier, the *Hornet*. For this dangerous and untested mission, Arnold needed an experienced pilot and one who could inspire others by example. With little hesitation, he selected then Lt. Colonel James H. "Jimmy" Doolittle. According to Arnold, "the selection of Doolittle to lead this nearly suicidal mission was a natural one. He was fearless, technically brilliant, a leader who not only could be counted upon to do a task himself if it were humanly possible, but could impart that spirit to others."[22]

Doolittle blended two backgrounds, being at once a superlative aviator and a highly trained aeronautical engineer who had made his name as an Army

Air Service test pilot and racing pilot. He also was no stranger to the classroom, having earned a master's degree and Sc.D degree from the Massachusetts Institute of Technology, receiving the first doctorate in aeronautical engineering ever awarded in the United States. Afterwards, he was assigned to work with the Daniel Guggenheim Fund for the Promotion of Aeronautics, during which, in 1929, he became the world's first pilot to take off, fly a set course, and land an airplane without ever seeing the ground—thus pioneering what was then called "blind flying." During the 1930s, he set a speed record flying the tubby but overpowered Granville brothers' *Gee Bee* racer, and had worked with Shell Oil to perfect 100-octane fuel, a critical factor in the Royal Air Force's victory over the *Luftwaffe*—which used less powerful 87-octane fuel—during the Battle of Britain.

Doolittle surveyed available aircraft for the carrier mission and selected the B-25B, a new twin-engine bomber as the best candidate for the job. He then established an elite team of pilots and mechanics and set to work with intensive training at what is now Eglin Air Force Base in Florida. The force then deployed to the West Coast, and, after loading their bombers on the USS *Hornet,* steamed through the Golden Gate Bridge and into history. On April 14, 1942, Doolittle's force of 16 B-25B bombers took off from the *Hornet* in the Western Pacific to bomb targets in Japan and then land in China. The bombers were successful in hitting their targets and, following the raid, fifteen of the aircraft reached China (although many crews were forced to bail out due to low fuel), while one aircraft landed at Vladivostok in the Soviet Union. All but seven of the 80 crew members survived the mission.

Doolittle's raid was a tremendous success in that the mission fulfilled the tactical goals set forth by the president and the Joint Chiefs and it presented a "severe psychological shock" to the leadership and people of Japan who previously had full faith in their invincibility. The raid's success also served to boost the morale of the American people at a time when it was most needed. Doolittle was awarded the Congressional Medal of Honor and promoted from colonel to brigadier general for carrying out this daring and ultimately successful mission. Later in the war, he was promoted to lieutenant general and commanded the 8th Air Force in Europe, taking it to the Pacific near war's end.

An interesting story that reveals another dimension of Jimmy Doolittle occurred at a dinner I once hosted for the Order of Daedalians in 1979 at the Travis AFB officer's club when I was commander of the 22nd Air Force. The dinner was to honor the elder surviving members of the Daedalians who had been officers and pilots during World War I. As we went around the tables sharing observations about the early days of flying, one member asked Doolittle about an experience that took place at a San Antonio airfield long ago. He and Doolittle had spent the day flying Jennies (Curtiss JN-4 biplanes) in the

Curtis JN-4H "Jenny" Biplane. First flight in 1915 with 6,813 produced. Many modified models were the backbone of American postwar trainers (Smithsonian Institution).

hot and muggy Texas weather and needed to cool off. Apparently, Jimmy suggested to this pilot that they take a few spins around the airfield with Jimmy seated on the landing gear axle between the wheels! When asked why he chose this unusual way to stay cool, he gave a simple answer—"It seemed like a good idea at the time!"

The next day, I escorted the general around the Travis AFB flight line. After a ground-level inspection of a C-5 Galaxy, I asked him if he wanted to climb up to the cockpit using the ladder, a three-stories high, lightweight ladder. Doolittle didn't even respond and immediately started up the ladder. We spent an enjoyable thirty minutes in the cockpit discussing every dial and switch. He was ready to fly! I wished we could have accommodated him.

General Carl Andrew Spaatz

General Carl Andrew Spaatz (USMA 1914) was the ideal model for any aspiring West Point grad. He was a very capable officer and was sought after both as a staff officer and commander. As noted in one of his biographies, he was a quiet man and portrayed as a "doer" and "problem solver" who achieved results. He was one of the first military pilots and shot down three German aircraft in World War I. Before he attended the command and general staff school in 1935 as a lieutenant colonel, he commanded three different groups and was a staff officer for the chief of the Air Corps. By 1941 he was ready for World War II with greatly increased responsibilities.

A quick review of his rapid career progression reveals that Spaatz became chief of staff for General Arnold, who then was commander of the Army Air Forces. General Spaatz became commander of the Air Force Combat Command followed quickly by command of our forces in Europe as they began to build up for the war. He then was commander of the 8th Air Force, followed by commander of the U.S. Army Air Forces in Europe. He next was assigned by General Eisenhower to be commander of Allied Northwest African Air Forces and later promoted to temporary lieutenant general and also commander of the 12th Air Force. He then advanced rapidly to become chief of all strategic air forces in Europe.

As an interesting side note, two of the men under his command were Major General Jimmy Doolittle and Major General Nathan F. Twining (USMA 1918). Twining later became chief of staff of the Air Force and subsequently chairman of the Joint Chiefs of Staff. General Spaatz returned from Africa to the European theater and was given command of all deep bombing missions against Germany. He directed the punishing, thousand-airplane raids against Germany in Dresden and Berlin, which later were criticized by some as too severe, but which helped end the war in Europe.

As war in the European theater came to a close, he was promoted to full general and moved to command of the Pacific. In the summer of 1945, Spaatz arrived on the island of Guam to assume command of the new U.S. Army Strategic Air Forces in the Pacific, which included the 20th Air Force under Major General Curtis LeMay. After an initial tour with LeMay's 20th Air Force, Spaatz sent a telegram to Arnold's Chief of Staff General Lauris Norstad (USMA 1930) who at the time was deputy chief of Air Staff at Army Air Forces Headquarters: "Have had opportunity to check up on Baker Two Nine [B-29] operations and believe this is the best organized and most technically and tactically proficient military organization that the world has seen to date."[23]

Spaatz immediately made LeMay his chief of staff and Jimmy Doolittle was assigned responsibility for the 8th Air Force based in the Philippines and Okinawa.

Through these experiences and from the broad scope of his responsibilities, Spaatz had effectively become commander of the strategic air forces later to be identified as the Strategic Air Command (SAC). Following directions from our political leaders, General Spaatz directed the massive strategic bombardment that applied the coup de grace of two atomic bombs dropped on Japan to bring World War II to its end.

Strategic airpower was just a concept in the early 1900s but by the 1940s and 1950s it had become a brutal reality. Spaatz had many admirers as well as critics, but he was given this new high-tech capability and directed by political leaders to fight and to win. He carried out these assignments and helped to lead the allies to aerial and total victory in Europe and the Pacific.

The Stage Is Set

These early years of military aeronautics were a time of concept validation and aircraft development leading to the demonstration of overwhelming military value during World War II. Billy Mitchell was most famous for his advocacy of air power and his strong argumentative positions which finally led to his court martial. In World War II, the new bomber and fighter aircraft put airpower on full display. Arnold pulled together this new military capability with its attendant industrial, organizational, logistical and political issues resulting in the establishment in 1947 of the U.S. Air Force, equal to the Army and Navy.

As World War II was winding down in 1946, the U.S. armed forces, including the Army Air Forces, underwent a massive and rapid demobilization. At the height of the war in the Pacific just before Japan surrendered, the AAF had 2,253,000 military and 318,514 civilian personnel. By May 1947, AAF military personnel had been reduced to 303,600 and civilian personnel to 110,000. The total number of airplane mechanics also was drastically reduced, from 350,000 to less than 35,000, having a severe impact on the aircraft "in commission" rate. The inventory of aircraft had fallen from 70,000 to 25,000, with only 4,750 of those combat ready.[24] Most of the discarded airplanes were cut up for scrap. The new defense budget called for an 85 percent reduction in military resources. At its height during the war, the Army Air Forces had 218 operational units—by the end of 1946 it was down to 55 air groups, only two of which were deemed combat ready.[25]

America's wartime ally during World War II, the Soviet Union, was fast becoming an adversary, sowing the seeds for the brewing Cold War. Based on this history, the stage was set for the early years of the U.S. Air Force. Aircraft capability and, in turn, air warfare doctrine had evolved in the Army Air Forces from reconnaissance of the battlefield and close air support of ground forces to interdiction of enemy supply routes and aerial defense of friendly forces. Finally, strategic bombing of enemy industry, transportation and civilian population became the primary Air Force mission. When the West Point classes of 1948–58 arrived on the scene, they entered a new, dynamic organization, albeit one much smaller than it had been during World War II. This new organization was shaped and impacted by constantly evolving technology. The competition between the three services—Army, Navy, and now

Air Force—over roles, missions and money, was in full force. But these graduates inherited a service that had been shaped in large part by those USMA graduates who came before them.

As described in Clarence Elebash's (USMA 1948) paper, "West Point and the Air Force":

> West Point graduates held many prominent positions in the early days of the independent Air Force. Congress passed the National Security Act on July 26, 1947, and the Air Force became a separate service on September 18 of that year. The October 1947 Air Staff organizational chart listed 27 principal staff officers. Of these, 11 were Academy graduates, including Chief of Staff Carl Spaatz (USMA 1914), Vice Chief Hoyt S. Vandenberg (USMA 1923), Assistant Vice Chief William F. McKee (USMA 1929), and Deputy Chief of Staff for Operations Louis Norstad (USMA 1930).

And as we will learn more in the coming chapters:

> all but three of the first thirteen [Air Force] Chiefs of Staff were West Point graduates. Two of the ten also served as Chairman of the Joint Chiefs of Staff. General Nathan F. Twining was JCS Chairman from 1957 to 1961 and General George S. Brown was Chairman from 1974 to 1978. As late as 1992, 45 years after the Air Force became a separate service, an Air Force USMA graduate was the Joint Commander-in-Chief of the Air Force Space Command and the North American Aerospace Defense Command (Donald Kutyna, USMA 1957).[26]

Chapter 2

Path to Independence

The U.S. Air Force became a separate military service on September 18, 1947. However, as we saw in the previous chapter regarding the early beginnings of U.S. military aviation, the seeds of a separate military service co-equal with that of the Army and Navy were planted well before this date. The concept of war being fought on other than land or sea took considerable justification and was a constant struggle with the Army, and especially with the Navy before it was accepted. While most saw a future for air power in the form of reconnaissance and close air support of Army and Navy operations, in the early days only a few airmen could visualize the concept of bombing deep in enemy territory, a concept that came to be known as strategic bombardment.

A confluence of factors during and shortly after World War II proved instrumental in convincing decision makers that an independent airpower service was needed. These factors included:

(1) rapidly advancing aeronautical technology that provided much greater payloads and striking range to enemy targets;

(2) atomic (fission) and thermonuclear (fusion) weapons;

(3) the hugely expanded military and industrial strength of the Soviet Union and

(4) an unprecedented global war, World War II, that provided the proving ground to drive home the realization that modern warfare would now require a strong strategic air force.[1]

It was these factors and the efforts of a few strong-willed advocates of airpower that ultimately justified a third independent military service. As noted earlier, as General Arnold said after Mitchell's court martial trial regarding Mitchell's strong advocacy of strategic bombardment, that "he was righter than hell and he knew it."[2] Unfortunately, as historian Herman Wolk wrote of Mitchell, "He was an air power prophet, but, like most prophets, he failed to persuade his contemporaries."[3]

Of course, the U.S. Army aviation units grew in size and importance as a function of the steady advances in airplane performance and as the growing possibilities for military usefulness became more obvious. At first, balloons and dirigibles had performance advantages over the fledgling mechanical aerial machines and, as noted previously, the Wright brothers had difficulty in selling their machine to U.S. or European countries. Finally, in 1909 after a series of successful flights in Europe, Wilbur Wright sold seven airplanes to the French. Within five years, the European nations and Imperial Russia had purchased more than 1,122 airplanes of many different types (the United States possessed just 40).[4]

The military organizations in Europe varied but only in Britain was an Army air service established, the Royal Flying Corps, later to become the independent Royal Air Force (RAF). However, even in England there was a constant inter-service struggle over money, manning, and aircraft as well as how best to manage this new capability.[5] A British committee was formed (the Smuts committee) to study these issues. The committee issued its report in 1917 (known by some as the Magna Carta of aviation) which noted that "as far as can at present be foreseen, there is absolutely no limit to the scale of its [airplane's] future independent war use…. It therefore recommended the creation of one unified air service."[6] But the conflict in Great Britain between generals and admirals continued into 1918 until, finally, in April 1918, the Royal Air Force was established by merging the Royal Flying Corps and the Royal Naval Air Force.

Air service independence took a similar path in the U.S. but was slower to be resolved. After the first Wright brothers flight in 1903, it wasn't until 1907 that Army Chief Signal Officer Brigadier General James Allen (USMA 1872) published the first specification for an Army airplane.[7] At the same time, General Allen issued a memo stating, "an aeronautical division of this office is hereby established … to have charge of all matters pertaining to military ballooning, air machines and all kindred subjects." He assigned Captain Charles deForest Chandler to run the division and then Lt. Colonel George Squier (USMA 1887), who later became the first commander of the Aviation Section. Three years later, in 1910, the first airplane was delivered to and flown at Fort Myer and, at Allen's direction, was boxed and shipped to San Antonio. After Foulois and his crew reassembled the plane in Texas, Foulois become the first military pilot to fly in the first military airplane.

The Army-Navy battle for control over air power began only seven years after the invention of the airplane when the Navy launched a Curtis-designed plane from a modified battleship. In 1911, a Navy pilot landed on a 119-foot wooden platform placed on a cruiser. The first Navy carrier, USS *Langley*, was commissioned in 1922 and included a catapult for launching.[8] This early Army-Navy competition in airplane development formed the backdrop for the decades-long drive for an independent Air Force.

The first predecessor organization of the Air Force began in 1907 with the creation of the Army Signal Corps' Aeronautical Division. Airplane performance improved rapidly over the next 30 years starting from speeds approaching 100 mph, altitudes of a few thousand feet, and ranges of about 500 miles which proved suitable for reconnaissance and close air support of ground and naval forces. However, with the technological advances made in the B-17, B-24 and, most dramatically the B-29 which could fly slightly over 2,000 miles (combat range) with 5,000 pounds of bombs and fighters such as the F-51 with a range slightly over 500 miles, long-range strategic air power became a reality. As a result of World War II, the Navy saw the future of the strategic nuclear mission and fought to use carrier-based airplanes for the mission. However, the relatively short range of carrier-based aircraft and the capability of long-range strategic bombers such as the B-29 had been clearly demonstrated. Nonetheless, the Navy continued to argue for the strategic bombing mission despite the new, even longer-range B-36.

Table 1. Predecessor Organizations of the U.S. Air Force

Aeronautical Division, Signal Corps: August 1, 1907–July 18, 1914

First Commander: Captain Charles deForest Chandler

(Note that General James Allen [USMA 1872] issued the first specification for a military airplane on December 23, 1907[9] and assigned Chandler as the commander.)

Aviation Section, Signal Corps: July 18, 1914–May 20, 1918

First Commander: Lieutenant Colonel George O. Squier (USMA 1887)

Division of Military Aeronautics, Army: May 20, 1918–May 24, 1918

First Commander: Major General William Lacy Kenly (USMA 1889)

Air Service of the American Expeditionary Force (AEF): September 3, 1917–May 19, 1918

Chief of Air Service: Major General William Kenly (USMA 1889)

Army Air Service: May 24, 1918–July 2, 1926

First Commander: Lieutenant Colonel Billy Mitchell

Army Air Corps: July 2, 1926–June 20, 1941

First Commander: Major General Mason M. Patrick (USMA 1886)

United States Army Air Forces: June 20, 1941–September 18, 1947

First Commander: Major General Henry H. (Hap) Arnold (USMA 1907)

United States Air Force: September 18, 1947 forward

First Chief of Staff: General Carl A. Spaatz (USMA 1914) through April 29, 1948

Second Chief of Staff: General Hoyt S. Vandenberg April 30, 1948–June 29, 1953

The Early Drive for Autonomy

Each military aeronautical unit prior to the establishment of the U.S. Air Force was a branch of the U.S. Army. In the early years, the War Department felt that the Air Service's primary role was either for reconnaissance or in support of ground or naval troops. As a result, it was subordinate to Army ground commanders. There were many studies and proposals at the time, including bills before Congress, regarding how best to organize and manage aviation within the Army. The resulting law, the Reorganization Act of 1920, recognized the Air Service only as a combat branch of the Army.

However, the concept and drive for air services autonomy on an equal footing with the Army and Navy began nearly concurrently with the formation of the Aeronautical Division. Debate continued over the ownership of the strategic mission for nearly 30 years before the official establishment of the U.S. Air Force in 1947. Throughout this period many organizations including the Army, the JCS and Congress examined the issues surrounding the Air Force's independence and the unity of command. Through our prism today, the notion of a separate air force seems almost a given, but as we have seen, it was not always so. Military aviation in the U.S. started as air support for ground forces, so gaining autonomy proved to be a challenging and often contentious matter. What is noteworthy is that at nearly every milestone along the path to independence, a USMA graduate, or graduates, played a key role. A few of the more notable initiatives for autonomy are outlined below.

1920—The National Defense Act of 1920

This legislation updated the National Defense Act of 1916 to reorganize the Army and decentralize the procurement and acquisitions process for equipment, weapons, supplies and vehicles. As part of the act, the Air Service was designated a combatant branch of the Army. In 1926, the Air Service was renamed the Army Air Corps, with Major General Mason M. Patrick (USMA 1886) as chief of the Air Corps. It was during this period that many advances in aircraft technology, including rudimentary development of new monoplane bombers and fighter aircraft were taking place.

1935—Creation of General Headquarters (GHQ) Air Force

The next major milestone in the march toward independence occurred in 1935 when the War Department established the General Headquarters (GHQ)

Air Force. After reviewing recommendations from two War Department review boards, it was decided to consolidate all flying units into a single aerial task force under one air commander. However, the review board rejected the proposal for an independent air force and a unified defense department concluding that "independent air missions have little effect upon the issue of battle and none upon the final outcome of war."[10] The board recommended that the GHQ Air Force be made up of air combat units capable of operating either independently or in cooperation with ground forces.[11]

Rather than being restricted to the traditional role of supporting Army ground troops on the battlefield, the scope of the new GHQ included long-range bombardment and observation to defend U.S. coastal areas and island possessions from attack by sea. However, at the time, the GHQ Air Force lacked an essential capability to fully carry out its mission—a long-range bomber.[12] Lt. General Frank Andrews (USMA 1906) was appointed by Army Chief of Staff Douglas MacArthur (USMA 1903) to command GHQ Air Force. General Andrews was a staunch supporter of the four-engine, long-range strategic bomber, particularly the B-17 Flying Fortress, which proved its worth in World War II. The Air Corps, headed by Major General Oscar Westover (USMA 1906), retained its role but now was responsible only for supply, airfields, and training. Both Andrews and Westover were killed in aircraft accidents.

Under General Andrews's leadership, GHQ Air Force was formed into three wings. Brigadier General Hap Arnold (USMA 1907) headed the 1st Wing at March Field, California, and because his Western wing was the largest, Arnold was promoted from lieutenant colonel to brigadier general[13]; Colonel Henry Conger Pratt (USMA 1904) commanded the 2nd Wing at Langley Field, Virginia; and Lt. Colonel Gerald C. Brant (USMA 1904) led the 3rd Wing at Barksdale Field, Louisiana. The chief of the Air Corps and the GHQ commander were at the same level of command so each reported separately to the War Department.[14] As later observed by Foulois, the GHQ Air Force was "the most important and forward-looking single step ever taken to secure a military unit of adequate striking power to insure to the United States a proper defense in the air."[15]

1935—West Point's Stewart Field

As a telling indicator of the Army's intent to retain the air force mission within the Army, in 1935 the Army began to acquire land 15 miles northwest of West Point for the establishment of an air field for the purpose of training USMA cadets how to fly.[16] In 1942, West Point's new air field was completed— Stewart Field was open for training and began basic flying training for 269 cadets. Those cadets who graduated from the flight training program would be second lieutenants in the Army Air Corps. At the opening ceremonies for Stewart Field, the USMA superintendent, Major General Francis B. Wilby (USMA 1905), stated, "This decision [to build and operate a flight training school] was one of the most momentous decisions in the history of the Military Academy, if not the life of our nation."[17] He went on to state that "the airplane has revolutionized methods of warfare." It is noteworthy that by 1943 significant numbers of cadets elected to participate in flight training: 43 percent of first classmen and 45 percent of second classmen (third and fourth classmen could not elect classes).[18]

With an investment in flight training of this magnitude, the Army at that time was focused on developing a trained cadre of pilots to serve as part of an Army branch providing reconnaissance and ground support for Army troops. The concept of strategic long-range bombardment within an independent air force had not yet been accepted.

1939—Expanding Role of the Army Air Corps (AAC)

With Adolf Hitler's Third Reich increasingly expanding its power over the late 1930s, President Roosevelt recognized the need for greatly enhancing U.S. military capabilities, particularly that of our airpower. In January 1939 he declared "that American defenses were utterly inadequate."[19] At the time, the AAC maintained only 1,700 aircraft. As Hitler's domain rapidly expanded, U.S. war plans for increased numbers of aircraft grew exponentially, with the president calling for up to 50,000 airplanes only one year later.[20] At the time such production figures seemed fantastically unrealistic, particularly given America's poor aircraft production record during the "Great War," when similar extravagant claims had proven embarrassingly illusory. But this time America had the civil-military industrial base and modern metal fabrication and assembly techniques to make it reality. Indeed, by the end of the Second World War, the U.S. would have produced nearly 300,000 airplanes, approximately 96,000 in a single year, dwarfing the production rates not only of the Axis, but the Allies as well. At the time of his call for 50,000 airplanes, Roosevelt recognized the need not only to build up American air power, but also to supply the air force needs of allies such as the British, French, and others.[21]

Compounding the challenge were conflicting views on exactly what the mission of air power was to be: Should it be long-range strategic bombers capable of striking behind enemy lines? Or close air support of troops on the ground? Perhaps air defense fighter aircraft? Possibly airlift of troops? Just reconnaissance and intelligence gathering? Or all or some of the above? In fact, the Army Air Forces would eventually fulfill all these missions, and many others as well.

Among the many military minds grappling with these issues were a number of West Point grads destined to play increasingly important roles in the coming years including Hap Arnold (USMA 1907), Carl A. Spaatz (USMA 1914), Hoyt S. Vandenberg (USMA 1923) and Lauris Norstad (USMA 1930). While all these were Air Corps pilots, not all who helped advance American military air power were airmen. Army Chief of Staff General George C. Marshall (VMI, 1901) and Dwight D. Eisenhower (USMA 1915) were just two of many other non-airmen who were perceptive and innovative, and thus accepting of this new and rapidly advancing military arm.

1941—Creation of the Army Air Forces

As the U.S. mobilized for war and with President Franklin D. Roosevelt's ordering of the massive buildup in U.S. air power to respond to Nazi aggression, the War Department formed the Army Air Forces (AAF) on June 20, 1941. This marked a major step toward air power autonomy. Air Force historian Herman Wolk has written that this "constituted the most radical change in War Department organization before World War II."[22] Major General Arnold became chief of the AAF, with responsibility for all U.S. air forces across four continents. He formed his own Air Staff as part of AAF headquarters which soon paved the way for organizational independence. The formation of the AAF within the War Department created an autonomous entity similar to the Marine Corps within the Navy Department, though the AAF had a much broader combat and administrative mandate.[23]

On August 14, 1941, Major General Arnold, as chief of the Army Air Forces, along with the chief of staff of the U.S. Army, General George C. Marshall (VMI 1901) and admirals Harold R. Stark (USNA 1903, chief of naval operations, 1939–42) and Ernest J. King (USNA 1901, commander of the Atlantic Fleet and later chief of naval operations in 1942) were the senior military participants at the Atlantic Conference in Newfoundland where President Roosevelt and British Prime Minister Winston Churchill met to establish the Atlantic Charter. The British air, ground, and naval chiefs accompanied Churchill, such that Arnold effectively served at this meeting as a member of the U.S. Joint Chiefs of Staff.[24] This served to firmly establish Arnold and the AAF as a full member of the high-level war planning efforts. At another important conference two years later in 1943 in Tehran, the first of the World War II conferences of the "Big Three" Allied leaders (the Soviet Union, the United States, and the United Kingdom) took place. Arnold was again a key member of the planning efforts taking place at this important strategic meeting.

In 1942, pursuant to Executive Order 9082, Lt. General Arnold's position was changed to commanding general, AAF. This made his position co-equal with the commanding generals of the other components of the Army. At the same time, the War Department abolished the Army GHQ and organized the Army into three autonomous components: the Army Air Forces, the Army Ground Forces, and the Services of Supply, each with a commanding general reporting to the chief of staff.[25] As noted in Herman S. Wolk's book, *Toward Independence: The Emergence of the U.S. Air Force, 1945–1947*,

> During World War II, because of its quasi-autonomous position within the War Department, the Army Air Forces held representation on all Joint Chiefs of Staff committees in Washington…. It was clearly in the interests of the common military effort, as it was clearly the intent of General Marshall, to preserve the system whereby the Army Air Forces exercised great influence in determining the way in which U.S. Army air units were employed.[26]

In July 1943, the AAF's independence was further solidified by the War Department's publication of Field Manual 100-20, "Command and Employment of Air Power," a doctrinal pronouncement rooted in the combat experience of the Royal Air Force and the AAF in the Middle East. The manual stated: "Land power and air power are coequal and interdependent; neither is an auxiliary of the other." It established the three priorities of AAF tactical operations that governed subsequent air employment during the liberation of Europe: first, air superiority; second, interdiction; and third, interdiction and battlefield air support.[27]

As the key architect of the new AAF, Arnold was quick to rely on trusted advisors, many of whom were West Point graduates. In addition to his Air Staff, during the war Arnold created a personal Advisory Council, which included four West Point grads who later became senior generals: Jacob E. Smart (USMA 1931), Fred M. Dean (USMA 1938), Charles P. Cabell (USMA 1925) and Lauris Norstad (USMA 1930). Each of these men made major contributions both to the combat history of the AAF (and later USAF), and to its capabilities.

1944—Creation of New Air Force Units

In the war in Europe, the independence of the AAF's war planning and execution was taken to a new level in February 1944 with the establishment of the U.S. Strategic Air Forces in Europe led by General Spaatz. This provided command and control authority in the AAF over all of Europe and was the unit responsible for the strategic bombardment of enemy targets throughout Europe. This was followed shortly in April 1944 with the creation in the Pacific Theatre of the Twentieth Air Force, a strategic bombing force led by General Spaatz under Arnold as executive agent of the Joint Chiefs of Staff.[28] This role effectively put the AAF on an equal footing with the ground forces under General MacArthur and naval forces under Admiral Chester W. Nimitz (USNA 1905) in the Pacific.[29] The Twentieth's mission was to conduct a strategic long-range bombing campaign directly against the Japanese home islands using the most sophisticated aircraft of its time, the Boeing B-29A Superfortress, a four-engine, turbocharged and pressurized bomber with remotely controlled defensive gun turrets, carrying up to a 10-ton bomb load. The Twentieth initially conducted high-altitude bombing raids on occupied Burma and Japan from remote bases in India and China. After American naval and land forces gained control of other Japanese-held islands such as Guam, Saipan, Iwo Jima and Okinawa, the Twentieth relocated to the Mariana Islands which furnished advanced launching bases for further bombing missions, and, in the case of Iwo Jima and Okinawa, for fighter aircraft that could both escort the B-29 force and contest the Japanese Imperial Army Air Force and Japan's Naval Air Force in their own skies. The Twentieth continued its bombardment campaign until the Japanese surrendered in August 1945, following extensive low-altitude fire-bombing raids and atomic bomb attacks on Hiroshima and Nagasaki, on August 6 and August 9, respectively.

Wolk considered formation of the Twentieth Air Force to be a "landmark event" in the Army air arm's drive for independence, for it "gave the Army Air Forces (AAF) what Arnold termed 'a Global Air Force.'" The Twentieth's strategic bombing campaign against Japan served as a precedent for the postwar establishment of the Strategic Air Command (SAC), which thereafter formed the core of America's strategic deterrent force—a force comprised initially of bombers, and later a mix of bombers, intercontinental ballistic missiles (ICBMs), and air-launched cruise missiles—during the long watch of the 40-year Cold War.[30]

1944—Postwar Planning

Though the issue of organization of the military services was postponed until after the war, it remained a thorny subject. The central role played by American air services in all theaters of engagement had firmly established the air forces as an important third dimension of the country's war fighting capability. But the question remained of how best to organize the military for optimum command and control and, ultimately, victory on the battlefield. A workable postwar structure was needed.

In April 1944, Congress formed the Woodrum Committee to address the Army's recommendation to the JCS that "for purposes of providing unity of command, of economy, and for the elimination of duplication and overlapping, there should be created a Single Department of War."[31] As part of the Committee's hearings, Assistant Secretary of War for Air Robert A. Lovett testified regarding the need for a separate air force while Undersecretary of War Robert P. Patterson and Lieutenant General Brehon B. Somervell (USMA 1914), chief of the Army Service Forces, testified to the existence of inefficiency in logistical support due to the lack of inter-service coordination. The Navy took an opposing position, largely to "maintain their primacy as the first line of defense, using new weapons (aircraft), but without the constraints of a unification scheme."[32] Undersecretary James V. Forrestal testified on behalf of the Navy, stating "that the question of military organization should be studied further, and it should not be assumed that a single department was agreed upon until completion of an objective study. No decision, even 'in principle,' on the unification of the departments could be taken until the war had concluded."[33]

By 1947, after a delay of more than two years, President Harry Truman directed the services to reach an agreement on the issue of unification. As a result, the Army appointed Lt. General Lauris Norstad (USMA 1930) to work with the Navy's Vice Admiral Forrest Sherman (USNA 1918) to develop a solution. After concluding a 10-month study by the JCS Special Committee for Reorganization of National Defense, they recommended establishment of three equal Cabinet-level departments for the Army, Navy and Air Force, together creating the Department of National Defense headed by a civilian secretary. Admiral James O. Richardson (USNA 1902), the senior Navy member of the committee, filed a minority report opposing the recommendation for a single Department of National Defense arguing that the plan was "theoretically better than any yet proposed, but from a practical point of view it is unacceptable."[34]

It is interesting to note that in part as a result of their successful collaboration in the unification challenge, both Norstad and Sherman went on to attain senior positions in their respective services. Norstad became a four-star general and supreme allied commander, Europe, and commander-in-chief, U.S. European Command. Sherman also attained four stars and became the chief of naval operations in 1949.

Another noteworthy collaboration that greatly facilitated the smooth transition to unification occurred between General Hoyt S. Vandenberg (USMA 1923) and Army Lt. General Joseph Lawton Collins (USMA 1917) who later became Army chief of staff. Vandenberg, working as Spaatz's deputy, worked closely with his Army counterpart, Collins, in resolving the many logistical challenges of separating Army Air Force resources into the new Air Force.

This included the allocation of service and supply personnel from the Army into the new Air Force. As noted in Phillip S. Meilinger's book on Vandenberg, "Their relations were so effective and amiable that complete agreement was reached on over two hundred basic items in a matter of weeks. President Truman was greatly impressed and termed the relationship a 'record of cooperation.'"[35]

Arnold's Advocacy for Air Force Independence

As explained in Wolk's book, Arnold and others saw that:

> World War II had ushered in a new era that would be dominated by air power, both conventional and atomic. Japan had been forced to surrender without invasion after atomic bombs had been dropped on Hiroshima and Nagasaki.... Thus, the most important lesson for America in peacetime was that "our security can in the future be threatened suddenly and with terrific destructive power. The new peacetime military establishment must be geared to deter conflict by maintaining adequate forces in-being."[36]

Supporting Arnold in the case for unified command and air force independence was the supreme commander of Allied Forces in Europe, General Dwight D. Eisenhower (USMA 1915) and President Harry Truman. Eisenhower testified before Congress in 1945 emphasizing the importance of unity of command, the critical role played by airpower in gaining victory and the need for creating a separate Air Force in the postwar world. As Wolk emphasized, "Eisenhower during the entire war saw the armed forces as comprised of three equal parts—ground, sea, and air. He constantly referred to 'our three great fighting arms.'" The armed forces, he explained, "should rest on a three-legged stool with each leg equally important—Army, Navy, Air Forces."[37]

President Truman, as commander-in-chief, "was convinced that a lack of proper command organization and faulty communications contributed to the Pearl Harbor disaster" and after the war "came out strongly for unification and establishment of a separate Air Force" as a "step toward insuring our future safety and preserving world peace."[38]

1947—Birthing the U.S. Air Force

The National Security Act of September 18, 1947, and the accompanying Executive Order 9877 established the new U.S. Air Force. This came about, in part, by the unprecedented power demonstrated by U.S. air forces during World War II as well as the strong airpower advocacy of General Arnold,

General Eisenhower and President Truman. It might be presumed that this brought to an end the forty-year struggle for military air service independence—but, in fact, it did not, and the final two years before establishment of the Air Force as an independent service proved to be the most contentious. In particular, the senior civilian and uniformed leadership of U.S. Navy persistently disagreed. They were determined to continue their fight to keep the Army Air Force as part of the Army, keep the Navy and Marines in charge of their own air services and maintain the Navy's direct access to the president, a privilege they had enjoyed for a dozen years with Franklin Roosevelt because of his fond attachment to the service. Truman, an Army artillery officer in the First World War, did not share the same warm feeling, complaining at one point that when he became president, the White House had seemed like a vast wardroom aboard a ship. However, the Navy saw an opening because the documents were written in general terms, allowing some degree of interpretation with unclear definitions of service roles and missions. Against continued strong resistance by the Navy, Secretary of the Air Force W. Stuart Symington and General Spaatz, chief of staff of the Air Force, faced a challenging task to gain full and equal inter-service status.

The first priority was to change the AAF organization from an Army support unit to a standalone air force with separate personnel system, base facilities, logistics support, etc. Competition for funds was severe in the environment resulting from the dramatic postwar demobilization and greatly reduced defense budgets. The long-standing issue of the military services' roles and missions were still not resolved. At the same time, the Air Force's strategic nuclear bombing mission was the main national defense against the expanding Cold War with the USSR despite a limited number of atomic bombs and B-29s configured to deliver them.

General Spaatz, the new CSAF, was the epitome of a senior Air Force officer with time-

General Hoyt S. Vandenberg (USMA 1923), CSAF during Berlin Airlift, Korean War and technology growth (U.S. Air Force photo).

honored credentials: he had shot down three German airplanes in World War I; he was the first to demonstrate in-flight air refueling; he commanded long-range strategic air forces in Europe and then in the Pacific; and he supervised the first atomic bomb attacks. However, Spaatz agreed with General Arnold that a new Air Force needed new, younger leaders who would focus on the future and not past accomplishments. Therefore, in less than a year, General Spaatz, who was ready to retire, was faced with the delicate task of picking a younger, highly qualified successor. He considered Generals Joseph T. McNarney (USMA 1915) and the younger candidate Hoyt S. Vandenberg (USMA 1923) to be the best candidates for the role. It was Vandenberg's broad experience, demonstrated combat leadership, political acumen, and diplomatic skills that gave him the edge. Marshall, Eisenhower, Arnold, Symington, Forrestal and Truman readily agreed to Spaatz's recommendation.

Vandenberg was sworn in as CSAF on April 30, 1948. He faced a daunting series of challenges: political controversy; inter-service rivalry, the unforeseen Berlin airlift and Korean War, and major ongoing R&D efforts for radically new aircraft as well as launching what became a national crash-program to develop "robot" cruise missiles and intercontinental ballistic missiles (ICBMs). A 1949 amendment to the National Security Act changed the national military establishment to the Department of Defense (DOD), making it a Cabinet-level organization with the three military services as departments with DOD having "direction, authority and control" over the three military departments. At the time, President Truman stated: "we finally succeeded in getting a unification act to have unification."[39] This legislation firmly centralized the U.S. military bureaucracy with the Air Force being not only independent, but also, since it was responsible for the strategic nuclear mission, a major player in national defense. The stage now was set for West Point's graduating classes of the late 1940s and 1950s to exert their influence on the USAF.

Chapter 3

The Class of 1950

On July 1, 1946, a mixed group of nearly a thousand eager, talented young men arrived at West Point to begin the first tortuous phase of cadet training: "Beast Barrack." A few of the lucky ones joined the group but reported about a month later. Some were barely 17 years old while some were as "old" as 21. Over a quarter had prior military experience. A few were combat veterans and some were officers with battlefield promotions; others had received Officer Candidate School (OCS) commissions. But regardless of the background, they all got the same treatment: "drop that bag, stand tall, chin in, chest out, roll that butt under, dumb smack!!!" Many in the group were shocked at the treatment they were receiving and were asking themselves, *What have I gotten myself into and do I want to be here?* Others just took it in stride. A few like Joe McCrane, 21, who had received five battle stars as a Marine rifleman in the Pacific war up through the battle for Okinawa thought that three square meals a day, a good bed at night and playing football with a national championship team was a pretty good deal. Most of the cadets with previous service under their belt leaned toward Joe's attitude. But no matter the background and personal feelings, the Class of 1950 was underway!

Each member of the entering class had led a successful life prior to entering West Point—best in high school academics or best in high school sports, and some had military service with outstanding records. Of course, all had earned a competitive appointment to the Military Academy. But the stakes were raised at West Point with this talented group. All of us were treated to an intense, four-year indoctrination in how to "do better" and adhere to the Academy motto: "Duty, Honor, Country." Competition—whether academic, athletic, or military—was the name of the game. The next four years would challenge and change all of us such that only 670 of those plebes would survive the four years and graduate.

Class of 1950 Memories Project

In anticipation of the celebration of the upcoming 50th anniversary of the West Point Class of 1950 that took place in May 2000, our classmate and class historian Joseph P. Buccolo issued an invitation to each living member of the class to respond to either or both of the following questions:

1. What was my most memorable experience at the U.S. Military Academy?
2. How [has] the influence of the total "Academy Experience" impacted my life?

Joe compiled a collection of responses entitled "Memories of West Point and its Impact on the Class of 1950" (*Memories Project*).[1] As Joe stated in his introductory letter, "It remains a goal that each member of the Class of 1950 leaves a legacy of memories and thoughts of their experiences at West Point and of their life's experiences."

Encouraged by the initial response, other classmates submitted responses over the ensuing years such that by 2005 the compilation had grown to four thick volumes. With no restrictions on the nature or length of their narratives, our classmates provided a rich tapestry of memories not only from their days at West Point but from their Army and Air Force careers that followed. Joe provided us this wonderful collection of memories to help bring to life the story of West Pointers but particularly members of the Class of 1950 who entered the Air Force and their impact on the Air Force.

Joe should be congratulated for his fine work on our class history. Since these memories probably have not changed over the past 15 to 20 years, many of them have been included here, with many quoted directly. Of course, after graduation came the unexpected Korean War, the first of three wars with which we contended during our military careers.

Distinguished Graduates

Our research into West Point grads' contributions to the Air Force produced considerable documented and intriguing history. However, we had more access to information, and a lifetime of personal experience with my own class and will therefore focus on what we considered to be their most notable and interesting moments. The *Memories Project* was a great resource and from there the West Point Association of Graduates with their distinguished graduates (DG) awards showed us where to start. The award is given to USMA graduates "whose character, distinguished service, and stature draw wholesome comparison to the qualities for which West Point strives, in keeping with its motto: 'Duty, Honor, Country.'"

It's interesting to note that the Class of '50 was the only class in West Point history to have seven four-star generals on active duty in its ranks (four in the Army, two in the Air Force and one in the Philippine Army—Fidel Ramos, who later became President of the Philippines). This was the only class to have three classmates serving concurrently as chief of staff of their respective services, the Army, the Air Force and the Philippines Army. The Class of '50 also was the first one to have eight distinguished graduates: Bill DeGraf, Fidel Ramos, Frank Borman, Charlie Gabriel, Dave Hughes, John Wickham, Dick Trefry and Wally Nutting.

Frank Borman

As one of the most recognized members of our class and a recipient of West Point's distinguished graduate award and the Congressional Space Medal of Honor, we turn to astronaut Frank Borman. Frank orbited the earth and, as commander of Apollo 8, circled the moon, making him, along with crewmates Jim Lovell and Bill Anders, the first of only 24 humans to do so. (Incidentally, of these 24 astronauts, five were West Pointers—Frank Borman, Mike Collins, Buzz Aldrin, David Scott and Alfred Worden.) Frank made the following contribution to the *Memories Project* regarding the impact that cadet life had on him:

> The concept of mission or duty. I learned and tried to carry out through my career the importance of subordinating one's desires to the successful completion of the overall mission—and [my] intense desire to succeed in the mission.
>
> The importance of being truthful and honorable in one's life and expecting the same in one's superiors and subordinates.

Frank has always been a no-nonsense, thorough, and decisive officer and a dedicated family man. We were classmates at Air Force flight training and flew together as test pilots at the Air Force Flight Test Center. He is an excellent lifetime pilot and still is active as a pilot at ninety-two years young, flying his own single engine prop airplane. Of course, he still passes his annual FAA flight physical!

Charlie Gabriel

Charlie Gabriel was a great guy with a small town, "country boy makes good" life story. Like Frank Borman, as a young boy he wanted to fly and both he and Frank certainly succeeded. They also were both fine high school football players, but Charlie went on in his sophomore year at Catawba College to be a star and lead the nation that year in total offense, running and passing. His athletic ability caught the eye of many college scouts including Herman Hickman, the fine Shakespeare-quoting assistant coach at West Point who had previously recruited Doc Blanchard, one of the greatest running backs ever at West Point. The Catawba coach was furious and even complained to President Truman about West Point's theft of his best player, but to no avail. Charlie wanted to play at West Point, so he became a relatively famous plebe with the chance to be a pilot. Unfortunately, an injury took away Charlie's edge as a football player, but he continued playing football as a fine halfback on the 1949 undefeated team. As a pilot he flew in the Korean War, first flying ground support missions in the F-51 and then finishing his combat tour in the F-86 with two MiG kills. In Vietnam he was an RF-4 wing commander and flew 152 combat missions. After tours of duty at Tactical Air Command (TAC) HQ, deputy commander of U.S. Forces in Korea and commander of USAF Forces in Europe he returned to the Pentagon for the fourth time to become the chief of staff of the Air Force (CSAF). Charlie was the first career fighter pilot to become CSAF.

General Gabriel was well known for his emphasis on taking care of people to ensure that an Air Force career provided an outstanding way of life. He also made an interesting point that "our personnel experts say that about

North American F-86A Sabre. It was the most produced Western jet fighter with 9,860 produced of all variants. The first U.S. swept-wing fighter. Very successful against MIG-15s in Korea (U.S. Air Force photo).

A USAF McDonnell Douglas F-4D Phantom over North Vietnam in 1972. A twin-engine, long-range, supersonic jet interceptor and fighter bomber used extensively in Vietnam by the USAF, Navy and Marines, there were 5,195 produced (U.S. Air Force photo).

70% of Air Force members make a career decision [to stay in or get out] based on the feelings of their spouse." Mrs. Dorothy Gabriel and Charlie both advanced this objective of "people first" with the total force including the Air National Guard and the Air Force Reserves.

Two classmates from 1950, Generals Wickham and Gabriel, both chiefs of staff of their respective services, recognized and acted upon the unique opportunity they had to improve upon the cooperation between and capability of Air Force support of Army ground forces. They commissioned a series of initiatives—31 to be exact—to enhance the effectiveness of joint combat forces and battlefield cooperation which was described in a detailed monogram published in 1987 titled *The 31 Initiatives: A Study in Air Force—Army Cooperation*, authored by the chief historian of the Air Force, Richard G. Davis. This book chronicles the close working relationship between these two West Point classmates and their separate services to improve our overall military capability. Following release of *The 31 Initiatives*, the two chiefs of staff institutionalized this bi-service innovation and cooperation process by establishing the Joint Assessment and Initiatives Office (JAIO) in the Pentagon.

Bill DeGraf

Classmate Bill DeGraf, with a battlefield commission prior to entering West Point and having earned many honors at West Point including being first academically in our class, regimental captain and first in service to our class over the years, provided a thoughtful summary in the *Memories Project* of what West Point did for him: "In the Army life that followed West Point training in honor, responsibility, mission accomplishment, logical thought and leadership, coupled with the friendships developed as a cadet, stood me in great stead in the various positions I held from platoon leader (in Korean war combat) to NSC staffer in the White House (under Henry Kissinger)." As our classmate, Lou Genuario has written, "Bill loves West Point and its traditions and has dedicate his life to its service. We as a class and as individuals, are the beneficiaries of that service."

After his career in the Army, Bill went on to work on military matters as assistant vice president at Science Applications International Corporation (SAIC) until 1987. Bill joined our many classmates in Korea and later went to the war in Vietnam as a brigade commander, earning a rare third Combat Infantryman Badge. As Genurario wrote, Bill has led our class activities over the years. More than thirty-five years and counting as class scribe and strong supporter of class reunions.

Incidentally, as reported by Lou, when Bill was a plebe he provided the best showstopper to a question from an upper classman. Rather than the mandatory "Yes sir, no sir, no excuse sir" response, Bill's exchange went: "Have you had any previous military experience, Mr. DeGraf? Yes sir! Where and when, Mr. DeGraf? Sir, I received my first commission on the battlefields of Europe in January 1945! [Long pause] 'Post, dumb smack!'"

Two DGs with whom I was personally involved were General Wally Nutting (USMA 1950), a classmate at the Navy War College Command and Staff course and a lifelong family friend and Lt. General Richard Trefry (USMA 1950). General Nutting served combat tours in Korea and Vietnam and completed his distinguished military career with command of the Southern Command and then Readiness Command. General Trefry served in Korea and Vietnam and for six years was the Army inspector general. After retiring in 1983 he co-founded Military Personnel Resources, Inc. and served as military assistant to President George H. W. Bush and director of the White House Military Office. In 2009, the Secretary of the Army presented Trefry with the first Lt. General Richard G. Trefry Lifetime Service Award for his service in the Army and his accomplishments as a civilian.

Coincidently, two of these DGs managed sports teams on which I played: Frank Borman on the football team and Dick Trefry on the hockey team.

Two members of the Class of '50 played important roles within the

Strategic Air Command. In 1981, General Bennie L. Davis (USMA 1950) then commander of Air Training Command (ATC) and Lt. General Lloyd R. "Dick" Leavitt (USMA 1950), vice commander of SAC, were in the running to be commander-in-chief of SAC (CINCSAC) upon the retirement of General Richard Ellis. Both were very well qualified for the job. However, during the job interview with the secretary of Air Force (SecAF), Leavitt questioned why the Air Force was pursuing the acquisition of the B-1B when the new stealth B-2 would also be available, albeit not as quickly the B-1B which had previously been tested in its former B-1A version but then cancelled by the previous Carter administration. However, because of the B-1B's readiness and in the interest of political expediency, President Ronald Reagan wanted "a new bomber on the ramp when he runs for reelection in 1984."[2] Leavitt later acknowledged in his biography that he "had never dealt with political decision making and was shocked, disappointed and a little angered by this explanation,"[3] as to why he could not support the B-1 over the B-2. In short, Leavitt had questioned the wisdom of a key Air Force acquisition priority. In part as a result of this interchange, Davis became CINCSAC and Leavitt soon after retired. This is yet another example of the possible consequences of "telling truth to power" as characterized by another West Point grad, General Robin Olds, based on his discussions with President Lyndon B. Johnson.

Rockwell B-1B Lancer. There were 100 produced. Supersonic, variable, swept wing strategic bomber later shifted to a multi-mission bomber (U.S. Air Force photo).

Northrop Grumman B-2 Spirit. Twenty-one of them were produced. Long-range, stealthy, flying wing strategic bomber (U.S. Air Force photo).

John H. Vanston (USMA 1950) has a unique position in our class in that he is the only classmate to the best of my knowledge to have firsthand experience in close proximity to an atomic blast. As a captain, he was placed in charge of 250 officers at a nuclear bomb test in Nevada and wrote an article about his experience, excerpts which follow:

The year was 1955, and the U.S. Army had embarked on a program of developing relatively small tactical nuclear weapons that could be used on the battlefield. A series of atmospheric tests in Nevada had convinced military scientists that properly trained soldiers could not only survive such explosions but also take part in maneuvers planned to exploit these weapons.

These hypotheses, however, had never been tested, and the atomic bomb had taken on very frightening connotations. So to demonstrate that the weapons were "safe," the Army decided to run a test with live soldiers. The purpose of the test was to teach troops that the bomb was just another weapon of war. As the time for the explosion approached, we all crouched in the bottom of the trenches with our arms over our eyes. We shivered slightly in our field jackets; the desert is cold at six o'clock in the morning. Finally the countdown started—sixty seconds, thirty seconds, twenty, ten, five, four, three, two, one—and then came a flash of unbelievable intensity. In the brilliant light I saw through my jacket—and through my arm—the pebbles at the bottom of the trench. (For many years I thought this must have been some type of optical illusion. However, I have recently learned that this is a real phenomenon, apparently caused by X rays induced by the explosion.) Contrary to my expectations, the flash lasted for a considerable time, more than a second. As I was recovering from the flash, the temperature changed from morning cold to well above that of the hottest day I could remember.

Then, as I was reconciling myself to the blast of heat, the earth suddenly jumped what felt to be about six feet in the air and then fell back and began to tremble violently. The thought rushed through my mind: They've miscalculated and blown up the whole world. After what seemed a very long time, I finally had convinced myself of the world's probable survival when suddenly a tremendous freight train roared directly over my head. This lasted about a second, and then all was quiet—until a few seconds later, when the train roared back going the other way.

Now all was quiet. I lay quivering at the bottom of the trench, the counting of seconds long forgotten, when the announcement came that it was safe to stand up. By now several minutes had gone by since the initial explosion, and the fireball had spread considerably. Even so, it was a remarkable sight. About half an hour after the explosion, we were allowed to walk toward ground zero, stopping about two hundred yards from the actual spot. Along the way we saw an assortment of obliterated military vehicles, weapons, and dummies. The most impressive item was a heavy battle tank that had been split in two by the blast, with the turret blown one way and the main body the other.

Contemplating my experiences in the trench, I realized that I was no longer concerned about nuclear weapons. I was now *terrified* by them. Later in my military career I took part in many map exercises and maneuvers in which commanders simulated the use of nuclear weapons, often rather casually. I listened to a number of armchair war hawks, as well as some very prim and proper ladies, advocate that we drop a couple of nukes on Hanoi or Baghdad or Pyongyang to show those people we meant business. I feel confident their opinions would have been different if they had been in the trenches [with me] at Apple H.

My last assignment in the Army was with the Defense Atomic Test Command in Albuquerque, New Mexico, where I was the test-group director for two underground nuclear tests. After I retired in 1970,I got a PhD in nuclear engineering from the University of Texas, and taught it there for several years before leaving to start my own business.[4]

Many politicians and senior generals have been involved in planning for the deployment of nuclear weapons. However, John's experience offers a good lesson for anyone contemplating use of a nuclear weapon.

Another classmate deeply involved in the theory of nuclear war and command and control issues was Kenneth Moll (USMA 1950). Like most of us in the Air Force, we wanted to fly, and Ken flew F-80 combat missions in Korea and the F-86 on alert in the Air Defense Command. However, he made his mark as an advanced planning officer for command and control requirements on the SAC, USAF and JCS headquarters' staffs. The Cold War with the new devastating nuclear weapons and ever-shorter time between launch and distant targets required rapid reaction and response. Ken was involved in highly classified planning for the airborne command post and the worldwide military command and control system. Rapidly improving high-tech reconnaissance and communication systems made future planning a necessity. When Colonel Moll retired in 1975, he was chief of the Worldwide Command and Control Requirements Division of the JCS. He also was a prolific writer on military command and control issues. Much of what Ken contributed during his career laid the foundation for today's sophisticated command and control systems and operations.

Korean War Experiences

As detailed in the *Memories Project*, "the Korean War came as a surprise to many people. It was a surprise to the United States Government and the United States Army, and it was a big surprise to the 670 newly graduated cadets who had on 6 June 1950 received their diplomas and commissions as second lieutenants after four years of hard work at West Point. When these new officers graduated, the world was at peace." Then, on June 25, 1950, North Korea launched its invasion of South Korea. Just five days later, on June 30, President Truman authorized use of American ground forces to defend South Korea. When these newly commissioned lieutenants reported for duty and their units were called up for the war, they immediately deployed to Korea. "The new second lieutenants went into battle with lots of enthusiasm and courage but little practical knowledge, for as a result of a decision to save a few dollars, the Class of 1950 went to their initial assignments without being sent to their branch basic officer courses. Forty-one members of the Class of 1950 died while serving in the Korean War, and another 84 were wounded. A total of 365 members of the class served in Korea from 1950 to 1953."

From his entry in the *Memories Project*, John Watson, Jr. (USMA 1950) described his experience in Korea, writing that that he was sent to Korea 15 days after the war began and his unit was soon after overrun by overwhelming numbers of Chinese communist troops and he was taken prisoner in North Korea for nearly three years. He reported that he survived during terrible times while seeing 38 percent of his fellow POWs die. At one point in his captivity, John came very close to death from beriberi and starvation. He stated that 7,140 servicemen were captured in the Korean War. Of these, 2,701 died in captivity. The memories that stick in his mind are the deaths from starvation and disease and the long death march and bombing by the U.S. Air Force. After he retired from the Air Force, he became an ordained deacon in the Catholic church.

John provided his thoughts on the cadet experience: "The West Point experience was a growing, on-going formative process which has continued throughout my life. West Point is rich in tradition, history and ideals which has shaped, guided, molded, and formed my actions, attitudes and outlook on life. I consider it an honor and privilege to have been selected to be associated with such an outstanding few who have served West Point and our country so well."

It's important to note that several cadets who did not receive the highest aptitude ratings as cadets went on to distinguished careers, some receiving the highest possible military honors. With great determination they developed into heroic combat leaders.

Michael DeArmond (USMA 1950), who also endured time as a POW in North Korea, wrote:

> As with most graduates, my four years at West Point influenced my life and character in a significant fashion. Besides an excellent education, military discipline, and my cavalier attitude towards it, were key factors in my development. As the only First-class private, king of the Area, receiver of a demerit load that left little margin for further transgressions, and a six-month room confined, I developed a fortitude and self-sufficiency that stood me well in later life. While deserving of retribution, preclusion from corps squad athletics rankled. [Michael was a member of the soccer, swim and track teams.] After being shot down over the Yalu River and captured by North Koreans, I quickly drew on the stoicism developed in me at the Point. I often relied in the fortitude and ingrained self-sufficiency to counter the despondency and survival uncertainty associated with 17 months in either solitary confinement or a 4'×6' isolation cell with one other POW. The reason being refusal to sign a germ warfare confession or, as the Chinese interrogator said, "something is twisted in your brain." While my objective at the Academy was to "stay in" and graduate, my objective as a POW was to survive and "get out." The fortitude and tenacity developed at West Point motivated two unsuccessful escape attempts, one from an isolation cell where a British Captain had been shot and killed attempting to escape a short time earlier.
>
> In summary, I believe that West Point's investment to make me a professional soldier was, as with most of my classmates, adequately returned. My most lasting and cherished memories from West Point are those of my classmates, living and dead, who served their country well.

Another example is my classmate in A-1 Company, Charlie Butler (USMA 1950), who later demonstrated extraordinary military valor in combat. Charlie risked his life in combat with enemy forces both in Korea and later in Vietnam, receiving the Distinguished Service Cross in Korea and the Silver Star in Vietnam where he was killed in action while serving as an infantry lieutenant colonel.

Another cadet from A-1 company and a football player, Samuel S. Coursen (USMA 1949), was awarded the Medal of Honor for extreme bravery in combat in the Korean War. As written in the Medal of Honor citation:

1st Lt. Coursen distinguished himself by conspicuous gallantry and intrepidity above and beyond the call of duty in action. While Company C was attacking Hill 174 under heavy enemy small-arms fire, his platoon received enemy fire from close range. The platoon returned the fire and continued to advance. During this phase 1 his men moved into a well-camouflaged emplacement, which was thought to be unoccupied, and was wounded by the enemy who were hidden within the emplacement. Seeing the soldier in difficulty he rushed to the man's aid and, without regard for his personal safety, engaged the enemy in hand-to-hand combat in an effort to protect his wounded comrade until he himself was killed. When his body was recovered after the battle 7 enemy dead were found in the emplacement. As the result of 1st Lt. Coursen's violent struggle several of the enemies' heads had been crushed with his rifle. His aggressive and intrepid actions saved the life of the wounded man, eliminated the main position of the enemy roadblock, and greatly inspired the men in his command. 1st Lt. Coursen's extraordinary heroism and intrepidity reflect the highest credit on himself and are in keeping with the honored traditions of the military service.[5]

I am forever inspired by the struggle, character, and courage under extreme duress that these classmates displayed. I also should note that a number of other West Point graduates serving in the Air Force received the Medal of Honor: Colonel Leon W. Johnson (USMA 1926), Brigadier General Frederick W. Castle (USMA 1930), Lt. Colonel Leon R. Vance (USMA 1939), and William A. Jones (USMA 1945).

Another example of courage under fire is General Robert C. Mathis, USAF (USMA 1948), a distinguished graduate who, as a lieutenant, was a temporary forward air controller with the Army during the Korean War. He was on a ridge line about 200 yards in front of the well dug-in friendly forces when during the night his position was overrun by a wave of Chinese forces. He was wounded but managed to escape while one of his enlisted men was wounded, another was killed, and the lieutenant with him was taken prisoner for three years.[6]

Classmate Paul Zavitz (USMA 1950) has one of the unique career progressions of any of his 167 classmates who entered the Air Force. He was commissioned in 1950 in the Army, served in Korea as an infantry lieutenant, resigned from the Army in 1953 and immediately joined the Air Force as a first lieutenant, thereby becoming the 168th Air Force member of our class. He served a full Air Force career as a pilot and retired as a colonel with a full career as an Air Force pilot and then a civilian pilot.

Classmate John Streit contributed a thought-provoking description of his experience as a POW in Korea for over twenty months after being shot down by ground fire in his F-51:

It might be instructive here to provide an overview of the POW environment as it had evolved and as existed at this time—early 1952. In the early months of the war, from June to September 1950, the North Koreans provided the facilities and administered the POW camps, such as they were. Numerous atrocities, summary executions and extreme brutality were not uncommon and many POWs died or were killed. After the Inchon landings in September and the retreat by North Korean forces deep into North Korea in the fall of 1950, Chinese Communist forces intervened on a massive scale, drove back down into South Korea and essentially took control of the war including the handling of the POWs.

Treatment did not noticeably improve under Chinese administration, plus they made concerted efforts to persuade POWs to support the Communist side. They also attempted to break down the military command structure within POW groups. For the remaining part of 1950 and most of 1951, treatment continued to be harsh, even brutal, with little food, clothing or medical treatment. Not surprisingly, many POWs, including our two classmates, died during this period, suffering from malnutrition and the various diseases which accompany it, especially dysentery, pneumonia, and beriberi.

By the end of 1951, however, conditions in the POW camps had improved somewhat, due primarily to the fact that Armistice talks, which convened in July 1951, had made progress. In fact, by December 1951 (before I was shot down), agreement had been reached on all points of the proposed Armistice Agreement except for the issue of the release of POWs. The Communist side insisted that every POW be returned to his own country. The UN side, having captured thousands of Chinese and North Koreans who wanted no part of their former homelands, insisted that the POWs be given a choice.

This issue was not resolved until well over a year later, in 1953, following General Eisenhower's election and inauguration as President of the United States. He sent a not too subtle signal of a likely major escalation of the UN war effort if final agreement was not reached without undue delay. Although there were some difficulties, agreement was finally completed on July 27, 1953. Hostilities ceased and the POW exchange subsequently took place on UN terms with those POWs who chose not to return allowed to stay with their captors. Over 20,000 Chinese and North Koreans chose to stay either in Taiwan or South Korea and there were a few UN POWs who stayed with the Communists, including 23 Americans.

During the 613 days that I was a POW, from 1 January 1952 until 6 September 1953, conditions were harsh, but had improved enough that they were seldom life threatening.

Years later at the National War College, Dick Leavitt told this story about how the Korean War *really* ended:

Dulles [John Foster Dulles, Secretary of State] later disclosed that he warned the Chinese–North Korean legation that America would use nuclear weapons if the war continued. The Panmunjon meeting resulted in an armistice, prisoners were exchanged, and the fighting ceased. In 1967, while I was a student at the National War College, Ex-President Eisenhower spoke to our class. One student asked Eisenhower whether he would have authorized the use of nuclear weapons to end the war, as Dulles implied. Eisenhower's answer was both presidential and enigmatic: "I didn't have to answer that question then … and I don't have to answer now!"

Statistical Summary of the Class of 1950

One quarter of the class of 1950 were young veterans of World War II who served in ranks from private to major. Such maturity in an incoming class is as Joe Buccolo said in his *Memories Project* entry "is to be without parallel."[7] The class went from World War II to another full-blown war in Korea shortly after graduation followed by the decades-long Cold War and then the war in Vietnam.

During the Korean War, nine classmates from the Class of 1950 withstood the traumatic POW ordeal with two of our Army classmates dying while captive. Four of the nine POWs were Air Force pilots as a result of the pilot and aircrew exposure to enemy fire while flying forward of friendly lines. This included John Streit in an F-51, Joe Green in an F-84, Ernest Dunning in an F-80, all brought down by ground fire, and Michael DeArmond shot down in his F-86 by a MiG-15. Pilots had received more than a year's worth of training prior to operational flying so they were late to the fight. The Korean War broke out only 18 days after graduation and 141 members of the class, mainly Army officers, went directly to combat units. In total, 365 members of the class saw combat in Korea with 41 killed in action and 84 wounded. This was one of the highest numbers of casualties and casualty rates of any West Point class during this century in the three-year period following graduation.

A total of 112 members of the 168 graduates who entered the Air Force became pilots. Seven of these pilots were killed in action in Korea as lieutenants: Thurston R. Baxter (1951, flying an F-51), Medon A. Bitzer (1952, flying an F-51), George B. Eichelberger, Jr. (1952, flying an F-51), Harry E. Rushing (1952, flying an F-51), John M. McAlpine (1952, flying an F-51), William B. Slade (1952, flying an F-80), and Gene A. Dennis (1952, flying an F-84). Two more, both lieutenant colonels, were killed in action in Vietnam: Carl B. Mitchell (1964, flying a B-26) and Bobby G. Vinson (1968, flying an F-4).

Fourteen others were lost in aircraft accidents: James W. Smyly III (1951, flying a T-6), Henry E. Tisdale, Jr. (1951 flying an F-80), John M. Garrett, Jr. (1951, flying an F-84), Elliot R. Knott (1951, flying an F-80), Russell E. Leggett (1951, flying a B-45), John A. Dille, Jr. (1952, flying an F-80), Thomas F. Casserly (1952, flying an F-86), Robert A. Williams (1952, flying an F-84), Anderson O. Hubbard (1952, flying a B-26), Lewis A. Page, Jr. (1953 flying a T-33), William S. Todd, Jr. (1955, flying a B-57), Eugene C. Etz (1955, flying a T-33), Robert D. Willerford (1956, flying a T-33) and George F. Vlisides (1965, flying an A-1E), recipient of the Distinguished Service Cross (DSC).[8]

General Charles Gabriel, chief of staff of the USAF and General Bennie Davis, commander of SAC, and 18 others of the 168 entering the Air Force advanced to the ranks of general officers. There were 43 colonels and 47 lieutenant colonels in this group of career Air Force officers totaling 110 or 65 percent of the 168 who served on active duty, serving from 20 to 36 years in the Air Force.

The last officer from the Class of 1950 to retire from active service was Major General William F. Ward. He was a combat veteran who was wounded in Korea and, in the Gulf War, served as commander of the Army Reserves supporting the war. He retired in 1991, 41 years after graduating from West Point.

West Point Athletics

The purpose of West Point's athletic program was firmly established by General Douglas MacArthur when he was West Point's superintendent from 1919 to 1922. General MacArthur mandated that all cadets receive expert athletic instruction leading to competition at the intermural and intercollegiate levels. "He wanted every cadet to be an athlete."[9]

As carved in granite at the south gymnasium, General MacArthur's belief was "upon the fields of friendly strife are sown the seeds that upon other fields, another day, will bear the fruits of victory." He had a preference for competitive college football and in 1959 when the National Football Foundation awarded him their gold medal for contributions to the college game over the years he said, "football has become a symbol of courage, stamina, and coordinated efficiency. In war and peace, I have football men to be my greatest reliance."[10]

My football experience during four years of football under Coach Earl Blaik (USMA 1920) and his meticulously selected coaching staff was a defining aspect of my cadet life, as I believe it was for many others. It was serious competition among the best football players in the country. As Bennie Davis wrote in his *Memories Project* submission:

> The first fundamental principle that I learned and which has served me well through my career is that "my word is my bond."
>
> The second major experience at West Point was my association with one of the greatest men I have ever known, Colonel Earl "Red" Blaik, my football coach. Col. Blaik taught us that less than our best performance should not be acceptable to us. That to be successful in any of life's endeavors you must be willing to make sacrifice—that you must be willing "To Pay the Price" to succeed—and at times that price is very high. Learning and practicing that principle has been a major force in my life.

Coach Blaik demanded discipline, attention to every detail of the game and its thorough execution. He consistently emphasized the need for complete preparation in order to win. He relished tough competition and fully understood the hard work and intensity required to win. The team record over our four years (31 wins, two losses, and four ties) tells the story.

My four-year roommate, Bill Henn, who came to West Point as a strong, but young, 17-year-old football player, steadily improved as a tackle under the coaching of Vince Lombardi and Blaik. At the end of his four years at West Point, he had become an excellent tackle. Coach Lombardi is reported to have said that with another year he would have been an outstanding player. Another fine football tackle, Phil Feir (USMA 1949), led a distinguished military career and later became West Point's commandant of cadets.

Yet another example of grit and determination learned on the football field was that of Matthew T. Henrickson. As Matt said in his *Memories Project* entry, although his smaller size (172 pounds) kept him from being one of "Blaik's Boys," his interest in attending West Point was primarily to play football. His four years of football were highlighted by having to play, as a member of the B-Squad, the national champions four days a week. Yet to enjoy playing the sport, he was being punished physically. He eventually became an A-Squad team member. It's worth noting that the A-Squad was the number one football team in the country in 1946 and the B-Squad ranked among the Top 20. As Matt said, these lessons learned on the football field influenced his behavior for the next 46 years. He served as a navigator in three combat commands and flew missions in Korea and Vietnam.

It is worth noting the effect that the gridiron experience, and the coaching of the country's finest football coaches had upon the future career success of those cadets who played on West Point's 1946–49 football teams. The following table is a snapshot of the record of the Class of 1950 football lettermen:

Class of 1950 Football Letterman Record (26 + manager)

Record

- Undefeated three years out of four, 1946–49
- Lambert Trophy in 1948 and 1949
- Beat Navy three out of four years, with a tie in 1948, won 38–0 in 1949
- Combined won-lost record of 31 wins, two losses, and four ties during 1946–1949

Captains of Corps of Cadets—5 (Borman, Dielens, Kuyk, Shelley, Yeoman)

"A Squad" Team Captains—5 (Galiffa, Irons, Kuyk, Trent, Yeoman)

Career officers

- 30+ years—6
- 20+ years—12

- General officers: 6
  - General Charles Gabriel—Chief of Staff, Air Force
  - General Bennie Davis—CincSAC
  - Lt. General Robert Lunn—Vice Cmdr. Army Material Command
  - Lt. General Jack Mackmull—Cmdr. XVIII ABN Corps.
  - Lt. General Skip Scott—Supt. Air Force Academy
  - Major General Charles Kuyk—Cmdr. 22nd Air Force MAC
  - Colonels—11

Combat Losses
- Killed in Korea
  - Bill Kellim
  - John Trent
- Killed in Vietnam
  - Bob Vinson
- Distinguished Graduates—2
  - Colonel Borman
  - General Gabriel
- Commander—First crew to circle the moon
  - Colonel Borman—awarded Congressional Space Medal of Honor

Numerous Awards for valor and exceptional service

I am a firm believer in the value of competitive sports. (My last competitive athletic event was in an eight-mile open water sculling race on Puget Sound when 75 years young.) History shows that a great sports team requires a great coach. In addition to Coach Blaik, West Point's track coach, Leo Novak, and lacrosse coach, Morris Touchstone, fully qualify as great coaches.[11]

Another classmate/competitor with whom I roomed at West Point as a plebe is Brigadier General Ted Crichton who wrote in the *Memories Project* that his most memorable experience as a cadet was having Coach Novak teach him that you need to have a "fire within" in order to win in competition.[12] Ted went on to write that "something else I am sure stands out as well with other classmates is that something that the Academy taught all of us was the importance of honesty and integrity in everything we do. 'Honesty, integrity, and winning comes together, of course, in combat.'" Ted had been an Air Force enlisted aircraft mechanic prior to West Point and graduated to be a pilot in the first jet bomber, the B-45, and test engineer during the B-58's development. He commanded airlift organizations up through wing and division level and flew 100 C-130 combat missions in Vietnam. After receiving a Master of Science in Engineering degree he served as an R&D officer on the

Air Staff and in the Air Force Systems Command (AFSC) at Electronic Systems Division (ESD).

During our four years as cadets, Coach Touchstone received many accolades and produced talented players who became fine leaders as officers. General Wally Nutting was one of them. General James Hartinger (USMA 1949) was co-captain of the 1949 lacrosse team and became an All-American lacrosse player. He went on to become the first commander of the Space Command and NORAD.

Class Reunions

The Class of '50 has retained its identity and friendships over the years with the help of many reunions. The purpose of each gathering, small or large, has always been to be with old friends who share much of the same history—tales to tell, memories of the past and to honor those departed. The largest gatherings are well-planned and organized events every five years at West Point with all its history and memories of cadet life. Many classmates, veterans of the Korean War, journeyed to Korea many years later for the unveiling of a memorial honoring our 41 fallen classmates. It was a sad but worthwhile reunion with our South Korean comrades in arms.

A happier reunion was in Colorado Springs at the Air Force Academy in 1986 to see what the long gray line of West Point grads had produced. This was an enjoyable, enlightening reunion of more than 350 classmates and their wives, elegantly led by our classmate Lt. General "Skip" Scott (USMA 1950), then the USAFA superintendent, and his wife, Sally. Skip gave us a detailed briefing on the academy followed with tours of the facilities, cadet rooms and activities, even glider flights. He finished the event with a grand party at the superintendent's house. While the two academies often compete on the playing fields, for us there was considerable pride from our involvement in the creation and development of this new military academy.

Perhaps not the first but definitely the most explosive reunion occurred during the opening year of the Korean War when classmate General Volney Warner, then a lieutenant, was leading his unit down the Korean peninsula in retreat from a fast-advancing Chinese force. There was one last bridge to cross before reaching U.S. lines and Lieutenant "Will" Henn was in position and assigned to blow up the bridge. After a rapid greeting and with the last U.S. soldier off the bridge, a thundering explosion celebrated the reunion and stopped the enemy's advance! This marked an unusual mini-reunion and one of the few not orchestrated by classmate Bill DeGraf. Incidentally, Will claimed to have blown up many more bridges in Korea than he had built as an engineer!

Another memorable reunion was in 1996 when 78 members of the Class of 1950 returned to Korea at the invitation of the government of Korea and the Korean Veterans' Association, 50 years after being sworn in to the Army and 46 years after graduating from West Point. For six days these graduates, who served in Korea mostly as platoon leaders or pilots, their wives, a number of widows of classmates and some of their children "made a pilgrimage to the place where the Class of 1950 received its baptism of fire, made its firsts sacrifices, and started on a lifetime of selfless service to deter and defeat aggression during the Cold War."[13] In addition to visits to the Korean War Museum, Panmunjom (the village where the 1953 Korean Armistice Agreement was signed), Gyeongbok Palace and other sites, they dedicated a bronze memorial plaque at the Korea Military Academy honoring their fallen classmates.

As we'll see in the following chapters, graduates from the Class of 1950 continued to interface with one another throughout their careers whether they served in the Army or Air Force. This included experiences as young officers in Korea, later as more seasoned officers in Vietnam, then the Cold War and ultimately at the highest ranks of the Army and Air Force, culminating in the earlier-described collaboration between senior classmates who became chiefs of staff of the Army (General John A. Wickham, Jr.) and Air Force (General Charles A. Gabriel). No other class had the same bonding opportunity to forge Army–Air Force connections since the Air Force had just been created three years earlier in 1947 and the Air Force Academy would not graduate its first class until 1959.

Chapter 4

Cultural Transitions

It could be said that the years in which the West Point graduates from the classes of 1948 through 1958 served in the Air Force, particularly during the '60s and '70s, were among the most turbulent in America's history. Sweeping changes in our society involving the roles of African Americans, draft-age young men and the status of women in the workforce were transforming not only the armed services but our society as a whole. Further unsettling the nation were an increasingly unpopular war in Vietnam and the ever-present specter of the Cold War's nuclear balance of terror hanging over the land. In reaction to all of this, and perhaps not surprisingly, thousands of Americans of all political stripes and persuasions took to the streets and organized dozens of sometimes violent protests, most of which were part of the anti-war movement.

These protests were dramatically highlighted during the Watts riots in Los Angeles and at Kent State University in Ohio where four students were shot and killed by National Guardsmen. John F. Kennedy and Robert F. Kennedy were assassinated in 1963 and 1968, respectively, and Martin Luther King also was fatally shot in 1968. The landmark Civil Rights Act of 1964 and Voting Rights Act of 1965, when most of these West Point grads were lieutenant colonels or colonels, outlawed discrimination in schools, employment and public accommodations based on race, color, religion, sex, or national origin. The Civil Rights Act was preceded by just a year with the passage of the Equal Pay Act that prohibited wage differentials based on sex. Rather than a piece of legislation that regulated industry or commerce, the Civil Rights Act sought to regulate the behavior of the American people.

Implementation of these laws in the military and the regulations they spawned (such as those by the Equal Employment Opportunities Commission, EEOC) became the responsibility of military leaders to develop policies and procedures for their commands. Many of these senior leaders were West

Point grads. For example, six out of eight of the Air Force chiefs of staff during this period were West Point grads and many of the major commands were headed by West Pointers. Much of the enforcement of these regulations fell to the officers from the graduating classes of 1948–58 who at the time were largely colonels and brigadier generals. These issues are addressed here according to each of the major societal challenges arising during the period: (1) mandatory racial integration of the armed forces; (2) a shift from the military draft to an all-volunteer force; and (3) mandatory integration of women into the armed forces. Each of these changes was directed by an executive order from the president.

Racial Integration in the Air Force

The transition from racial *segregation* to racial *integration* within the military services was a very significant change impacting the early years of the Air Force. The military buildup for World War II brought increasing numbers of African Americans into the military, although few were officers, and most served in supporting roles. As General George Marshall, chief of staff of the Army said, "society dictated that it was absolutely necessary for the War Department to follow a policy of segregation."[1] Thus, "separate but equal" was the prevailing standard for the military in order to avoid any disharmony with the greater American society. Then, in 1940, President Franklin D. Roosevelt ordered the AAC to organize a new flying unit made up only of African Americans. This led to the creation of the 99th Pursuit Squadron. To train African American pilots and mechanics for the new squadron, the Air Corps opened a new training base in Alabama at the Tuskegee Institute. By the spring of 1941, the first 13 African American pilots supported by enlisted aircraft mechanics entered training.

In September 1941, West Point graduate Captain Benjamin O. Davis, Jr. (USMA 1936), the first African American to solo an aircraft in the AAC, became commander of the 99th Squadron. As a colonel, he later commanded the 332nd Fighter Group which included the 99th and three other squadrons. The unit became well known as the "Tuskegee Airmen." In April 1943, the 99th Squadron was deployed to North Africa to join the allies and was promptly followed by the rest of the 332nd Fighter Group. It flew its first combat mission on June 2, 1943, and a month later, on July 2, 1st Lt. Charles B. Hall shot down the first of 112 German airplanes eventually credited to the Tuskegee fliers.[2] Throughout World War II, African American pilots and airmen demonstrated that they could fight with the same bravery, tenacity, skill, and distinction as other fighter squadrons and thus set the stage for racial integration in the AAC.

With Davis as their combat leader, the 99th Squadron flew 1,491 missions totaling more than 150,000 sorties over North Africa, the Mediterranean, and Europe and escorted countless Allied bombers into enemy territory, flying Bell P-39 Airacobras, Curtiss P-40 Warhawks, and then, successively, Republic P-47 Thunderbolts and the North American P-51 Mustang. An assessment by Air Force historian Daniel Haulman found that during 179 bomber escort missions "the [332nd Fighter Group] lost significantly fewer bombers to enemy airplanes than other fighter groups in the Fifteenth Air Force."[3] On January 27–28, 1944, the 99th shot down thirteen German airplanes while protecting Allied invasion forces at Anzio, Italy. They destroyed more than 250 enemy aircraft in the air and another 150 on the ground; the most memorable mission was on March 24, 1945, when, while escorting B-17s bombing Berlin, three Tuskegee airmen each shot down a Messerschmitt Me 262 jet fighter. But the 355 Tuskegee fighter pilots who deployed overseas were just the tip of the iceberg; overall, counting support and maintenance personnel, and other aircrew assigned to bombers and other duties, there were at least 14,632 Tuskegee Airmen.[4] As combat leader, Davis was awarded the Silver Star, the Distinguished Service Cross and several air medals, and in October 1943, he assumed command of the 332nd Fighter Group. The group itself earned a Distinguished Unit Citation, and of its pilots, 95 earned Distinguished Flying Crosses (one receiving two). Eighty-one of the 355—approximately 23 percent—died in accidents or in combat, and 31—approximately 9 percent—were taken prisoner after having been shot down over enemy territory. In October 1945, the 332nd Fighter Group was deactivated.[5]

Then, on July 26, 1948, President Truman issued an executive order to all military services to racially integrate their ranks.

It is distressing to note that while at West Point, General Davis was shunned by his white classmates, none of whom spoke to him outside the line of duty. He never had a roommate. He ate by himself. It is likely that his classmates hoped this treatment would drive him out of the academy. But this "silent treatment" had the opposite effect—it made Davis even more determined to graduate. And in the process, he earned the respect of his classmates, as evidenced by the biographical note beneath his picture in the 1936 West Point yearbook, the *Howitzer*: "The courage, tenacity, and intelligence with which he conquered a problem incomparably more difficult than plebe year won for him the sincere admiration of his classmates, and his single-minded determination to continue in his chosen career cannot fail to inspire respect wherever fortune may lead him."[6]

Based on his experience at West Point and with the Tuskegee Airmen, General Davis fully understood the extent of the racial issue in the Air Force. As a colonel, he was assigned to help draft the Air Force's racial integration plan which, when put into action, resulted in the Air Force being recognized by many as the leading military service to racially integrate its ranks. In 1959, while serving in Germany, he was promoted to major general, the first African American to attain that rank in any of the military services. General Davis not only had a very successful career as a staff officer but after command at squadron and wing level, he was promoted to lieutenant general and became commander of the 13th Air Force at Clark Air Force Base in the Philippines.

General Davis was the first African American to attend the Air War College, command an integrated unit, be promoted to brigadier general in the Air Force (his father was the first African American brigadier general in the Army) and command a numbered Air Force. Twenty eight years after Davis's military retirement, Pres-

Lt. Gen. Benjamin O. Davis, Jr. (USMA 1936), commander of Tuskegee Airmen (U.S. Air Force photo).

ident Bill Clinton advanced him to the rank of general in 1998 saying, "General Davis is here today as living proof that a person can overcome adversity and discrimination, achieve great things, turn skeptics into believers and through example and perseverance can bring truly extraordinary change."[7] In recognition of his exemplary service, in 1995 he received the West Point AOG Distinguished Graduate Award.

In 2017, after a rigorous memorial naming selection process by the USMA, the Army, and the assistant secretary of the Army, a new cadet barracks at West Point was officially named the Benjamin O. Davis, Jr., Barracks (the "Davis Barracks"). Notably, the USMA command historian has written that in honoring General Davis, his selection "magnified the significant and relatively untold story of West Point's contribution to military aviation."[8] In this book we hope to help rectify this omission.

Another outstanding African American leader devoted to the Air Force's racial integration effort was General Daniel "Chappie" James, Jr., with whom I worked when he was vice commander of the Military Airlift Command (MAC). I considered it a real honor to work with such a fine officer and leader.

The Tuskegee Airmen were the first African American military aviators, 1941–48 (U.S. Air Force photo).

General James graduated from the Tuskegee Institute in 1942 and was commissioned in the AAC after flight training in 1943. He flew just over 100 F-51 and F-80 combat missions in Korea. As vice commander for Colonel Robin Olds's McDonnell F-4 Phantom II fighter wing in Vietnam, he flew 78 additional combat missions into North Vietnam. In the early 1970s he was appointed deputy assistant secretary of defense (public affairs) before becoming the vice commander of MAC in 1974. He was promoted to four-star general and assigned as commander-in-chief, NORAD/ADCOM at Peterson Air Force Base in Colorado in 1975. In these dual capacities, he had operational command of all United States and Canadian strategic aerospace defense forces. In 1977, he became the special assistant to the chief of staff. Throughout his career, General James was recognized by military and civilian organizations for his motivational speeches on American values and patriotism. He became the first African American four-star general of any U.S. military service.

Marcelite Harris, one of the first two female AOCs (air officer commanding) at the Air Force Academy, was another African American history maker who had an outstanding career as a maintenance officer in Vietnam, Japan, and bases in the U.S. She rose to the position of director of maintenance at HQ Air Force. She later became a White House aide for Presidents Ford and Carter. As a major general, she was the highest-ranking female in the Air Force and Department of Defense.

One example of the explosive nature of racial friction that existed in the military was at McGuire AFB in 1971 when a colonel was physically attacked by a group of enlisted African Americans. Just a few days later at McChord AFB where I was vice commander and the acting senior officer while the commander was away, a large group of African American airmen gathered and demanded to be heard regarding their allegations of unequal and unfair treatment. I immediately contacted my equal opportunity master sergeant and security police and arranged to immediately meet with the group to hear their concerns. Out of this meeting, we compiled a list of their grievances and assured them that their grievances would be addressed in a prompt manner. Tensions were reduced and relations were gradually restored.

Unfortunately, as we write this, the issue of racial integration still haunts the country. In August 2017 in Charlottesville, Virginia, a group of marching white supremacists wearing body army and carrying weapons were confronted by counter protesters resulting in a violent melee with one protester killed and thirty injured. The president made a statement to the nation regarding this incident in which he equated the actions of the white supremacists to those of the protesters. In rapid response, the five chiefs of the armed services—Army, Navy, Air Force, Coast Guard, and National Guard—each posted statements on social media condemning the president's position in uncompromising terms. As stated by the Army chief of staff, General Mark A. Milley: "The Army doesn't tolerate racism, extremism or hatred in our ranks. It's against our values and everything we've stood for since 1775."[9] As this statement indicates, the U.S. military has been at the forefront of racial integration where it remains today.

The All-Volunteer Force

Another major factor impacting all military officers was the end of the military draft and the shift to an all-volunteer force in 1973, shortly after the end of the Vietnam War. The question of a volunteer military force had been an issue of fervent debate during the 1960s, especially during the Vietnam War. Active demonstrations by college students opposed to the draft and the war also contributed to the lowering of the voting age from 21 to 18 and to the end of the draft. The transition to an all-volunteer force was finally enacted by President Nixon's executive order in 1973. However, it remained a hot issue for some time. That same year General Westmoreland declared that "as a nation we moved too fast in eliminating the draft." Four years later Senator Sam Nunn claimed, "the all-volunteer force may be a luxury that the U.S. can no longer afford." Among Senator Nunn's concerns was the high cost of an all-volunteer force which was driven by the higher salaries and other benefits needed to incentivize individuals to join the armed services.[10]

A primary argument for the draft was that, by exposing, whether directly or indirectly, all U.S. men to military service and the hazards of war rather than just a relatively small population of volunteers, the U.S. population would think very carefully about the cost—in people and resources—of war. The draft provided a huge pool of potential recruits, however draftees (as opposed to volunteers) often were reluctant to serve, served only for a short time, and frequently were not highly motivated. In addition, draftees posed significant challenges to military leaders tasked to train and motivate these young men to productively serve in the military. Exacerbating the situation were the many deferments granted candidate draftees for a variety of reasons such as medical issues, marriage and college enrollment that allowed many to avoid military service, creating considerable inequities in the process.

By contrast, the all-volunteer force was able to provide an adequate number of recruits who were typically motivated to serve, easier to train and usually stayed in the service longer, many for an entire career. Recruits also were also incentivized by the potential to earn college credits which, with the job skills gained, would aid transition to a civilian career. These factors contributed to a more skilled, better trained military force that was needed to maintain and operate the increasingly sophisticated high-tech military equipment.

The characteristics of an all-volunteer force resonated particularly well with the Air Force in contrast to the Army and Navy. The Air Force was perceived by many as the high-tech military service where education received and skills gained during military service would either contribute to a military career or transfer into the civilian sector. These factors, as well as the Army's much larger force and higher ratio of enlisted men to officers, made implementing the all-volunteer force easier for the Air Force than, particularly, the Army and to a lesser degree the Navy.

As asserted by noted journalist, historian, and political commentator Theodore White, "Blacks and youth had won their entrance to equality by violence in the street as much by appeal to conscience. The next group, the women of America, would win by appeal to conscience alone, victories that may be even longer lasting."[11] I would add that persistence and professional job performance also were key factors in the integration of women. In both cases, the military's need for motivated and trainable recruits was a driving factor in integrating African Americans and women into the military.

Integration of Women

Women in the military air service got their start during World War II as flight nurses when women's support of the military was driven by an increasing need for their specialties during time of war. With new airlift capability, air evacuation and fast treatment of wounded warriors became feasible, driving the demand for more flight nurses. Nurses who had not even finished their flight training were called into action during the North Africa invasion before the first class of Army Nurse Corps flight nurses graduated in 1945. Medical evacuation ("medevac") flights in combat zones were especially vulnerable to enemy attacks because aircraft used for evacuation could not display their non-combat status. Over the course of the war these flight nurses attended to over a million patients.[12]

The Women Air Force Service Pilots (WASP) program was created in August 1943, graduating over 1,000 pilots that year. WASP pilots were assigned to a variety of missions such as flight training instructors, glider tow pilots, towing targets for air-to-air and anti-aircraft gunnery practice, engineering test flying, and ferrying aircraft. One of them, Ann Baumgartner, became the first American woman to pilot a jet airplane when, on October 14, 1944, she flew a twin-engine Bell P-59A Airacomet at Wright Field, Ohio, while assigned to its Flight Test Division.[13]

One year after the formation of the Air Force, President Harry Truman signed the Women's Armed Services Integration Act, accepting women as a permanent part of the military, but with restrictions regarding numbers, combat participation and rank. It was the beginning of the Women's Air Force, and for the next 30 years it would represent a separate part of the Air Force.

During the Korean War (1950–53), the only Air Force women permitted to serve in the battle zone were medevac nurses. Servicewomen who had joined the reserves following World War II were involuntarily recalled to active duty as Women in the Air Force (WAF). In Vietnam, WAFs served in hospitals, frontline hospitals (MASH units), in headquarters offices, intelligence units, and a variety of personnel positions. I note that my mother shipped over to Europe as a Red Cross volunteer to support the troops during World War II.

In 1968, 20 years after Truman's executive order in 1948, the passage of Public Law 90-130 lifted many of the previous restrictions including the numbers of women who could serve, how and in what capacity they could serve (such as in combat) and ranks they could attain. It also allowed women to enlist in the Air National Guard. In 1969, Air Force Reserve Officer Training Corps (AFROTC) was opened to women.

Jeanne M. Holm, who was commissioned in the Women's Auxiliary Air Corps in 1942, was appointed director of Women in the WAF in 1965 and

Four female pilots leaving their B-17 *Pistol Packin' Mama* circa 1944. They were members of a group of Women Airforce Service Pilots (WASPS) trained to ferry military aircraft. From left: Frances Green, Margaret (Peg) Kirchner, Ann Waldner and Blanche Osborn (U.S. Air Force photo).

held the position until 1973. In 1971, she became the first woman in the USAF promoted to brigadier general. Two years later she became the first woman in all the military services to be promoted to major general. After retiring from the Air Force, in 1975 she became special assistant to President Ford in the Office of Women's Programs. She had a significant influence on women's progress in the military throughout her successful career.

In 1975, the chief of staff of the Air Force established a test program for future Air Force women pilots. A test group of 10 women joined their male counterparts in pilot training in 1976. These women not only earned their wings but excelled in the program. Over the ensuing years these women became instructor pilots and aircraft commanders of KC-135 (tanker), C-9 (medevac) and C-141 (transport) aircraft. As noted by one of the new pilots, their entry into the world of flying was not easy, with many facing resistance from instructors, male classmates and even complete strangers. In 1976, the

Air Force Reserve also selected the first woman for undergraduate pilot training.

In 1979, Colonel Duane H. Cassidy, one of my MAC 22nd Air Force wing commanders assigned a woman to command an all-women C-141 crew on a week-long MAC cargo/passenger mission through the Pacific. In 1986, SAC assigned two all-women aircrews on the KC-135 and KC-10 tankers that refueled FB-111s during the raid on Libya. Also in 1986, SAC assigned the first women-only Minuteman missile crew to alert duty.

As noted in 1979 by Antonia Chayes, undersecretary of the Air Force: "In the past decade the number of women has increased from approximately 12,000 to more than four times this amount."[14] At the same time, the total active duty personnel in the Air Force declined by about 300,000 to 560,000 personnel. During this period there was also a shortage of skilled, trainable manpower due to the sophisticated weapons to be maintained and operated. In Undersecretary Chayes's words: "It is not sensible to shut out 50% of a dwindling manpower pool."[15] More women were now working in maintenance and "moving into unit-level command positions." Undersecretary Chayes stated to Congress that "we intend to maintain this momentum in the 1980's and grow from 1.4% to 18% women in the active duty Air Force by the mid–1980's."[16] Its noteworthy that Undersecretary Chayes's overall evaluation of gender integration in the Air Force was that the performance of women "showed no significant overall quality difference from the males." She added that "the Air Force was committed to more progress and deserves credit for the positive attitude based upon the favorable results in the field."[17]

In 1974, the Air Force graduated its first female flight test engineer from the prestigious Air Force Test Pilot School, then Captain Jane L. Holley. In 1980, the first women graduated from the service academies. Among the members of the first class of women graduating from the Air Force Academy in 1980 were Susan J. Helms and Janet C. Wolfenberger. Helms was a mission specialist on the crew of five space shuttle flights. She lived in the space station for five months and jointly holds the world record for longest spacewalk at nearly nine hours. After 12 years as an astronaut with NASA she returned to the Air Force and become a lieutenant general and commander of the 14th Air Force Space Command at Vandenberg AFB. Wolfenberger became the first female four-star general in the Air Force. She began her career in weapon system acquisition as an engineer and held a variety of assignments at headquarters Electronic Security Command and AFSC. She held several positions in the F-22 System Program Office, served on the F-22 program at HQ USAF, and was the B-2 system program director for the Aeronautical Systems Center. She also commanded ASC's C-17 Systems Group.

In 1988, the Air Force selected the first woman pilot to undergoing training at the USAF Test Pilot School, Captain Jacquelyn S. Parker (who subsequently graduated with Class 88B). Another graduate of the Test Pilot School and C-141 pilot was Colonel Eileen Collins. In 1995, she became the first woman pilot to fly the space shuttle (Space Transportation System or STS). In 1999, she was the first woman commander of a U.S. spacecraft (space shuttle *Columbia*). She flew four missions in the shuttle and spent more than 38 days in space. She also served at the Air Force Academy as an assistant professor of mathematics.

Colonel Jeannie Leavitt finished pilot training at the top of her class in 1992. At that time, she was not allowed to fly in combat aircraft. In 1993, the secretary of defense removed the restrictions on women flying combat missions and Leavitt became the first woman fighter pilot. After flying 2,500 hours including 300 combat hours in the F-15 in Afghanistan and Iraq, she was assigned as the first woman commander of a fighter wing.

Other notable advancements of women in the Air Force include the first woman secretary of the Air Force, Heather Wilson (USAFA 1982) and Arizona Senator Martha McSally (USAFA 1988).

Incidentally, 1985 marked the year when West Pointers from the 1948–58 graduating classes had completed their military service with the exception of just five senior leaders still on active duty: General Gabriel, chief of staff of the Air Force (retired 1986), General Bennie Davis, SAC commander (retired August 1985), Lt. General "Skip" Scott, USAF Academy superintendent (retired 1987), General Michael J. Dugan (USMA 1958, later chief of staff in 1990) and General Donald J. Kutyna, who became commander-in-chief of the North American Aerospace Defense Command and the U.S. Space Command in 1990, retiring in 1992. Also, in 1986, for the first time, the Air Force Academy's top graduate was a woman (Terrie Ann McLaughlin).[18]

Once women were successfully integrated into the Air Force, West Point grads were officers and commanders leading the implementation effort. Like U.S. society in general, this integration effort was challenging and, to many, painfully slow. These West Point grads helped lead the successful integration of women into the Air Force and set the model for equal treatment and advancement of women in all missions of the Air Force.

Chapter 5

Focus on Advancing Technology

The Air Force—both past and present—has been shaped by steady and sometimes revolutionary advances in a wide variety of technologies. Indeed, it could be said that the Air Force owes its very existence to advances in technology. Like the other military services, it has been impacted by the ever-changing threats to national security, politics, budgetary constraints and inter-service rivalries. But these influences have not altered the basic fact that the Air Force is first and foremost the product of scientific advances and the application of those advances to the many dimensions of aerospace power. And though, with a few exceptions, the West Point grads were not in the laboratories and universities where many of these advances were created, they played a central role in defining technology requirements, testing and evaluating scientific advancements, collaborating with civilian scientists and engineers, and ultimately applying and managing these new weapons systems in the interests of national security.

As these young officers graduated into the newly formed Air Force, they entered an organization shaped by the lessons of World War II and its aftermath with a dramatic reduction in force and funding. The Air Force pursued programs to develop improved weapons systems, including jet aircraft, rockets, missiles, sensor systems, communication systems and eventually space-based systems. These advancements drew upon a unique marriage of great scientific minds and farsighted military thinkers and managers, some of whom graduated from West Point.

Although World War II, according to Army Air Forces Commanding General Hap Arnold, was won by logistics, the development of radical new technologies during the war left a lasting imprint on the AAF leader. Radar, atomic bombs, jet aircraft, and rocket propulsion made it clear that the next war would look very little like the last. After the war, Arnold ensured that the AAF would foster relationships with the scientists and engineers who would create the technologies needed to win the next war. He had the vision and leadership to push new science and technology within the Air Force—characteristics that earned him the title "Architect of the Air Force."

As Arnold stated in his memorandum to Dr. Theodore von Kármán when initiating a long-range development program for the Air Force: "I believe the security of the United States of America will continue to rest in part in developments instituted by our educational and professional scientists…. While our scientists do not necessarily have the questionable advantage of basic military training, conversely our AAF officers cannot by necessity be professional scientists."[1]

While the interaction between scientists and Air Force officers has been and continues today to be an ongoing collaboration, we've chosen to highlight just a few examples where scientific inquiries under Air Force direction led to highly effective advancements in aerospace power.

AAF Scientific Advisory Group (1944)

In November 1944 as part of a long-range development program, General Arnold commissioned the formation of a Scientific Advisory Group (SAG). This body was made up of some of the country's leading scientists working under the direction of Dr. Theodore von Kármán, who, after the death of Germany's Ludwig Prandtl in 1953, was universally recognized as the world's greatest living authority in fluid dynamics and aerospace science. This group was the predecessor organization to the USAF's Scientific Advisory Board (SAB). Dr. von Kármán served as the chairman from 1944 to 1955. The third chairman of the SAB during the period 1956 to 1959 was Major General Jimmy Doolittle.[2]

In general terms, Arnold commissioned the group to assess the current state of airpower and aeronautical R&D programs among the world powers of World War II, and to provide recommendations as a guide for future AAF R&D programs. Prior to World War II there was little formal integration of science and technology with military needs and Arnold sought to cure that situation. One author noted that Arnold "saw the future as an age of missiles, robots and weapons of super-destructiveness. When the war was over and the nation demobilized, how could the military retain a pool of talented scientists? The answer was the Air Force's Project RAND."[3] RAND (an acronym for Research and Development) was established in 1948 as a non-profit corporation with one client—the U.S. Air Force—to maintain a connection between military planners and R&D developments. Since then RAND has grown into one of the world's leading research institutions, providing ideas and solutions to thousands of clients.[4]

In a similar vein, Lt. General Jimmy Doolittle saw the SAB as the organization through which American science could learn more about Air Force challenges and assist in their solution. And General Twining (USMA 1918) relied upon guidance coming to the Air Force from the SAB as essential for new ideas and a way to refine military thinking.

In his letter to Dr. von Kármán dated November 7, 1944, Arnold provided background and mission objectives for the group, stating: "I am asking you and your associates to divorce yourselves from the present war in order to investigate all the possibilities and desirabilities for post-war and future war's development as respects the AAF."[5]

At least two of the questions Arnold raised in his letter to von Kármán are instructive, especially considering current day issues and technologies:

What proportion of available money should be allocated to research and development?

Is it not now possible to determine if another totally different weapon will replace the airplane? Are manless [sic], remote-controlled radar or television assisted precision military rockets or multiple purpose seekers a possibility?

Von Kármán's report, produced just a year after Arnold's request, was made up of 12 volumes containing 32 scientific monographs. It was developed through the collective effort of scientists from every field of research bearing on air power. One of the early chapters, authored by Dr. von Kármán himself, was titled, "Science—the Key to Air Superiority." The title alone speaks volumes about the group's view of the relationship between science and air power.

Many of Dr. von Kármán's findings and recommendation are of special interest, particularly regarding his observations on the role of technology in the two world wars as they might impact future wars:

In the First World War, victory or defeat was decided mainly by human endurance. Science and technology played an important but to some extent a secondary role.... The second war had, from the beginning, a technological character.... This new element was the decisive contribution of organized science to effective weapons.... [N]ever before have such large numbers of scientific workers been united for planned evaluation and utilization of scientific ideas for military purposes. Outstanding results of such planned cooperative research are, on our side, radar and atomic bombs, and on the German side, jet-propelled missiles.[6]

A few of the recommendations that he submitted concerned how the Air Force, industry and the scientific community could best work together, including:

- Cooperation between science and the Air Forces
- Adequate facilities in the Air Forces for research and development
- Scientific and technological training of Air Force personnel

As these inquiries and recommendations illustrate, from the earliest days of its formation, technological advancement has been a defining characteristic of the Air Force and its leadership. The need for a close working relationship between scientists and Air Force leaders was best summarized in von Kármán's report:

> He [von Kármán] warned that it would not be possible to relegate scientific problems and officers to one niche and military problems and officers to another, noting that *"scientific results cannot be used efficiently by soldiers who have no understanding of them, and scientists cannot produce results useful for warfare without an understanding of the operation."* [emphasis added] He charged Air Force leadership with the task of creating and maintaining a climate of mutual respect and cooperation between the scientists and military planners ... and only a constant inquisitive attitude toward science and a ceaseless and swift adaptation to new developments can maintain the security of this nation through world air supremacy.[7]

As noted aviation historian Walter J. Boyne, a former director of the Smithsonian National Air and Space Museum, stated: "In all the history of aviation there has never been a more productive alliance than that of von Kármán and General Henry H. 'Hap' Arnold. The results of their efforts did much to bring the United States Air Force to its current state of unmatched capability and power."[8] It was from their collaboration that a strong working relationship between military leaders and scientists was forged leaving its imprint on U.S. air power for decades to come.

Bernard A. Schriever

One of the most important decisions of Arnold's postwar actions to ensure U.S. technological superiority was to place a little-known colonel with combat experience and a master's degree from Stanford in the new position of scientific liaison to the SAB. The choice of Colonel Bernard A. Schriever to be the Air Force's scientific point man would prove to be a master stroke.

As scientific liaison, Schriever would meet some of the nation's most brilliant scientists, who after World War II would move into prominent positions of influence.

> Schriever promoted two major ideas: *that scientifically-driven innovation was crucial to the Air Force, and that management of these innovations required leadership and authority just as much as the operational Air Force.* [Emphasis added]

General Bernard A. Schriever. He and Wernher von Braun were architects of the U.S. ballistic missile and military space program (U.S. Air Force photo).

Inspired by the scientists' vision of technical change, Schriever with unprecedented authority and top priority led the Air Force's development of ballistic missiles, and then its push into space. His career showed that the Air Force need not wait for technical development, but could lead and direct it.[9]

After World War II, Schriever and these scientists became strong allies with access to leaders at the highest levels of government. Schriever would consistently rely upon their scientific expertise.

In 1959, Schriever became commander of the Air Research and Development Command (ARDC), later in 1961 organized as the Air Force Systems Command (AFSC), itself based upon Schriever's original design. (AFSC and its subordinate units are discussed in a later chapter.)

In 1963, he directed "Project Forecast," one of the most comprehensive long-range assessments of military science and technology. The multi-volume report was based on the work of a large gathering of specialists from federal agencies, universities, corporations and nonprofit organizations.[10] From these initiatives and the later achievements of the Air Force's missile and space programs it becomes clear that the choice of Colonel Bernard Schriever as the Air Force's military point man at the dawn of the missile age was indeed a masterstroke.

Edward Teller of Lawrence Livermore Laboratory (1976)

A good example of the close interaction between scientific minds and Air Force applications comes from the work of Dr. Edward Teller. Dr. Teller issued a series of memoranda in 1976 to the SAB regarding remotely piloted vehicles (RPVs). Dr. Teller strongly advocated the use of RPVs which "could introduce a new age in American defense policy."[11] Dr. Teller succinctly articulated the benefits, both strategic and economic, of using RPVs in warfare, particularly RPVs with "full military utilization of electronics" where the U.S. maintained a significant technological advantage over the Russians. In another memo he strongly advocated arming the B-1 bomber with a variety

Air-launched cruise missile (AGM-86 B/C/D). Speed: 550 mph; range: up to 1,500 miles; payload: nuclear or conventional warhead (U.S. Air Force photo).

of cruise missiles which would be either preprogrammed or remotely controlled. It is remarkable how prescient he was in light of today's cruise missiles with the capability of flying at high subsonic speeds using self-navigation at extremely low altitude.

About the same time (mid–1970s), an engineer by the name of Sam B. Williams, who later became the founder of Williams International, was engineering and marketing an extremely small jet engine. He paid me a visit when I was the director of requirements on the Air Staff to pitch his new engine to the Air Force after having previously presented his concept to the Marines and the Navy who were not particularly impressed. We arranged a demonstration for the Air Force that took place on the parade ground at Fort Myer—the very site that Orville Wright had demonstrated his flying machine in 1908. The demonstration consisted of a flight by Mr. Williams's test pilot, wearing a jetpack, who flew at an altitude of approximately 50 feet around the parade field. The Office of Secretary of Defense (OSD) later considered that a subsonic cruise missile with this engine launched from a B-52 was a possible alternative to the B-1.

The culmination of further tests was the development of the air-launched cruise missile (ALCM) and the Air Force's procurement of 1,750 AGM-86 ALCMs followed by continued development of improved cruise missiles with stealth, greater speed, navigation and greatly improved accuracy.

Importance of Advanced Education

As first recommended by von Kármán, senior Air Force leaders saw the need for what is now called STEM—scientific, technology, engineering and math—education in the Air Force. Officers were encouraged to gain advanced engineering and other degrees at some of the country's finest colleges and universities. But this integration didn't exist only at the highest ranks. Rather, the key architects of a technologically driven Air Force recognized the need to extend scientific knowledge to many Air Force officers with leadership responsibilities and to encourage these officers to gain advanced engineering and other degrees. Based on his research of West Point graduates from the classes of 1948–58, Colonel (Ret.) Clarence Elebash (USMA 1948) found that approximately 53 percent of these graduates obtained advanced degrees, many of which were masters of science or doctorate degrees in aeronautical engineering and related subjects.[12]

The following is a table of a few senior West Point graduates and other notable figures with advanced degrees in aeronautical engineering and other related disciplines who helped lead the development of many of the Air Force's groundbreaking technologies.

Table 2. Advanced Engineering Degrees of Selected Air Force Leaders

Name	USMA class	Key Position	Degree	University
Jimmy Doolittle	N/A	Lt. General; Chair of SAB and consultant	MS—Aeronautical engineering; ScD—Aeronautical engineering	MIT
Dr. Hans Mark	N/A	Secretary of Air Force	PhD—Physics	MIT
Lew Allen, Jr.	1946	General; Air Force Chief of Staff	MS, PhD—Nuclear physics	Illinois
Brent Scowcroft	1947	Lt. General; Deputy to the President	PhD—International Relations	Columbia
James R. Allen	1948	General; Air Force Chief of Staff	MS—Business administration	Denver
Robert C. Mathis	1948	General; Vice Commander AFSC, TAC	PhD—Electrical engineering	Texas
Robert E. Pursley	1949	Lt. General; Military Assistant to three SecDefs	PhD—Economics	Harvard
Robert T. Marsh	1949	General; AFSC Commander	MS—Aeronautical engineering	Michigan
Abner Martin	1949	Lt. General; Dir. B-1 SPO; Dir. Defense Mapping Agency	MS—Engineering	MIT
John G. Albert	1949	Lt. General; Gemini Launch Director; Dep. Space Defense, SAMSO	MS—Aeronautical engineering	Michigan
Richard Henry	1949	Lt. General, Commander SAMSO	MS—Aeronautical engineering	Michigan
John E. Kulpa	1950	Major General; Dir. Special Projects for Secretary of the Air Force	MS—Aeronautical engineering	AFIT
Archie Wood	1950	Colonel; Dep. Asst. Secretary of Defense for Strategic Forces	MS—Aeronautical engineering; MBA	MIT
Charles L. Gandy, Jr.	1945	Colonel	MS—aeronautical engineering	Princeton
Frank Borman	1950	Astronaut	MS—Aeronautical engineering	CalTech
Buzz Aldrin	1951	Astronaut	Doctor of Science—Astronautics	MIT
Ed White	1952	Astronaut	MS—Aeronautical engineering	Michigan
Dave Scott	1954	Astronaut	MS—Aeronautics/Astronautics	MIT
Donald Peterson	1955	Astronaut	MS—Nuclear engineering	AFIT
Alfred Worden	1955	Astronaut	MS—Aeronautical engineering	Michigan
Donald J. Kutyna	1957	General; Space Commander	MS—Aeronautical engineering	MIT

It is important to underscore that the emphasis upon educating senior leaders on advances in weapon systems technology has been a key feature of the Air Force since its very beginning. Indeed, since its founding in 1919,[13] the Air Force Institute of Technology (AFIT) has been a primary academic institution of higher learning for Air Force officers and through which many of the above officers received their advanced academic training, either directly through AFIT or sponsored by AFIT at other leading universities.

It also should be noted that many of the senior decision makers in the Air Force during this period, including General Lew Allen, Jr., as chief of staff of the Air Force, General Robert Mathis as vice commander of AFSC and later served on the staffs of the secretary of Air Force and Defense, and Harold Brown and Hans Mark as secretaries of the Air Force all had PhDs in various scientific disciplines. This stands in contrast to the other military service secretaries who came from the ranks of business, law or politics. During the period 1965 to 1981, there were seven Air Force secretaries with extensive engineering or scientific backgrounds: Harold Brown (1965–69), Robert C. Seamans, Jr. (1969–73), John L. McLucas (1973–75), James W. Plummer (1975–76), Thomas C. Reed (1976–77), John C. Stetson (1977–79), and Hans Mark (1979–81). And during this period there were six chiefs of staff of the Air Force with considerable R&D experience and education. Furthermore, of the West Point graduating class of 1950, 11 received advanced engineering degrees through AFIT, primarily master's degrees in aeronautical engineering.[14]

One way to explain its history and mission is to draw directly from AFIT's website:

AFIT's Mission

The Air Force Institute of Technology, AFIT, is the Air Force's graduate school of engineering and management as well as the Air Force's institution for technical professional continuing education. A component of Air University and Air Education and Training Command, AFIT is committed to providing defense-focused graduate and professional continuing education and research to sustain the technological supremacy of America's air and space forces. Since resident degrees were first granted in 1956, more than 17,500 graduate and 600 doctor of philosophy degrees have been awarded. In addition, Air Force students attending civilian institutions have earned more than 12,000 undergraduate and graduate degrees in the past twenty years.

It is interesting to note that a predecessor of AFIT was founded in 1919 by a West Point graduate, Colonel Thurman Bane (USMA 1907) and Colonel Edwin Eugene Aldrin, astronaut Buzz Aldrin's father. Under Bane's leadership, AFIT's predecessor organizations were established to provide training to Air Service pilots.

Another early leader at AFIT was Lt. General Laurence Craigie (USMA 1923). Craigie spent his early career in the Army Air Service as a pilot. In 1935, he started his R&D career graduating from the Air Corps Engineering School at Wright-Patterson AFB, and then was promoted to chief of the Aircraft Projects Branch. While in this test pilot position he became famous as the first armed forces pilot to fly a jet, the XP-59, on its initial flight. In 1948, he was reassigned as commandant of AFIT, a position he held until 1950 when he went to the Korean War as vice commander of Far East Air Forces in Tokyo. Craigie serves as an excellent example of the career path followed by many Air Force leaders involving a rotation from operations into R&D and then into senior levels of management.

Other examples of this policy of rotating career officers between operational assignments and R&D positions to gain broader real-world experience include the following:

- Colonel USAF (Ret.) Richard Lorette (USMA 1950)—with two combat tours, Korea and Southeast Asia, an MS degree from AFIT in management, a Project Officer in the B-52 SPO, followed by a PhD from Harvard and then an AFIT instructor.

- Lt. General USAF (Ret.) Tom Stafford (USNA 1952, Honors graduate). Tom was an interceptor pilot flying the F-86Ds until entering the Test Pilot School where he graduated in 1958, first in our class of 58C, and stayed as an instructor before being selected for the NASA Gemini and Apollo programs. He piloted the first rendezvous in space and then assisted in the development of basic theory, techniques and mission planning for future rendezvous. On his fourth Apollo mission he was commander of the Apollo-Soyuz rendezvous and hookup in space with the Russian capsule. His understanding and leadership of operating in space is recognized by space agencies throughout the world. After his distinguished career in space travel, he completed his Air Force career by rotating back to command the Air Force Flight Test Center followed by a tour at DCS R&D HQ USAF where he supervised development of the fighter, bomber and cruise missile stealth programs.

- Lt. General Richard C. Henry (USMA 1949)—General Henry's career path provides a great example of job rotation within different Air Force functions. He started with a tour in B-50s with a nuclear bomber mission, followed by several years in jet fighters flying 207 combat missions in F-4s in Vietnam. He went on to earn an MS in Aeronautics and Instrumentation at the University of Michigan followed by a return to the Strategic Air Command as a staff officer for the Thor IRBM deployment in England. From 1960 until 1966 he had assignments with both military and NASA space projects including manned spaceflight systems for Gemini and Apollo. He then had headquarters assignments at the Tactical Air Command (TAC) and USAF Air Staff followed by command of a fighter wing.

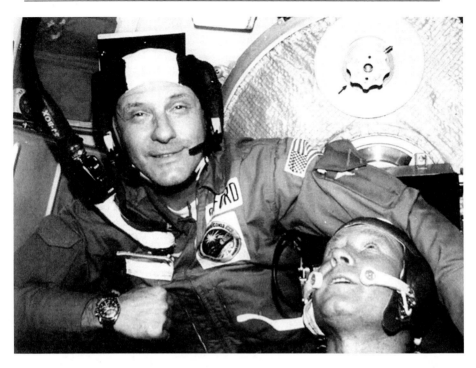

NASA astronaut Tom Stafford and Russian cosmonaut Alexei Leonov with the Apollo and Soyuz rendezvous in space, July 17, 1975 (NASA photo).

After two previous years as vice commander of Space and Missile Systems Organization (SAMSO) (later named Space Division) he became commander in 1978 and held the position until retirement in 1983. General Henry received distinguished service awards from the Air Force, DOD and NASA.

• Hans Mark, former secretary of the Air Force and a former deputy administrator of NASA, received his PhD in physics from MIT and also taught graduate courses in physics and engineering at MIT and other universities. A strong advocate of imparting scientific knowledge to the Air Force, when he was undersecretary of the Air Force he taught a short class on applied physics to a small group of junior general officers on the Air Staff at that time, including myself.

In 1978, General David C. Jones, then chief of staff of the Air Force and later to become chairman of the Joint Chiefs of Staff, directed a one-week AFIT course for senior Air Staff personnel to expose them to potential contributions of technology to future air and space weapons systems. As noted in a letter to the class from the AFIT commander: "The course presents fundamental principles of key technologies and scientific methods, their applications to current weapon systems, and future projections.... We believe this course will focus your attention on areas where advanced technology can provide us with qualitatively superior capabilities."[15]

The story of advances in technology with new materials, concepts, and designs that gradually resulted in a useful weapon system is long and complex. Scientists and engineers create the building blocks of what is possible, and others push the envelope of requirements to create better and even unique weapon systems. During our military careers there was an explosion of new technologies and weapon system capabilities. The challenge for our generation and others to follow was what, how, and when to develop a new weapon system or improve upon an existing system while staying on budget and still maintaining a fully operational Air Force. There were many decisions made along the way and many extended analyses would slow or even stop a program. Some Air Force cynics termed this "paralysis by analysis."

I will share an anecdote that illustrates this. In my experience as director of requirements on the Air Staff with oversight responsibility for the B-1, in

Boeing B-52D Stratofortress dropping bombs over Vietnam. Long-range, subsonic strategic bomber. First flight, 1952. There were 744 produced. More than 60 years of continuous service. B-52Ds flew combat in Vietnam with 60,000-pound payload dropping up to 108 bombs including 500- and 750-pound bombs. Twenty years later, the B-52H models launched cruise missiles against Iraq (U.S. Air Force photo).

1977 I accompanied my boss, then Lt. General Alton D. "Al" Slay, to inform General Jones that President Carter's administration had just canceled the B-1 program. After about a minute of thoughtful consideration, the chief observed, "So be it. We work for and obey our civilian leadership." Soon after the next presidential election, President Reagan's team restarted the B-1 program, naming it the B-1B. At the time, two factors likely influenced the B-1 decision: First, a Presidential Foreign Intelligence Advisory Board (PFIAB) adamantly disagreed with the CIA's estimate "that the Soviet air defense missile shield was impenetrable" and therefore that a new bomber was useless.[16] Second, two retired Air Force colonels, both West Point grads, Archie Wood (USMA 1950) and Alton H. Quanbeck (USMA 1948), who then were working for the Brookings Institute, had written a detailed cost-effectiveness analysis, *Modernizing the Strategic Bomber Force, Why and How*, which concluded that the present bomber force, armed with long-range cruise missiles, would be adequate for the near future instead of the costly new B-1. Did either or both these analyses affect the cancellation decision? I don't know. However, it is interesting to note that the B-52H with cruise missiles and the B-1B both are still part of today's strategic bomber force, despite the nation's investment in "low observable" radar-confounding technology that led to the Northrop B-2A Spirit stealth bomber.

B-52G Stratofortress with AGM-86B Air-Launched Cruise Missiles (ALCMs) (U.S. Air Force photo).

Another Air Force leader who rotated among operational and R&D assignments was Lt. General Brent Scowcroft (USMA 1947). He began his Air Force career as a pilot and then gained a master's degree, served a stint as a faculty member at the Air Force Academy, then earned a PhD in international relations from Columbia University. He moved from assignments with the Joint Chief of Staffs (JCS), HQ, USAF and the Office of the Assistant Secretary of Defense (SecDef) for International Affairs. In 1972 he became military assistant to the president and in 1973 he became deputy to the president until he retired as a lieutenant general in 1975. He was assistant to the president for national security affairs from 1975 to 1977 and from 1989 to 1993, during which time he mentored a number of individuals who went on to serve in senior national security positions, most notably Soviet studies expert and future Secretary of State Condoleezza Rice. He was certainly a highly respected American statesman when in 1995 he was designated a West Point AOG distinguished graduate.

Colonel Bill DeGraf (U.S. Army, USMA 1950), another class of 1950 distinguished graduate, was a member of the president's National Security Council (NSC) and assisted such prominent White House executives as Secretary of State Henry Kissinger in the security decision-making process. He earned a MS in nuclear physics from Purdue University and in retirement he continued to work military matters with the civilian organization SAIC.

Next, as we move across the Potomac to the Pentagon, it is worth acknowledging two West Point graduates and Air Force officers assigned to the Office of the Secretary of Defense (OSD). Lt. General Robert E. Pursley (USMA 1949) started his career as a pilot in Korea where he flew 50 combat missions in the B-26 Invader (aka Night Intruder). He then went to Harvard for an MBA in economics followed by five years on the USAFA faculty teaching economics. He then spent two years on the OSD staff as a systems analyst before going to the Air War College as a student and part-time instructor. His next assignment was most significant as he spent six years as military assistant to three secretaries of defense: McNamara, Clifford, and Laird. Lt. General Pursley's last position prior to retirement was commander, U.S. Forces, Japan, and commander, Fifth Air Force.

As an interesting aside, 30 years after his retirement, Pursley joined retired Secretary of Defense Laird in publishing a 2006 opinion article in the *Washington Post* in rebuttal to several retired general officers who had complained that Secretary Rumsfeld should resign based on his overly authoritarian style, disregard of military advice and poor decision regarding the war in Iraq. In their opinion piece, Laird and Pursley claimed that this group of general officers may have been speaking with a narrower view when criticizing Rumsfeld, who had a broader view of international affairs and U.S. interests. In addition, while these officers had many chances to speak up while on active duty, they did not, and to complain now, while it might be considered a reasonable debate, could be considered by the enemy as a sign of U.S. weakness and lack of resolve. Laird and Pursley concluded that their only valid argument is that "our democracy is designed to favor civilian control of defense decisions." Considering the severity of the national debates and books that are considered "reasonable debates," Pursley was likely strongly influenced by his many years in OSD and the power struggles within the Pentagon.

Colonel (Ret.) Archie Wood (USMA 1950) started his career with a tour in Korea and experienced a most unusual event, that of being forced to parachute from a disabled transport aircraft. Surviving that, his next assignment was at MIT to study weapon system engineering where he received an MS degree followed by engineering tours at Wright-Patterson AFB, Ballistic Missile Division, and then the Minuteman System Program Office (SPO) as the program was just getting started. As a side note, both authors of this book were involved with the Minuteman program, one as a launch control center in Wyoming next to a pair of critical keys that, if turned, could have changed the world as we know it and the other was in the Pentagon pushing a pencil!

Colonel Wood returned to MIT to the Sloan School of Management for another master's degree before going to OSD as an analyst in the Strategic Forces office, the start of almost nine years in what he described as "the higher realms of defense policy." He next attended the National War College and went on to be SPO chief for the AGM-86 air-launched cruise missile (ALCM), the first long-range cruise missile which was a questionable new weapon system for the Air Force because it presented competition for the traditional penetrating strategic bomber. As director of requirements on the Air Staff and advocate of a new Air Force weapon system, I was sent on a challenging mission to brief the SAC commander and his staff on the attributes of a bomber launching long-range standoff cruise missiles. These were interesting assignments for both Colonel Wood and me. Colonel Wood retired in 1971 but returned to the OSD as assistant for arms control and later became deputy assistant secretary of defense for strategic forces. Archie writes in the Class of 1950 *Memories Project* that he was privileged to work on some of the most important strategic forces policy issues: negotiation of the ABM Treaty with the Soviet Union, ballistic missile air defenses, the decision to proceed with the Navy Trident program and initiation of the long-range cruise missile program. As mentioned earlier, he addressed many of these same issues while working for the Brookings Institute.

The Process of Weapon System Acquisition

In understanding the role played by West Point grads in defining, developing, acquiring, testing and operating many of the Air Force's major weapon systems, it is useful to have a basic understanding of the DOD's acquisition process. Many West Point graduates served in a variety of roles up and down the acquisition chain, particularly in defining system requirements, managing R&D and, later, testing the systems and bringing them to operational readiness.

The history of the Air Force's acquisition process began quite simply with the Army Signal Corps' purchase of the Wright Military Flyer from the Wright Brothers in 1909 for $25,000 with a bonus for each mile per hour flown over 40 mph! Orville Wright and Benjamin Foulois made the final check flight before the sign-off by Army Major George Squier (USMA 1887). These two officers established the aircraft's requirements, evaluated the proposal, flight tested and purchased it. Only two men did the entire job! Later, Foulois took the plane to Fort Sam Houston by rail, reassembled it in Texas and finished his flying instruction by correspondence with Orville Wright. This acquisition process stands in stark contrast to the process that we experienced during our military careers in the '50s through the '80s and the process that exists today. (As an interesting side note, in 1977 I flew a partially disassembled A-10 Thunderbolt in a C-5 Galaxy from the factory in New England to Edwards AFB in California, to be reassembled for the flight test program—not unlike Foulois's train trip with the Wright Military Flyer!)

Ever-advancing technology and ballooning costs caused the acquisition process to become a lengthy, complex, and highly regimented process. In some cases, decisions affecting weapon system acquisition were made at the highest levels of government including the sitting president. For example, President Eisenhower was directly involved in decisions concerning the acquisition and operation of U-2 reconnaissance aircraft and the first reconnaissance satellites. The decision to cancel the production of the B-1 bomber in 1977 and then to restart the program in 1981 were made by two different presidents. These decisions were authorized by Congress, the OSD and finally implemented by the Air Force. A far cry from the first aircraft acquisition by two men for $25,000!

By the time of the B-1 acquisition, careful consideration was required to address national defense policy as well as the political and economic impact resulting from contractor selection. In some cases, these decisions impacted the economic well-being of entire regions of the U.S. The cost of major projects ran into billions of dollars with many weapon systems experiencing multi-decade life spans requiring expensive modifications to remain mission effective. This evolution in the acquisition process took place in a relatively short period of time and, as it evolved, West Point grads played a role at all levels of the process.

Congressional committees with strong backing by their regional lobbyists pushed for ever-more-detailed information on new programs. In the late

Fairchild Republic A-10A Thunderbolt II (aka Warthog). Introduced in 1977, 716 of this twin turbo-fan engine, close air support and forward air controller support aircraft were produced (U.S. Air Force photo).

'70s I recall assisting my boss, Lt. General Alton Slay, DCS HQ USAF, in preparing to brief congressional committees regarding our Air Force R&D programs. In order to be fully prepared we would brief him on the details of each program, and he would assemble literally a grocery cart full of viewgraphs to take with him for the briefings to Congress. His aide, a major, was fully prepared to immediately present the desired chart as requested. Congress wanted oversight, and they got a "fire hose" full of it from General Slay!

One apt description of the acquisition process for military aircraft comes from a paper authored by Jacob Neufeld of the Office of Air Force History in 1974 when describing development of the F-15 Eagle:

> Military aircraft seldom, if ever, leap unchanged from the drawing board to flight line; rather, they evolve slowly, each stage of development influenced by such diverse factors as technology, economics, politics, enemy threat and just plain chance. These varied forces interacting—not the planner's original vision—frequently dictate the end result. The history of aircraft is studded with examples affirming this thesis; what began as a fighter evolved into an interceptor; an attack plane into a fighter-bomber; and a commercial airliner into a military transport.[17]

When Robert McNamara was SecDef from 1961 to 1968, he centralized the weapon system acquisition process at OSD, introduced system analysis to the process and established a planning, programing and budgeting system (PPBS) for defense department procurement. He instituted policies to examine R&D programs based on performance, schedule, cost and technical risk for determining whether to begin, terminate or continue programs. He also eliminated the "fly-before-buy" concept and introduced the system acquisition policy known as total package procurement (TPP). In general, TPP was a method of procuring the total weapon system, performance, development, production, schedule commitments and support needed to introduce and sustain the system in operation.

TPP was applied to several Air Force, Army and Navy acquisitions but it proved to be unsuccessful on a number of projects. As a result, TPP was eliminated in 1970 under the next administration. In 1965, I was involved as a member of the Air Force Source Selection Board (SSB) regarding the selection of the Lockheed C-5 transport which was selected by the OSD Source Selection Authority (SSA) over the recommendations of the SSB. The Lockheed C-5 proposal was the lowest cost bid and the SSA choice served to prove the wisdom of the phrase "pay now or pay later." The C-5 soon developed major wing defects requiring either severe operational limitations or extensive multi-billion-dollar modification.

In addition to working with the SSB on the C-5, I was a C-5 wing commander (at Dover AFB) and later at the Pentagon I was the senior Air Staff officer representing the C-5 aircraft and its infamous problems. So it was no surprise to me when, in about 1977, I was assigned to accompany the AFSC commander, General William J. Evans (USMA 1946) to testify to Congress in support of the two billion dollar C-5 wing modification program. During that testimony, we reported that the Air Force was pleased with the performance of the C-5 but the structural integrity of the wings was a major issue, forcing the expensive modification at 8,000 flying hours rather than at 30,000 hours as specified. In fact, the C-5 received wing modifications and over the next 40 years continued to provide vital airlift capability for loads up to 80 tons and outsized equipment such as Army battle tanks. In 1973, it provided nearly half of the U.S.'s airlift support for the struggling Israelis in their fight against the invading forces of Egypt and Syria.

A few West Point graduates in the Air Force served at the highest levels regarding weapon system acquisitions, from senior advisors at the White House on the staff of the OSD or the SecAF's staff, but of course most worked within the uniformed ranks including in management within AFSC and the AFSC product divisions.

Air Force Systems Command (AFSC)

In 1950, then CSAF Hoyt S. Vandenberg (USMA 1923) made the decision to consolidate the Air Force R&D mission into a separate new command, Air Research and Development Command (ARDC), with equal status to the operational commands. He also established a DCS/R&D unit at Air Force headquarters. This new command was extremely busy and quite successful during its first years developing aircraft such as the F-86, B-52, C-130, and U-2 aircraft. Four years later in 1954, ARDC established the Western Development Division (WDD) in Inglewood, California, under the command of Brigadier General Bernard A. Schriever. Among its many accomplishments, WDD contributed enormously to the development of intercontinental ballistic missiles (ICBMs), particularly with the first ICBM, the Atlas, which became operational in 1959. In part as a result of the highly successful Atlas program and assignment of the space mission to the Air Force, in 1961 ARDC was redesignated as the Air Force Systems Command (AFSC) and based at Andrews Air Force Base 20 miles from the Pentagon. AFSC was given responsibility for all the Air Force's R&D programs as well as weapon system acquisition. Lt. General David M. Schlatter (USMA 1923) was the first ARDC commander followed by General Earl E. Partridge (USMA 1924). It is interesting to note that earlier in their careers these two officers played a role in the Normandy invasion along with other notable grads.

ARDC and later AFSC had a combined 15 commanders during the period 1950 to 1984. Seven of these commanders were West Point grads. Two AFSC Commanders became chief of staff of the Air Force (CSAF): General George S. Brown (USMA 1941) who later became chairman of the Joint Chiefs of Staff, and General Lew Allen, Jr. (USMA 1946). Brief summaries of their Air Force careers are as follows:

- General George S. Brown (USMA 1941) gained his flight experience flying B-24s during World War II. He went on to assume leadership positions in a number of Air Force units including those devoted to troop transport, pilot training, and weapon system testing. He became commander of AFSC in 1970 before assuming his role as chief of staff of the Air Force. This experience provided General Brown with firsthand knowledge of the many space and missile systems under Air Force responsibility. This, coupled with his leadership experience in air combat, pilot training and weapon system testing, provided the broad background suitable to his new position in 1973 as chief of staff and later in 1974 as chairman of the Joint Chiefs of Staff.

- General Lew Allen, Jr. (USMA 1946) gained his flight experience as a

B-29 and B-36 bomber pilot. He then earned a PhD in nuclear physics from the University of Illinois before being assigned to the U.S. Atomic Energy Commission's Los Alamos Scientific Laboratory as a physicist in the Test Division. Allen conducted experiments concerning the physics of thermonuclear weapons design and the effects of high altitude nuclear explosions as would be used for ballistic missile defense. He worked in a variety of positions in the Office of the Secretary of the Air Force regarding ballistic missile and space programs. He became commander of AFSC in 1977. He became the chief of staff of the Air Force in July 1978 and after his retirement from the Air Force in 1982 he became director of the Jet Propulsion Laboratory.

General Lew Allen (USMA 1946), PhD. Director NSA, commander AFSC and CSAF (U.S. Air Force photo).

The amount of aircraft systems developed and procured during the 1960s and 1970s through ARDC and its successor AFSC are numerous, but a few notables include fighter aircraft such as the F-15 and F-16; bomber aircraft such as the B-52, FB-111, B-1, and B-2; cargo aircraft such as the C-130, C-141 and C-5; and reconnaissance airplanes such as the U-2 and SR-71. AFSC also played a key role in the early development of ICBMs and space systems. During the Vietnam War, AFSC greatly expanded its R&D efforts regarding radar, communications and electronic warfare with modifications and new uses for several older airplanes such as the C-119 gunships, the KC-135, EB-66, and others.

Among the product divisions of AFSC were the Aeronautical Systems Division (ASD), Electronic Systems Division (ESD), and Space Systems Division (SSD). In 1967, the Ballistic System Division (BSD) and SSD were inactivated and consolidated at one location in Los Angeles under the Space and Missile Systems Organization (SAMSO) of AFSC.

Top: Formation of McDonnell Douglas (Boeing) F-15C Eagle aircraft. Twin-engine, high performance, air superiority fighter. First flight in 1972 with continuous upgrades to include day and night ground attack. *Above:* General Dynamics F-16 Fighting Falcon. Single-engine, supersonic fighter. More than 4,600 were produced and operated by the U.S. and many foreign countries. (both U.S. Air Force photo)

Aeronautical Systems Division (ASD)

The Aeronautical Systems Division (ASD) located at Wright-Patterson AFB was established in 1961 upon the combination of ARDC with the Air Material Command (AMC). It was redesignated as the Aeronautical Systems Center (ASC) in 1992 and later deactivated as a unit as a result of the Air Force's reorganization. ASD was the Air Force's leading R&D division responsible for the acquisition of new aeronautical systems and the upgrade and modification of existing aircraft systems to support the Air Force. ASD's mission was consistent with that of its successor organization, ASC, as described in its website: "The center designs, develops and delivers dominant aerospace weapon systems and capabilities for U.S. Air Force, other U.S. military, allied and coalition-partner warfighters, in support of Air Force leadership priorities."[18]

ASD was led by nine commanders during its period of operation, two of whom were West Point graduates: Lt. General Thomas H. McMullen (USMA 1951) and Lt. General George H. Sylvester (USMA 1949).

- Lt. General Thomas H. McMullen (USMA 1951)—Lt. General McMullen completed fighter combat crew training at Nellis AFB and then was assigned to a fighter-interceptor squadron in South Korea where he served as a flight commander flying combat missions in F-86s. He went on to receive a Master of Science degree in astronautical engineering from AFIT after which he transferred to the Space Systems Division in Los Angeles as project officer in the Gemini Launch Vehicle System Program Office. After flying 450 combat missions in Vietnam he returned to serve as the assistant mission director of the Apollo program, assisting in the preparation of Apollo space vehicles for flight and for training ground and flight crews for missions 6 through 13. In 1973, he was assigned as the system program director of the A-10 close air support aircraft where he managed the program through development and initial production phases. Following other assignments at AFSC and then TAC he was commander of ASD, receiving several awards for outstanding service.

- Lt. General George H. Sylvester (USMA 1949)—Lt. General Sylvester earned his pilot wings and was assigned to the Military Air Transport Service, MATS (later the Military Airlift Command, MAC, then Air Mobility Command, AMC) serving in a series of assignments before returning to West Point as an assistant professor of government. During the Vietnam War he flew combat missions in F-4Cs over North Vietnam becoming commander of Da Nang Air Base in 1966. In 1970, he became the assistant director, tactical systems test and evaluation for the Office of the Director of Defense, Research and Engineering, Office of the Secretary of Defense.

In 1973, he transferred to ASD, serving as vice commander until 1976 when he became commander. He later became vice commander of AFSC.

Electronic Systems Division (ESD)

The Electronic Systems Division (ESD) was established in 1961 at Hanscom Field in Bedford, Massachusetts, as part of the newly created AFSC. ESD's primary mission was to develop radar, command and control, and communications systems for the Air Force. ESD was responsible for developing the Semi-Automatic Ground Environment (SAGE) air defense system, which contributed to the development of modern-day air traffic control systems. The threat of Soviet nuclear-tipped ballistic missiles prompted the development of the Ballistic Missile Early Warning System (BMEWS) and a survivable new command center for the North American Air Defense Command in the underground Cheyenne Mountain Complex in Colorado. ESD also contributed to the development of greatly improved airspace surveillance in the E-3 Airborne Warning and Control System (AWACS) which entered service in 1977 and in the 1980s with development of the Joint Surveillance Target Attack Radar System (Joint STARS). As described in a recent Air Force magazine article, AWACS "instantly changed the whole regime of air combat. AWACS could direct the battle so adeptly that it multiplied the effectiveness of the forces it controlled…. The commander of the Tactical Air Command pronounced it the most significant single tactical improvement since the advent of radar."[19]

Throughout the period of ESD's existence as an operating division there were 10 commanders, five of whom were West Point graduates:

- Major General Kenneth P. Bergquist (USMA 1935)—Bergquist was assigned in 1958 to Hanscom Air Force Base as deputy commander (Air Research and Development Command). There, he was responsible for defense systems integration. In 1960, he became commander of the Command and Control Development Division. When the Air Force Systems Command and the Air Force Logistics Command were established in April 1961, the organizations at Hanscom were consolidated and renamed the Electronic Systems Center, with Bergquist as the ESC's first commander.

- Major General John B. Bestic (USMA 1939)—Following World War II, General Bestic served as chief of the Communications Division in the Directorate of Communications, Headquarters USAF and in 1949 was assigned to the Joint Chiefs of Staff as deputy director for communications-electronics. In 1950, he was named chief of communications-electronics at Headquarters SAC. After further telecommunications assignments in 1966 he was assigned additional duty as deputy director, DCA. He became commander of ESD in 1967.

Boeing E-3 Sentry. Airborne Warning and Control System (AWACS) aircraft. Used to detect aircraft, ships and vehicles at long ranges and conduct command and control of the battlespace by directing fighter and other aircraft strikes, there were 65 produced. Deployed by the USAF and other countries (U.S. Air Force photo).

- Major General Albert R. Shiely, Jr. (USMA 1943)—General Shiely served as a B-24 aircraft commander, instructor pilot and operations officer in World War II with several heavy bombardment groups. He served overseas as a B-24 aircraft commander and flight commander with the 15th Air Force in Italy. He later attended the University of Illinois, graduating in 1947 with a master's degree in electrical engineering and began a long period of service in Air Force research, development and engineering. From 1947 to 1954 his assignments included planning and management of electronics research for the Electronics Subdivision, Air Materiel Command at Wright-Patterson Air Force Base where he was active in the early research and development of electronic digital computers. In 1954, General Shiely was assigned as the USAF engineering manager for three major electronic air defense systems: SAGE for control of all U.S. air defense weapons; the Distant Early Warning (DEW) Line deployed across Arctic North America for warning of air attack; and the White Alice Communications System (WACS) to provide communication for defense of Alaska. These programs pioneered the application of many new technologies to military requirements including conversion of radar information to digital form, the first extensive use of the tropospheric scatter communication technique, and the first use of large-scale computers for real time control of weapon systems. General Shiely became commander of ESD 1971.

- Lt. General Robert T. Marsh (USMA 1949)—Lt. General Marsh joined the Armed Forces Special Weapons Project as an atomic weapons assembly officer at Sandia Base, New Mexico. He later earned an MS degree from the University of Michigan under the AFIT program in instrumentation engineering and aeronautical engineering. He later was assigned to Headquarters USAF in 1965 in the Office of the Deputy Chief of Staff, Research and Development, as a staff officer in the Directorate of Reconnaissance and Electronic Warfare. He then became chief of the Projects Division in the Directorate of Space. Following assignments at AFSC, in 1977 he became commander of ESD, where he served until 1981 when he became Commander of AFSC.

- Lt. General James W. Stansberry (USMA 1949)—Lt. General Stansberry served from 1950 through 1954 in the Armed Forces Special Weapons Project at Albuquerque, New Mexico. After graduating with an MBA through AFIT in 1956, he was assigned to the Northern Air Materiel Area, Pacific, as chief of production at the Kawasaki-Gifu Contract Facility at Gifu, Japan. He transferred to the Office of the Assistant to the Secretary of Defense (Atomic Energy) in Washington, D.C. This tour of duty culminated in his appointment as deputy assistant to the secretary of defense (atomic energy), where he served until July 1971. After assignments at AFSC and HQ USAF in project acquisition and procurement policy positions, he later was appointed deputy chief of staff for contracting and manufacturing at AFSC. He became commander of ESD in 1981.

Another grad who played a key role in the development of one of ESD's most successful programs was Major General Ken Russell (USMA 1945). Armed with an MS in nuclear physics from Purdue University through AFIT and an MBA from George Washington University, he served at ARDC as a nuclear weapons effects officer and later was named chief of the Weapons Effects Section, Directorate of Development. He then served at ARDC's Ballistic Missile Division in the evaluation of alternative intercontinental ballistic missile concepts. With this background he was assigned duties as director, Airborne Warning and Control Systems (AWACS) at ESD, a post he held for five years, a relatively lengthy period in the career of Air Force officers. He then transferred to HQ USAF as director of development and acquisition.

Space Systems Division (SSD) and Space
and Missile Systems Organization (SAMSO)

The other unit of the Air Force's missile and space program, the Space Systems Division (SSD), made significant advances in the development of many space systems. The division supported NASA programs such as Mercury and Gemini by procuring and modifying the Atlas and Titan II boosters and providing launch services at Cape Canaveral. Later, SAMSO worked closely with NASA on the NASA-managed Space Transportation System (STS). NASA was responsible for developing the space shuttle—a manned, reusable launch vehicle that would be the key element in the system. SAMSO was responsible for developing the Inertial Upper Stage (IUS) that would be used with the shuttle to place payloads into high altitude orbits. It was also responsible for activating the launch and landing site for the shuttle at Vandenberg AFB, California. Full-scale development of the IUS began in April 1978, and ground breaking at the Vandenberg launch site occurred in January 1979. As will be seen in later chapters, many West Point grads served in critical roles within the Space Systems Division and its successor organizations in the development of the country's military and civilian space systems.

System Program Offices (SPO)

The System Program Office (SPO) was the key organizational unit and focal point within AFSC, providing management and coordination of the Air Force's R&D activities for each major weapon system. The SPO director was tasked with developing and acquiring new weapons systems according to the requirements and budgetary constraints set forth by the Air Staff and Congress. SPOs also acted as the lead interface between the Air Force and contractors manufacturing the systems. The SPO was the integrator between the Air Force and the contractors. Many West Point grads served either as SPO directors or staff members within a SPO.

It is at the SPO level where the Air Force's emphasis upon the integration of technological advances in weapon systems was most apparent. For example, while many SPO directors and staff started their careers as rated pilots, they then went on to receive advanced engineering degrees. In a few cases, SPO chiefs had no flying experience and instead brought technical engineering and management skills to the table. This was because many systems installed on the aircraft (also known as "the platform") were the key features to be developed and integrated. An excellent example of this career path is General Marsh, discussed earlier, who, as a non-rated general officer became the commander of ESD and later commander of AFSC.

Launch of the space shuttle *Columbia*, STS-1 on April 12, 1981. Served from April 1981 through July 2011. First reusable spacecraft carrying astronauts and cargo into earth orbit (NASA photo).

It is noteworthy that in about 1973, Secretary of Defense Melvin Laird extended praise to the Air Force through Undersecretary of Defense Dr. John L. McLucas regarding the successful management of four specific aircraft acquisition programs. Each of these programs were managed by West Point grads: the F-15 fighter aircraft under SPO Chief Ben Bellis (USMA 1946) and later Robert C. Mathis (USMA 1948); the A-10 attack aircraft under SPO Chief Tom McMullen (USMA 1951); the E-3 AWACS program under SPO Chief Ken Russell (USMA 1945); and the B-1 Bomber under SPO Chief Ben Martin (USMA 1949).[20]

Other West Point grads who served in SPOs included:

• Major General John E. Kulpa, Jr. (USMA 1950)—General Kulpa devoted much of his career to the development of new weapon systems within AFSC and, later, as director of the highly classified Office of Space Systems on the Air Staff. Details of his contributions to the space mission are provided later in the Space chapter.

• Brigadier General Guy M. Townsend—General Townsend (Texas A&M) deserves mention because of his tremendous experience as a test pilot and his involvement in numerous aircraft during his career, including his role as SPO chief for the C-5 and B-1 and test force director for the B-70. Remarkably, Townsend was the first Air Force test pilot to fly the B-47, B-50, B-52, and the 367-80 prototype of the KC-135. Later as a civilian manager with Boeing, he worked in Los Angeles with Northrop's B-2 program to ensure the smooth integration of the B-2 wings, manufactured in Seattle by Boeing.

• Lt. General Abner "Abe" Martin (USMA 1949 and MS in weapons systems engineering from MIT through AFIT)—General Martin completed flight training in 1950 and later became an instructor and flight commander with the Air Training Command. In 1958, he began an eight-year association with the Air Force Ballistic Systems Division, AFSC. He also was the SPO director for the B-1 from 1974 to 1977. He went on to manage the development and procurement of guidance systems for the Atlas and Titan missiles and served as chief of the Airborne Integration Division in the Minuteman SPO. He finished his career as the Director of the Defense Mapping Agency.

• Lt. General Benjamin Bellis (USMA 1946)—General Bellis (USMA 1946, and MS in Aeronautical Engineering from University of Michigan in 1952) was responsible for a variety of weapon system programs including roles as deputy director and, later, director of the YF-12/SR-71 Systems Program Office. In 1968, he became deputy commander for reconnaissance and electronic warfare at ESD and in 1969 was appointed SPO Director for the F-15 program. Bellis went on to became commander of ESD in 1974.

A Time of Technological Transition

Our Air Force careers spanned a period that witnessed the most dramatic growth in technology the world has ever seen. We lived on the frontier of a new era that included the jet age for airplanes, nuclear bombs, and rocket engines carrying payloads for both peaceful and military purposes. We experienced a tremendous evolution in our weapons and military capabilities. But then in the late 1950s and early '60s, even greater change occurred with the introduction of semiconductors and microchip technology leading to greatly enhanced computing power as well as tremendous advances in ICBMs and space. As described by Fred Kaplan in his book, *1959—The Year that Changed Everything*, Texas Instruments introduced "a new device that would change the world as profoundly as any inventions of the twentieth century—the solid integrated circuit, or, as it also came to be known, the microchip."[21] The ability to produce faster, smaller, lighter, and more reliable systems for information processing had arrived, but the cost was very high. As Kaplan noted, "Miniaturization was every electronic firm's mantra. Rockets, missiles, and spaceships were seen as the jackpot markets of the future."[22] But he added that computers needed to become smaller and cheaper to satisfy those markets.

During this period, Brigadier General Schriever and his team at the Western Development Division put the new, lighter payloads into space using increasingly reliable rocket engines contributing to the development of ICBMs. The military provided the initial market demand for ICBMs which, along with innovation in manufacturing, steadily brought the cost down.

Kaplan observed that IC (integrated circuits) didn't take off quickly. That wouldn't happen until the beginning of the sixties, when President John Kennedy ordered production of the Minuteman II missile—which required tiny, reliable circuits for its guidance system. It was missiles and space that created the large demand. As Kaplan noted, the space race and the arms race—twin prospects of infinite expansion and instant annihilation—spurred America and the world into a lightning-flash new era.

Thus, the confluence of factors including improved technologies in electronics, rocketry and thermonuclear devices coupled with demand from the military's requirements for ICBMs led the way into space, both for military and civilian applications.

The USMA graduates of this era (1940s through 1980s) served their country at a time of unprecedented growth in technology and military aerospace capabilities. We were fortunate to be involved and in some cases leaders of the dramatic changes that occurred. We helped to define new weapon system requirements, to manage system development and in some cases to operate some of these greatly advanced systems. Many of these weapon systems remain in service today while others became important steppingstones for transitions to still greater capabilities. Among these transitions were the following:

- From ground and sea combat to ever-increasing air power and military missions in space
- From subsonic to supersonic to hypersonic to manned flight in space
- From aircraft detectable by radar to stealth aircraft
- From aerial engagement over enemy territory to aircraft with standoff rockets and missiles
- From manual operation of equipment to high-speed computer/digital operation making UAV/drones and satellite operations feasible
- From aerodynamic propulsion to rocket propulsion making feasible ICBMs and access to space with worldwide navigation, surveillance, and communications
- From saturation bombing using many unguided bombs to precision munitions achieving extremely high levels of accuracy, some approaching zero CEP (circular error probability)

(When in 2018 the author, with 12,000 pilot hours and having flown over fifty types and models of airplanes, flew in the pilot seat of a propeller-driven recreational airplane, then in an executive jet and finally in the simulator of a rocket ship for flying into space [SpaceShipTwo (SS2)], all with multiple switches, computers and strange displays, I knew that my era in aeronautics had passed. Technology has taken us into a new age of "switchology" and aerospace power.)

The record of Air Force aircraft with operational lives far beyond initial expectations is part of the legacy of these grads. These aircraft underwent major modifications in some way to aircraft structure, engines, avionics, navigation, or other systems during their operational lives and many were used for significantly different missions. The following table illustrates the long-lasting legacy of these aircraft which we, our children and possibly our grandchildren have flown or will fly. All these airplanes are in use today by the U.S. Air Force and, in some cases, by foreign air forces.

Aircraft	First introduced	Years of Service as of 2020
C-130 Hercules (transport)	1954	66
B-52 Stratofortress (bomber)	1955	65
U-2 Dragon Lady (reconnaissance)	1957	63
KC-135 Stratotanker (tanker/AWACS)	1957	63
T-38 Talon (trainer)	1961	59
C-5 Galaxy (transport)	1970	50

Aircraft	First introduced	Years of Service as of 2020
A-10 Thunderbolt (fighter)	1972	50
F-15 Eagle (fighter)	1976	44
F-16 Fighting Falcon (fighter)	1978	42
B-1 Lancer (bomber)	1986	34

Each of these aircraft has a long and complicated history of reacting to changing enemy threats, competition from other aircraft and weapon systems, and the availability of advancing technology providing the basis for modifications with still greater capabilities. Also, these advancements in capabilities allowed for a steep reduction in the numbers of aircraft being manufactured and deployed, albeit at a much greater cost per unit. A view of the number of strategic bomber aircraft produced together with their unit costs during the 1940s through 1980s highlights this point[23]:

Era	Aircraft	Number Produced	Years in Production	Unit Cost ($ Then)
WW II	B-24 Liberator	19,256	1940–45	297 K
WW II	B-17 Flying Fortress	12,731	1936–45	238 K
WW I, Korea	B-29 Superfortress	3,970	1943–46	639 K
Cold War	B-36 Peacemaker	384	1946–54	4.1 M
Cold War	B-47 Stratojet	2,032	1951–65	1.9 M
Cold War	B-58 Hustler	116	1960–70	12.4 M
Cold War, Vietnam	FB-111 Aardvark	563	1967–98	10.3 M
Cold War, Vietnam, Post-Cold War	B-52 Stratofortress	744	1952–62	14.4 M
Post-Cold War (before 1991)	B-1 Lancer	100	1973–88	283.1 M
Post-Cold War (after 1991)	B-2 Spirit	21	1987–2000	737.0 M

From this data it is easy to see the dramatic reduction in the numbers of aircraft from World War II through the Cold War and thereafter brought about by vastly expanded capabilities in range, avionics, refueling capability and weaponry in each aircraft as well as the greatly increased cost per unit.

In summary, the expansion of new technology and engineering in the fifty years from 1942 to 1992 was immense and produced the foundation for a new warfighting Air Force. In World War II when the U.S. targeted German oil, power and transportation systems, Nazi Armaments Minister Albert

F-117A Nighthawk Stealth fighter. First operational stealth aircraft from Johnson's Skunk Works, 2002 (U.S. Air Force photo).

Speer wrote that "a new era in air war began. It meant the end of German armaments production."[24] These bombing raids were massive, thousand bomber raids with primarily city-busting accuracy. Fifty years later, when defeating Iraq, the USAF was armed with entirely new weapons—a few stealthy F-117s launching precision guided munitions and the Air Force and Navy delivering extremely accurate cruise missiles hundreds of miles away from the target to initiate the devastating air attack on key targets. The new aircraft requirements during this 50-year period went from higher and faster to very low, terrain-following aircraft and missiles capable of penetrating enemy defenses. In the 1970s, stealth aircraft and standoff bombs and cruise missiles became the order of the day. Longer range aircraft and air refueling supported the expansive U.S. global mission. Miniaturization of new sensors, electronics and computers allowed space assets for surveillance, navigation and communication. AWACS aircraft were used against enemy airborne aircraft and JSTARS provided airborne observation and control of ground activity. Accurate target identification and strike became a reality with a circular error probability (CEP) from several thousand feet in World War II to less than 10 feet with precision-guided munitions. Technology fulfilled General Arnold's most ambitious vision of air power and aerospace power became a dominant reality in warfare.

Chapter 6

Flight Tests and Test Pilots

The Air Force process of bringing a weapon system through the R&D stage to that of initial operational capability (IOC) was and is a dynamic and lengthy process, but one that aims to produce a fully functional and combat-ready weapon system. The steadily increasing complexity and cost of developing aircraft and related systems from the Air Force's first, very basic military airplane flown by the Wright Brothers and Generals Foulois and Arnold (USMA 1907), the first military test pilot, to the advanced aircraft flown and tested by some of these West Point grads has only added to the time and expense of development. But this evolution in weapon system technology has produced vastly superior systems despite the long, torturous environment of ever-changing requirements, steadily advancing technology and greater political involvement in the process.

The final result after ten years or more of continuous concept analysis, engineering and development is an airplane ready to fly. The manufacturer's test pilot gets the honor of being the first to fly the aircraft to prove basic air worthiness. However, in two-pilot aircraft, an Air Force test pilot typically accompanies the company pilot as co-pilot. Then, as the flight test program proceeds, Air Force test pilots put the system through its paces, testing its air worthiness, performance, stability control and the many aircraft systems to determine if the total aircraft weapon system meets Air Force requirements.

From the pioneering days of the Wright Brothers and Foulois to tests of today's highly sophisticated aircraft, the overall objective of flight testing is still the same: to answer the question, can the airplane do its job?

On one occasion in 1961, General Foulois visited Edwards AFB to witness the current state of airplanes and aircraft technology. As a young Captain at the time, I had the privilege of leading the general on a tour of the Flight Test Center flight line. Despite his calm demeanor, the advances in aviation and the complexities and capabilities of the many new technologies must have staggered him. However, I recall that he was fascinated by the new technology and with few words he very calmly took it all in. On a later occasion he met with General Halloran, commander of the SR-71 strategic reconnaissance unit and was particularly interested in the tremendous capabilities of the SR-71. In his lifetime he had lived to see an almost unimaginable advancement in aeronautics.

Another example of interaction between a West Point grad and the early pioneers of flight took place when cadet Hoyt S. "Sandy" Vandenberg, Jr. (USMA 1951) flew as a passenger in a military transport bound for Europe, with his father, General Hoyt S. Vandenberg (USMA 1923 and second chief of staff of the Air Force) and with Charles Lindbergh on board. Sandy had the opportunity to visit with Lindbergh during the entire night flight because apparently Lindbergh was too nervous to sleep when flying across the Atlantic, when he was not the pilot! This example of how very different was the Air Force that we entered from the other services which had over two hundred years of history before these young officers graduated from West Point. In our case, we had the opportunity to spend some meaningful time with the very pioneers of flight whereas our other classmates at West Point and those of Annapolis entered services with very long histories and established bureaucracies.

While we were cadets and young lieutenants during the years 1945 to 1955, the Air Force developed 33 fighter and 22 bomber prototypes based on an underlying philosophy that included flight testing on a competitive fly-off basis, the winner being selected for production. This prototype process was not new because after a slow start in U.S. aircraft development during World War I, by 1918 many new American airplanes were being built and ready for flight test. By the 1930s, despite the national depression, the number of prototype flights per year increased to 12 and has never been higher before or since.

The selection of pilots to test these new aircraft also underwent significant change. It evolved from selecting the best "stick and rudder" pilots to one where pilots also had solid aeronautical education. In the earliest days of flight testing there was no formal test pilot training and the procedure amounted to the original cavalry procedure to just mount the horse/machine and become acquainted with its capability and tricks by actual trial. The accident rate soared and caused some to say that the losses from ill-prepared Army airmen was tantamount to legalized murder. The guts to brains ratio was clearly out of balance. In 1919, Colonel Thurmond H. Bane (USMA 1907) had taken the first rudimentary step to increase flight safety by signing a memorandum instructing 16 safety procedures to follow during flight test. The third procedure stated: "Pilots will make sure that they understand the operation of all controls especially the engine controls before taking off." Good advice to this day! Instruction number 8 stated, "Pilots will remain within gliding distance of McCook field at all times." (In 1927, the McCook Field operation was moved to Wright Field, now Wright-Patterson Air Force Base.) This advice is not very practical today except, for example, the X-15 and space shuttle. Let's just say that in those early years, airplanes and the pilots that tested them had a long way to go.

Early Days of the USAF Test Pilot School (TPS)

In 1944 at Wright-Patterson AFB, the Army, inspired by the UK's Royal Air Force (RAF) Empire Test Pilot School (RAF TPS), established a formal program to train flight test professionals in airplane performance, flight stability and control, flight test theory and piloting techniques. The increased focus on engineering theory was followed by practice in flight with various aircraft such as the AT-6, P-51, B-17 and B-25. The early classes of the U.S. Air Forces' TPS were filled with World War II veterans. For example, the TPS classes of 1944–45 had many fighter aces from World War II—Major Richard Bong with 40 kills, Major Dominic "Don" S. Gentile with 26 kills and Colonel Francis Stanley "Gabby" Gabreski with 28 kills and 6½ more to come in the Korean War. Major Bong also was a Medal of Honor recipient for his "aggressiveness and daring resulted in his shooting down eight enemy airplanes."[1] Major Bong was killed in August 1945 while taking off on a test mission in a P-80A shortly after graduation from TPS.[2]

Lt. Colonel Fred Ascani (USMA 1941) had returned from a tough B-17 combat tour in Europe to this new flight test organization. He graduated from TPS in 1946 along with Chuck Yeager, who had returned from a memorable fighter combat tour in Europe with more than 11 aerial kills and escape from capture after being shot down. Another member of that TPS class was Brigadier General Pete Everest, who had six aerial victories in Europe before he had a failing engine and was shot down and became a longtime prisoner of war.

Another 1946 TPS class member, Bob Hoover, had been shot down in his Spitfire in Europe and taken POW. After 16 months with many failed attempts to escape he finally broke free by stealing a German FW-190 and flying to safety in the Netherlands. Later, as a civilian pilot, he revolutionized modern acrobatic flying and was known as the "pilot's pilot." He later flew an F-80 photo chase airplane during the historic Mach 1 flight by Chuck Yeager, taking what is now the iconic photograph of the aircraft as it passed him in flight. Hoover was noted for his tremendously impressive airshow routines in P-51, F-86, F-100, T-39 and Rockwell Shrike Commander aircraft, making particular use of incredibly precise energy management. Not without reason did Jimmy Doolittle, along with many other pilots, identify Hoover as "the greatest stick and rudder man who ever lived."

Another World War II double ace and exceptional pilot from the class of 1946 was Spiros "Steve" Pisano. Born in Greece, he emigrated to the U.S. as a teenager by working on a tramp steamer. When interviewed by then war correspondent Walter Cronkite about his combat flight experience, Pisano explained the essence of being an ace. He was quoted as saying: "It happens too fast to think and worry. Luck, concentration, guts and accurate shooting is what it's all about!"

Two other World War II aces who were still active at Edwards during the 1960s were Chuck Yeager (Double Ace) and Bud Anderson (Triple Ace).

Other 1946 TPS classmates were General Robert L. "Bob" Cardenas and Guy Townsend (Texas A&M 1941). Cardenas was the Air Force project test pilot for the prototype YB-49 flying wing project, the forerunner of the B-2.

Brigadier General Charles E. "Chuck" Yeager standing in front of an F-15 Eagle in 1997, the 50th anniversary of his becoming the first man to break the speed of sound (U.S. Air Force photo).

Prior to entering the TPS, Cardenas had flown combat missions in the B-24 during World War II in Europe and was shot down but escaped to Switzerland. (Captain Glenn Edwards from the first TPS class at one point temporarily replaced General Cardenas and was killed flying this most-dangerous airplane. Edwards AFB was later named in his honor.) Cardenas later flew the new YB-49A across the country in record time of four hours and five minutes. As a result of this feat, he was invited to meet with President Truman, who asked him if he could make a low-level flight down Pennsylvania Avenue—which he did with great pleasure!

Guy Townsend had returned from a B-29 combat tour in the Pacific and then went on to make the first flights of the B-50, B-47 and B-52 with the Boeing test pilots. He later became the SPO chief for the C-5 and B-1. Generals Ascani and Townsend both became chief of bomber flight test at Wright Patterson AFB (a position I held 20 years later) and my TPS classmate Ted Sturmthal later held that position at Edwards AFB.

From Wright Patterson to Edwards

In 1946, Colonel Alfred Boyd became chief of the Flight Test Division. Unlike many from earlier days, he demanded disciplined flying with close tolerances. Test flying was changing from a glamorous, dangerous adventure to a more exacting science requiring precision flying.

By 1951 as aircraft performance increased, the school was transferred to Edwards AFB with its clear weather, 15,000-foot runway and enormous dry lake beds suitable for emergency landings. While at Edwards AFB, Generals Boyd and Ascani had a close working relationship in bringing flight testing into the modern age. General Boyd, like many of his contemporaries, began his flying career as an aviation cadet and from there he gained extensive flying experience and flew more than 700 unique military aircraft models including every Air Force type at that time in 1954. He was from the old school. This was in marked contrast to those who followed in the world of flight testing who, at a minimum had graduated from college and many of whom had advanced academic degrees, often in aeronautics. This occurred over the 1940s through the 1960s during the transition from World War II pilots with superior stick and rudder skills and outstanding combat records to a more educated and highly trained group of professional test pilots. General Boyd's contributions to Edwards were recognized by the designation of the TPS building as Boyd Hall in the 1980s.

Even when I was assigned to Flight Test Ops at Edwards AFB in 1958, my three bosses, Fitz Fulton, Bud Anderson, and Chuck Yeager, had all started as aviation cadets and immediately went to war. As noted above, two (Anderson and Yeager) were World War II fighter aces. Fitz Fulton, a bomber cargo pilot, flew B-26 missions in Korea, took part in the Berlin Airlift and later as a test pilot flew the new supersonic B-58, SR-71 and B-70 aircraft and was referred to by many as "the father of modern flight testing."

General Ascani (USMA 1941) while at Edwards as Boyd's deputy, flew many of the X series research aircraft. In 1953, Ascani left for the Air War College and then to Germany as a fighter-bomber wing commander before he returned to R&D at Wright Patterson where he was a leading member of a committee responsible for solving the challenge of reducing the time required to convert new technologies into useable weapons. Ascani then played a key role in the reorganization of Wright Field's science, engineering and management procedures to address this challenge. He later was assigned as the first director of systems engineering at Wright Field. He went on to an influential career in systems engineering at Wright Patterson, then the B-70 SPO director, followed by commander of the Wright Field system engineering group and, as a last assignment in 1970, as senior Air Force member of the OSD Weapons Systems Evaluation Group (WSEG) in the Pentagon.

Charles Lindbergh, Al Boyd, Chuck Yeager, and many other pilots are good examples of the earliest approach to flight testing. Together they flight tested more than 300 types of military aircraft, providing their assessments to eagerly awaiting engineers, military commanders and company owners. In Lindbergh's case, he went to Germany and the Soviet Union in the 1930s and reported back what he saw to the American government, the Air Corps—he was a reserve Air Corps colonel—and the aircraft industry. Later, at the end of the Second World War, he was sent back to Germany to investigate Nazi aeronautical and rocketry developments. Lindbergh later tested U.S. fighter airplanes and flew combat missions in the Pacific to show U.S. forces how best to utilize their airplanes. On one such mission he shot down a Japanese airplane.

But with new aerodynamic designs, powerful engines, and new materials, flight envelopes expanded with higher speeds and altitudes finally breaking the sound barrier and then the heat barrier. In addition, a few test pilots, including Neil Armstrong and Joe Engle (TPS Class of 1961), both of whom later became astronauts, flew the X-15, the first true "trans-atmospheric" airplane, capable of flying at hypersonic speeds into space and then returning to make a precision approach and landing on Rogers Dry Lake. You might say the sky was now the limit when, in 1961, President Kennedy set the goal of a man on the moon with safe return to planet earth in the 1960s.

It is important to note that Joe Engle (University of Kansas, 1955)—later Major General Joe H. Engle—after his experience as a test pilot at Edwards, became one of the first astronauts in the Space Shuttle program. In 1977, during the program's Approach and Landing Tests (ALT), he commanded the

North American X-15. First flight in 1959. Three were produced, and broke many speed records for manned aircraft, including the still-standing speed record of Mach 6.7 (4,520 mph). Thirteen flights at above 50 miles qualified the eight pilots who made them as astronauts (NASA photo).

space shuttle *Enterprise* when it was launched from an altitude of 25,000 feet from the top of a Boeing 747 commanded by Fitz Fulton and released for a glide flight to landing. As a former X-15 pilot, Engle was able to provide valuable observations about the handling and landing characteristics of the shuttle. His experience as an X-15 pilot contributed greatly to his selection by NASA in 1966 for the Apollo program. He later became commander of the second orbital test flight of the space shuttle *Columbia* in 1981. Engle is unique in that he became the only pilot to have flown two types of winged vehicles in space, the X-15 and the space shuttle, and is the only astronaut to have flown the shuttle manually through reentry and landing. As Joe said,

> The information and techniques developed in the X-15 program literally laid the groundwork for the Space Shuttle. Hardware, flight control systems, operational flight techniques, physiological data, crew operations with full pressure suit, data monitoring of both aircraft and biological parameters, simulation, and real-time mission control were all direct beneficiaries of the X-15 program. But

perhaps the most significant contribution was the airplane's demonstration of the ability to routinely manage energy of an unpowered low lift to drag winged vehicle through re-entry from space to a precise touchdown on a runway or lakebed."[3]

Because the lift-to-drag final approach angles and the approach pattern and touchdown speeds of the X-15 and the space shuttle were nearly identical from Mach 5 to touchdown, these concerns were "answered and put to rest.[4]

TPS Class 58-C

Test piloting of the newest experimental airplanes during the "glory years" of flight testing at Edwards AFB had great appeal to me and many others. After four years on the front lines of the highly regimented and seniority-driven SAC life, I was ready to give flight test a try. I passed the first step which was gaining entry to the Test Pilot School and the challenge of flying four different aircraft (T-28, B-57, T-33, and F-86) which I had never flown before. Competing with a class of highly talented and motivated mainly fighter pilots was a challenge. Down the flight line from the school was test operations ("Test Ops") with the much sought-after jobs alongside World War II fighter aces and pilots testing new supersonic aircraft pushing the frontiers of aviation and even space flight. Our class of 58-C was a fine group of 15 pilots, most with combat experience, one with a speed record and one who had bailed out of a failing aircraft. I had Strategic Air Command experience, some as a lead or select crew member, considerable high-speed, low-level flying followed by bomb delivery using the LABS ("Low Altitude Bombing System") maneuver with the B-47, which was originally designed for high altitude bombing. Just after my crew and I became combat ready with this procedure, it was cancelled the same day due to accidents caused by structural failure and pilot disorientation while flying inverted with minimum air speed at the top of the maneuver.

The school was competitive, fast, fun and paced by this outstanding and ambitious group. Six members were West Point grads who knew competition and relished this opportunity (Class of 1949: Joe Guthrie; Class of 1950: Harvey Prosser, Charlie Kuyk; Class of 1951: Jack Craigie, Murt Guild, Sully Johnson). Of these grads, four had MS degrees, five had Korean War combat experience, and one, Colonel Harvey Prosser (MS in math and calculus instructor at both West Point and the Air Force Academy) did a fine job of teaching calculus to our class as that subject is applied to aeronautics while still competing as a fellow pilot.

I was fortunate to have Joe Guthrie, who previously had flown all the school's airplanes, some in combat, fly with me on weekends so that I could

Top: Class 58-C on an F-86 at the Test Pilot School at Edwards AFB. Six West Point grads were in this class: Jack Craigie, Joe Guthrie, Sully Johnson, Mert Guild, Harvey Prosser, and the author, seated on the wing. *Above:* Boeing B-47E Stratojet. Strategic nuclear bomber. First flight 1947. There were 2,032 produced. Foundation design for high altitude, subsonic aircraft. First swept wing, multi-engine bomber using JATO rocket for assisted takeoff, drag chute for assist in stopping. A Lockheed F-80 served as its chase plane (both U.S. Air Force photos).

gain experience with the school's airplanes. What a deal to have two former West Point football players from the outstanding '46 to '49 teams flying F-86s cross-country in formation!

The class of 58-C had two notable graduates with significant pioneering influence on aircraft performance and space flight—Tom Stafford and Pete Knight. Tom Stafford (USNA 1952 and first in our TPS class), along with Fred Haise, another TPS graduate, became the fastest men in the world in their space capsule with a 24,270 mph return from space to earth, a record which I believe still stands. Later, Stafford was commander of the 1975 Apollo-Soyuz mission, with its first joint U.S.-Soviet rendezvous and join up in space. General Stafford later returned to the Air Force from his tour with NASA and became the Air Force Flight Test Center commander and then a lieutenant general as DCS R&D at Air Force HQ. The author worked for Stafford as director of requirements.

Colonel Pete Knight (BS in aeronautical engineering at Purdue through AFIT in 1958) was a test pilot for five supersonic Century series fighters before flying the X-15 and becoming the fastest man in the world, flying a winged airplane at 4,520 miles per hour (Mach 6.70), a record that still stands today. He became one of the first astronauts by exceeding 50 miles altitude in the X-15. Knight went on to 257 combat missions in Vietnam in the F-100 and returned to Wright Patterson, where he was test director for the F-15 and then back to Edwards as vice commander of the Flight Test Center and test pilot for the F-15. He was one of six test pilots selected to fly the later-cancelled X-20 Dyna-Soar (for "dynamic soaring"), slated to become the first winged orbital space vehicle capable of reentries and conventional landings (discussed later in the Space chapter). After retiring from the Air Force, Knight later served as mayor of Palmdale, California, then as a member of the California state senate—and, proving that public service ran in the family, his son Steven served as a member of the U.S. House of Representatives, during which he was a tireless advocate for advanced aerospace research.

Ted Sturmthal was a test pilot and often the project pilot responsible for the flight testing of a wide variety of aircraft including the B-57F, B-52H, C-130, B-1 and B-70. Sturmthal flew the first test flights of the B-1 in 1974 later taking it to supersonic speeds for the first time. He became the B-1 Joint Test Force Project Director. During the Korean War, Sturmthal flew combat missions in the B-26 and later in Vietnam was commander of a reconnaissance wing, flying nearly two hundred combat missions. At Edwards AFB he served as chief of the bomber/transport section. He was one of seven pilots to fly the Mach 3.2 XB-70 and along with Fitz Fulton flew the last flight of the B-70 to its resting place at the Air Force Wright Patterson museum.

Joe Guthrie was a Korean and Vietnam War combat veteran. He flew combat missions in Douglas B-26 Invader light bombers (not to be confused

North American XB-70A Valkyrie, 1966. Prototype version of the planned B-70 nuclear-armed strategic bomber. Capable of cruising for thousands of miles at Mach 3+ at 70,000 feet (U.S. Air Force photo).

with World War II's Martin B-26 Marauder bomber) in Korea and secret reconnaissance missions during the Cold War in RB-57 aircraft. In Vietnam, he was the squadron commander of an A-1 (a 1940s propeller-driven airplane) close air support attack squadron supporting the very dangerous "Jolly Green Giant downed airmen" rescue missions that made many miraculous rescues in enemy territory. When the downed pilot or crew was located, the A-1s would fly a very low-level perimeter defense around the location, often under intense enemy ground fire, while the rescue helicopter lowered a cable to the downed airmen to make the pickup. These rescues often became a raging battle as enemy ground forces closed in. His squadron rescued one of my EB-66 crews who had been shot down over North Vietnam. In order to thank him and his squadron and to gain more familiarity with their mission and the A-1's performance, I joined them on a close air support mission with one with one of his pilots. Toward the end of his command in Vietnam, one of his A-1 pilots, Lt. Colonel William A. Jones (USMA 1946) was awarded the Medal of Honor for his heroic contribution to the successful rescue of a downed F-4 pilot in North Vietnam.

Douglas A-1E Skyraider. First flight, 1945. With 3,180 produced, they provided heavy payload and endurance for close air support, search and rescue (U.S. Air Force photo).

Following his tour in Vietnam, Lt. Col. Guthrie was assigned as Chief of Test for the C-5 at the SPO in Wright Patterson. He flew a variety of USAF and British aircraft during his career. At Edwards, he served for nearly four years (1972–75) as the TPS commandant during the major transition from the Aerospace Research Pilots School (ARPS) aimed at training test pilots and astronauts back to the original Test Pilot School with the addition of flight test training to navigators and flight test engineers. As noted in his obituary, "He was known by friend and foe as a man of honor, a man who made the tough calls, a gruff man with a sense of humor and an iron clad sense of duty and he was a great story teller."

As noted earlier, Joe commanded the USAF Test Pilot School during the transition of the school back from the USAF aerospace research pilot school which had been commanded by Buzz Aldrin (USMA 1951). Since NASA had assumed responsibility for astronaut training, in this transition the Air Force reverted to its original mission as a Test Pilot School. In addition, non-rated officers, both men and women, serving as flight test engineers now became students in the new Test Pilot School. Guthrie retired after 28 years of military service as a pilot and then became a civilian test pilot for 14 more years. In 1984, he served as president of the international Society of Experimental Test Pilots, a tribute to his reputation in the field.

Fortunately for me, when our TPS class graduated, a bomber pilot was needed at Flight Test Operations and I was selected for the job. My first assignment was testing the B-52G with Lt. Colonel John Carlson (who later flew A-1 aircraft rescue missions in Vietnam with Joe Guthrie) and then with Toby Gandy (USMA 1945). My first project was evaluating the B-52G carrying two Air-launched GAM-77 "Hound Dog" missiles that gave SAC the first real standoff missile with up to a 500-mile range versus the existing 80-mile range of the SRAM (short-range attack missile) missile. Incidentally, this experience served as a forerunner for my future role on the Air Staff as the advocate for cruise missiles with a standoff range up to 1,500 nautical miles. While I was flight testing the B-52 with Hound Dog missiles, my classmate Colonel Jack Kulpa (USMA 1950) was at the project office at Wright Patterson responsible for introducing these missiles to SAC. Later, I was the test pilot leading a team of Flight Test Center pilots and engineers with SAC crew members in weapon system evaluation of the long-serving B-52H. This included extensive low-level, high-speed flying under a hood to evaluate the newly designed terrain following radar ("TFR") for flying at night and in adverse weather.

B-52H aircraft armed with long-range missiles are still flying 60 plus years later and are forecast to be useful for many years to come if given adequate maintenance, upgrades and, probably, expanded capabilities.

At the same time B-52 tactics were being evaluated, there were two high-altitude, high-speed programs under way to replace the B-52. The supersonic B-58 Hustler first flew in 1956 with IOC in 1960. It was a high-altitude bomber with limited payload range, difficult to fly and with high maintenance costs. One-hundred-sixteen B-58s were delivered and 26 were lost to accidents. The B-58 was retired after 10 years. I had the experience of a few test flights in the aircraft at the Flight Test Center.

General LeMay argued for the higher-flying Mach 3+ B-70, but this aircraft had a tortuous life in many respects—politically, technologically, and financially. The Cold War philosophy of bomber penetration to target from the U.S. at high altitude and high speed with a nuclear weapon was coming to an end in the face of more capable enemy defenses. The B-70 bomber program came to a dramatic end during flight tests with a midair collision between the second of two XB-70As built and a NASA F-104 chase airplane during a formation flight for General Electric publicity photographs. Regrettably, both the F-104 pilot, Joe Walker (a former X-15 pilot who held the record—354,200 feet [67 miles]—for the highest-ever X-15 flight) and Major Carl Cross, the XB-70A copilot, died in that crash. The remaining XB-70A went on to several years of productive life in flight test research of the many challenges of sustained Mach 3 flight. Like the B-58, destruction of enemy targets defended with SAMS and advanced fighters, accurate standoff missiles, and the new alternatives of ICBMs, and later, stealth aircraft, dramatically changed the operational environment and requirement for the B-70. However, sustained high-altitude, Mach 3 reconnaissance flight was moving ahead at Lockheed in Kelly Johnson's Skunk Works.

In 1961, when the Air Force was planning its own manned space programs (which became the Boeing X-20 Dyna-Soar and the Manned Orbiting Laboratory, "MOL"), the TPS was developing a course for astronauts and the school name was changed to the Aerospace Research Pilot School. Frank Borman and Jim McDivitt were TPS school instructors, future astronauts and members of a four-man team tabbed to develop the first space-oriented curriculum while simultaneously participating in their new program. Future astronauts Mike Collins (USMA 1952), Ed White (USMA 1952) and Dave Scott (USMA 1954) later took this astronaut course as did Don Kutyna (USMA 1957, who in 1987 become a general in command of the new Space Command and NORAD organizations) who then became a staff director at the school. When the man-in-space program was turned over to NASA and the two Air Force programs were cancelled by 1969, the school reverted to its original mission of training future flight test pilots and the name returned to the Test Pilot School. Interestingly, over the years four West Point graduates were commandants of the TPS—in order, Eugene Deatrick (USMA 1946), William J. Campbell (USMA 1953), Buzz Aldrin (1951), and Joe Guthrie (USMA 1949).

Other Flight Tests

As a test pilot, I was involved with two significant strategic bomber challenges: how to get off the ground faster and safely to avoid incoming ICBMs and, second, how to penetrate enemy defenses at low level at night during conditions of poor visibility. I was assigned these projects because of my SAC experience flying the B-47 at low level and high speed. We experimented with various methods of getting the maximum number of aircraft off the runway in minimum time, known as MITO, minimum interval takeoff. The project name, "Hurry-Hurry," started with B-47 aircraft and, after establishing the best procedure, we proceeded testing with the B-52, KC-135 and KC-97. We used Flight Test Center and SAC aircrews on these projects and later SAC used the procedure to complete tests with SAC test crews and the B-58.

The final proof of concept was performed with six B-47s at night, with maximum gross weight and all with JATO-assisted takeoff which created a huge amount of smoke and debris, resulting in extremely limited runway visibility. We taxied on to the runway at the minimum interval obtainable—six to ten seconds between aircraft—and immediately continued with the takeoff roll. Because of limited visibility, the runway had been marked with a two-foot wide painted yellow stripe at the turn and down the runway. The turn and runway were barely visible due to the night-time conditions and previous planes' JATO smoke. I piloted the last of six B-47s. At the computed refusal speed (go-no/go speed), the co-pilot Colonel Russell Schleeh, a senior test pilot and chief of Air Force Safety at Norton AFB, cut off an outboard engine (of the six engines) and we struggled safely into the air. One of the JATO bottles was reported from the ground to still be burning after takeoff, so we jettisoned the JATO rack which assisted our climb with only five engines. Flight tests of the remaining three aircraft types were less harrowing. The tankers (KC-135 and KC-97) were underpowered such that no engines were cutoff during testing and the B-52 with seven engines at full power after one was cut off was easy to manage.

The second test project for SAC involved the new terrain avoidance ("TA") radar which was designed to allow B-52s to make low-level, high-speed, all-weather penetration of enemy defenses. The radar looked ahead to reveal terrain which allowed terrain avoidance and a roller coaster low-level flight over mountainous terrain. After returning from one very turbulent low-level flight, the vertical stabilizer on our B-52 was observed to have a significant wrinkle along a rivet line indicating it had been severely overstressed. This information was communicated to Boeing, but the company was hesitant to acknowledge a significant structural problem. A few weeks later, Boeing, while conducting a similar low-level flight in mountainous terrain, encountered severe turbulence and the vertical stabilizer broke off along the same structural line as we had experienced. The Boeing pilot expertly brought the airplane back for a safe landing. Consequently, the major problem was addressed, and the vertical stabilizer was strengthened on future B-52Hs.

Edwards AFB Flight Tests

The X-15 paved the way for flight into space with the next generation, fixed-wing aircraft, the space shuttle. The X-15 was launched at 45,000 feet from under the wing of a modified B-52. As one of the B-52 pilots for several of these flights, I can say that it was a thrill to see the rocket-propelled X-15 accelerate away from us after launch and soar ahead climbing at about a 45-degree angle toward space, leaving a long white exhaust trail. During one record-breaking flight to Mach 4, Bob White (NYU, 1951, who, later as a major general, commanded the Flight Test Center) was the X-15 pilot; two West Point grads, myself and Frank Cole (USMA 1946) piloted the B-52. Bob and other X-15 pilots went on to set additional speed and altitude records exceeding Mach 6 at altitudes above 50 miles to become astronauts. I also had the opportunity to be a B-52 launch pilot for six of the twelve X-15 pilots:

the original North American Aviation Company X-15 pilot Scott Crossfield, Neil Armstrong from NASA (the first man to step on the moon), Joe Walker from NASA, Major General Bob Rushworth with the greatest number of X-15 flights (34), Major General Bob White, and Admiral Forrest Petersen USN. It was truly history in the making.

But experimental flight testing was not without risk. For example, Major Michael Adams died in the only crash of an X-15. Joe Walker later died in the XB-70A crash. And Captain Iven C. Kincheloe, while preparing to be the first USAF pilot to fly the X-15, died in an F-104 accident in 1958.

President Kennedy awarded Scott Crossfield, Joe Walker and Bob White the Harmon Trophy in 1961 honoring their flights in the X-15 program. This prestigious award was given to other test pilots mentioned in this book including Lindbergh, Doolittle, Yeager, Fulton and Borman. At the same award ceremony, President Kennedy also honored the four Mercury astronauts.

In test operations at Edwards, there often was the opportunity to accompany any pilot flying tests in a dual cockpit airplane. In fact, it was encouraged to give pilots experience in a wide variety of aircraft types, each with its unique good and bad characteristics. The benefit of "been there, done that" was substantial because as the old saying goes, "Flying is not inherently dangerous, but it is very unforgiving!"

By way of example, one day Chuck Yeager was about to fly a two-place F-100F with an empty back seat. I jumped at the chance to join him. As I observed earlier, General Yeager is a very talented aviator and with many hours in the F-100. But even when he flew with me during a B-52H air refueling, he demonstrated the same smooth, confident control notwithstanding his lack of experience in that aircraft. Furthermore, neither the B-52G or H models have ailerons but use spoilers for role control. This makes their flight control, particularly for something as delicate as air refueling, quite different from other aircraft. Nevertheless, Yeager stayed in contact with the KC-135 tanker even during a 180-degree turn. He said afterward, "Don't worry about all that plane behind you, the stick and rudder are the same!"

On another occasion, Bob Rushworth had an empty F-104B back seat when he was about to practice simulated X-15 approach and landing in preparation for his next X-15 flight. He took me along to observe the crucial final stage of an X-15 test flight involving a no-power, low-lift, high-drag, rapid descent to landing. It was quite an experience. We started from an altitude of 15,000 feet, reduced power to a minimum and came down like a rock, but Bob put it down on the spot every time!

Another exciting flight test involved "spin testing" where the pilot tests a plane's behavior while entering and recovering from a spin. Spin testing can be a hazardous procedure and many pilots first review techniques for entry and recovery in the T-37 trainer before attempting these tests in more

North American F-100 Super Sabre. First flown in 1953, there were 2,294 produced. First supersonic jet fighter. Initially it was the Air Force's primary fighter-bomber in Vietnam, later replaced by the F-105 and F-4 (U.S. Air Force photo).

advanced aircraft. I took every opportunity to fly along on these tests and it was quite an educational experience for a bomber/cargo pilot where spins hopefully never occur.

One of my T-37 spin testing experiences was with Captain Carl Cross. He had just been assigned to evaluate a prototype executive aircraft proposed for the Air Force. He was selected as project pilot because of his airlift experience. Because there was concern that the aircraft to be tested might experience spins, he conducted some spin training with me in the T-37. After undergoing this T-37 spin training, he was well prepared to spin test this new aircraft. However, while flying with the company test pilot he performed an "approach to stall" flight test and the aircraft fell off into a spin. After more than 10 spinning turns and many unsuccessful spin recovery attempts by Carl, the company pilot deployed the ground-braking chute to stop the spin. In actuality, the chute was installed for unadvertised spin recovery. Much later, Carl's luck unfortunately ran out when his ejection capsule failed, and he was killed in the XB-70A accident that also claimed NASA's Joe Walker.

Also, several fighter aircraft and U-2 pilots joined me on B-47 and B-52 flights to gain firsthand experience in how to handle bicycle landing gear common to these aircraft. This is a relatively uncommon landing gear con-

Top: Cessna T-37B Tweet. Small, twin-jet aircraft and a primary military trainer. First flight in 1954. There were 1,269 produced from 1955 to 1975. Retired in 2009. *Above:* Northrop T-38 Talon. First supersonic trainer. Twin jet. First flown in 1959. There were 1,146 produced and in service for more than fifty years (both U.S. Air Force photos).

figuration that features two main gear along the centerline of the aircraft, one forward and one aft of the center of gravity, and two small outrigger gears mounted near the wingtips. Unless the aircraft is slowed to near stall speed when landing, the front wheels touch down first, causing the aircraft to bounce back into the air. This poses a somewhat awkward flight situation due to the combination of slow speed and very low altitude (that is, very near to the ground) which can become quite dangerous. Even top-notch X-15 pilots were surprised by their first bounced landing in a B-47.

The C-133 and C-130 turbo prop aircraft also have their individual characteristics and I learned them all when flying with Doug Benefield, who was a real experienced test pilot in flying these aircraft. Unfortunately, Doug was later killed in a B-1 flight test accident.

In summary, the Test Pilot School class of 58-C and the test activities at Edwards played an important role in at least three major technological breakthroughs that would transform U.S. air power and carry us into space. These advances included hypersonic flight up to a speed of Mach 6 at the edge of space; long-range (standoff) cruise missiles launched from the B-52 and initial preparations for space operations and man-in-space.

Wright Patterson Flight Testing

Wright Patterson AFB is the focal point of Air Force aeronautical research and development. It includes Headquarters Aeronautical Systems Division (ASD), System Program Offices (SPOs), multiple laboratories, a variety of flight test aircraft, AFIT and the wonderful Air Force aeronautical museum. The flight test mission revolves around support for flight testing of various laboratory projects such as sensors, photography, Zero G, low visibility landing systems, support of high altitude anti-ballistic missile tracking systems and extreme weather operations of new aircraft. An interesting side note is that while I was stationed at Wright Patterson in the 1970s supporting anti-ballistic missile systems by flying C-135s carrying sensors to track reentry vehicles fired from Cape Canaveral or Vandenberg AFB, then Lt. Colonel Grayson Tate (USMA 1950) was actively involved in testing ballistic missile systems. He later became the first commanding general of the U.S. Army's Ballistic Missile Defense Systems Command.[5]

Zero G Program

The Zero G program conducted at Wright Patterson AFB in a modified KC-135 gave astronauts an opportunity to experience, for a short period, what it was like to operate in a gravity-free environment. As a pilot firmly secured in the pilot's seat, we first dove to pick up speed and then pulled up to fly a very precise zero gravity arc lasting about 35 seconds with the plane then regaining air speed with a steep dive and accompanying 2.5 G pullout. Not unlike a roller coaster! The rapid change in G forces at entry and then recovery to gain zero gravity conditions at the top of the parabola caused the plane to be called by some "the vomit comet." In addition to the precise instrumentation monitored by the pilots, we would watch a TV screen trained on the cabin where a crew member would release an unrestrained medicine ball when zero gravity was reached. We sought to keep the floating medicine ball in the center of the cabin to maintain its weightlessness. A somewhat crude but effective measure. On one flight astronaut Ed White (USMA 1952), in full pressure suit, was attempting, at zero gravity, to get out of and then back into an Apollo capsule mounted in the back of the plane. After several tries, he still was unable to get back in the capsule. (As a top-notch West Point swimmer, he had broad shoulders.) Failure to exit and reenter the capsule during space flight (at zero G) meant that he would not be able to walk in space. He was quite discouraged, so we took a break and he came up to the cockpit and told me the story. As former West Point athletes, I gave him a pep talk—"Just think small and be strong—go do it!" He did it and later during the Gemini

Astronaut Christa McAuliffe on the KC-135 for zero-G training (U.S. Air Force photo).

IV mission became the first American to walk in space. Unfortunately, he later died in the tragic Apollo I capsule fire on the launch pad.

My two test pilot tours of duty at Edwards Air Force Base and then as commander of bomber flight test at Wright Patterson, were a tremendous experience. They provided a chance to work with and support a talented group of people, including many West Point grads, all with a "can-do" attitude working at the frontiers of aviation and space. It is very gratifying in retrospect to look back and see the lasting results of our efforts.

It is interesting to note that because of the various design and performance issues with new airplanes, test pilots often were used in many key positions later in their careers. For example, regarding issues associated with the C-5, test pilots such as Guy Townsend, Joe Guthrie (USMA 1949), Jesse P. Jacobs, Jr., Harry Spillers (USMA 1949), Click D. Smith, Jr., Warner E. Newby and the author (USMA 1950) all served in different capacities regarding the selection, operation and evaluation of the C-5. The author also led a three-month study of the C-5's overall operational capability, including a detailed analysis of the C-5's wing modifications.

Chapter 7

Aerial Reconnaissance

Intelligence gathering through strategic aerial reconnaissance was a relatively low priority after World War II during the huge U.S. military demobilization. But in the late 1940s and 1950s as the Cold War with the Soviet Union intensified and the need for intelligence gathering increased, reconnaissance capabilities expanded dramatically. The U.S. policy of containing massive and aggressive Soviet land forces with primarily a limited nuclear bomber force required detailed knowledge of Soviet offensive and defensive capabilities. This need was recognized particularly by Brigadier General Paul T. Cullen, commander of SAC's long-range photo mapping and electronic reconnaissance wing who, in 1948, recommended that a thorough study of reconnaissance tactics, techniques, and operations be conducted.

General Earle E. Partridge (USMA 1924), then director of training and requirements at HQ USAF, added a memo to General Cullen's recommendations urging a fundamental rethinking of the Air Force's strategic aerial reconnaissance mission. Soon after the letter was issued, the position of chief of Air Force intelligence was filled by Major General Charles P. Cabell (USMA 1925) who had transferred to the AAC in 1931 and served primarily in observation positions leading to photographic and intelligence assignments. He became director of the staff for the JCS and while still on active duty as a major general, also served as deputy director of the CIA.

Past failures to detect and provide warning of surprise attacks such as those at Pearl Harbor and Korea helped persuade decision makers of the need for improved intelligence gathering capabilities. Indeed, the greatest fear in the early years of the Cold War was the possibility of a surprise Soviet attack. As a result of this growing recognition of the need for timely and detailed intelligence information, the reconnaissance mission was upgraded in priority and redefined to include aerial radar scope photography, target verification and mapping photography, bomb damage assessment photography, weather information and electronic intelligence (ELINT). B-29s, RB-50s and later RC-135s along with various Navy aircraft were all modified for electronic intelligence gathering and these missions later were defined as "ferret missions."

In addition, since World War II the United States had based its war plans on the existence of an atomic monopoly. However, on August 29, 1949, the Soviets shattered this assumption by exploding their first atomic bomb, first detected by Air Force reconnaissance aircraft. The news of the Soviet atomic bomb startled the U.S. military establishment and changed the perceived balance of power significantly. Most importantly, this surprise detonation of a Soviet atomic device underscored the importance of aerial reconnaissance.

By 1950, the JCS had formalized the goals and operating procedures of ferret missions, which had the objective of obtaining "the maximum amount of intelligence concerning foreign electronic developments." These missions were flown along the borders of the Soviet Union to locate and analyze enemy air defenses. President Truman's approval of the program proved to be a landmark in the history of aerial reconnaissance because no longer would military considerations alone determine ferret operations—now, political ramifications played a major role. As a result, reconnaissance activities henceforth received scrutiny not only from the military services but up to the office of the president as well.

As noted, ferret missions during the early 1950s employed older World War II Air Force and Navy aircraft modified to collect, primarily, ELINT regarding enemy early warning and ground-controlled intercept (GCI) radar information. These missions required that reconnaissance aircraft fly along the borders of the USSR, China and Korea to collect and analyze information about radar sites and signals. However, even without overflying enemy territory, these aircraft were vulnerable to attack by enemy fighters (typically MiGs) and surface-to-air-missiles (SAMS). In 10 separate attacks during the 1950s, 75 Air Force and Navy aircrew members were killed flying reconnaissance missions.

My classmate Dick Newton (USMA 1950) flew as a reconnaissance pilot during the 1952–58 period, first flying RB-29s and then RB-47Es. As he said in a letter to me, based on this experience he developed a pilot's appreciation for reconnaissance missions for two primary reasons: (1) reconnaissance missions were more varied and interesting than flying in a bomber stream over North Korea and he enjoyed living the reconnaissance adage, "alone, unarmed and unafraid"; and (2) you normally returned to home base (RTB) to deliver your film or other data for laboratory processing in order to complete the mission. During the Korean War he served in reconnaissance units that also used RB-45s, RB-50s and B-29s dropping propaganda leaflets over North Korea and China to "educate" citizens about the fallacies of communism and the advantages of freedom and democracy. Of course, these missions also included the collection of weather and enemy radar information to aid bombing missions. But these missions were along the international borders of these enemy countries, and only occasionally with short flyovers. Other short-range reconnaissance missions were flown during the Korean War with some overflights over enemy territory by West Pointers including Joe Guthrie (USMA 1949) in RB-57s and Bryce Poe (USMA 1946) in RF-80s.

Dick provided details of his July 1953 mission to locate and assist in the rescue of an RB-50 crew shot down over the Sea of Japan by Soviet MiG-15s. He was flying in heavy clouds at 500 feet above the water when he spotted several surface lights and went down to get below the clouds and nearly landed on a group of Soviet fishing boats. Bad choice! (Or, as Dick described it, "the worst decision I ever made!") As it happened, Capt. John Roche, the RB-50 co-pilot, was the only survivor of the 16-man crew. Dick was in communication with a U.S. Navy destroyer and assisted them in locating the fishing boats so that the Navy destroyer could initiate rescue operations.

In another anecdote, Dick described a reunion with Frank Borman and family during a maintenance layover at Clark Field in the Philippines where Frank was assigned to a fighter-bomber squadron. Dick said that Frank, in usual fashion, took every opportunity to fly as many aircraft as possible, including the F-80, T-33, T-6 and C-45. At one point, Frank took Dick along on a T-33 flight which turned out to be Dick's first jet flight, with a few aerobatics thrown in. During that layover, Frank also took Dick on his last T-6 flight, the same aircraft in which our class and many others had learned to fly.

The primary problem faced by Air Force pilots flying reconnaissance missions was vulnerability to enemy defenses. This severely limited or prevented overflight of enemy territory. Several different solutions to this problem were attempted by the Air Force in order to "do better" and gather overflight reconnaissance information.

For example, in an effort to penetrate enemy territory and collect photographic images, the feasibility of using a modified B-36 to carry and launch a reconnaissance fighter aircraft (RF-84) was developed and flight tested. Colonel Clarence E. "Bud" Anderson, later my boss at Edwards AFB and a World War II triple ace fighter pilot, was the test pilot for this concept of using a B-36 bomber as an airborne carrier platform. He describes these experiences in his fine book, *To Fly and Fight—Memoirs of a Triple Ace.* Another concept he later tested involved the use of two modified fighter airplanes coupled to each wing of a B-29 during transit to the enemy border, where they were to be launched for the overflight reconnaissance mission and then recovered for the return trip to home base. This wing-tip join-up and coupling was a very challenging and dangerous maneuver and after an inflight collision resulting in the loss of the bomber and one fighter, the concept was dropped. Colonel Anderson observed in his book that the program should have been canceled before losing his good friend and pilot John Davis.

The Air Force also was evaluating other aircraft to improve reconnaissance capability. Starting in 1947, four-engine straight-wing B-45s were produced, becoming the first operational jet bomber and part of the nuclear deterrent force. In the 1950s, 38 B-45s were modified as RB-45Cs to carry out reconnaissance missions. Ted Crichton (USMA 1950) was a B-45 bomber pilot at that time with a primary nuclear bomber mission. Several of the RB-45Cs were shot up, and one was shot down while attempting overflights of enemy territory. The airplane served only until 1959 when it was overtaken by the swept-wing, six-engine RB-47 which could fly at higher altitude, higher speeds, and for longer distances.

My experience with aerial photography missions first took place at Wright-Patterson AFB where we flew a variety of different cameras and film types for the reconnaissance laboratory. I will always remember flying a B-47 on a photo test mission in 1965 up and down the Hudson River, from West Point to New York City, at various altitudes from 5,000 feet and higher, while the new photographic equipment was making images for later evaluation. This flight took place in the autumn, so we captured the beautiful Hudson River fall foliage and a historic photo of West Point. One framed photo was presented to General Mark Bradley (USMA 1934), commander of Air Force Logistics Command (AFLC), at his retirement party at Wright Patterson while another still hangs in my study.

I also flew a B-52 photo mission for the space program from Wright Patterson AFB to the Pitcairn Islands in the South Pacific just west of South America and returned with one air re-fueling in order to obtain downrange photos for a satellite launch to the south from Vandenberg AFB in California. (As an interesting side note, many years later as a Minuteman III crew member, my son Charlie Kuyk III [co-author] and his crewmate launched a successful test of a Minuteman III ICBM from Vandenberg to Kwajalein Island.)

While assigned to bomber flight test at Wright Patterson, one of my RB-57D photo reconnaissance aircraft experienced a structural wing failure at high altitude and crashed near the base. The pilot, Tony Lyvere (not to be confused with Anthony "Tony" LeVier of Lockheed test pilot fame), was able to successfully eject and land. We had a good beer call that night! Finally, I flew a hundred missions over Vietnam in the Douglas EB-66 Destroyer ECM/reconnaissance aircraft collecting ELINT data and jamming enemy radar for our F-105 fighter wing and other fighter-bombers to counter the heavy enemy air defenses.

But the reconnaissance challenge remained and in 1954, President

Republic F-105G Thunderchief at the National Museum of the United States Air Force. First flight, 1955. There were 833 produced. Large, single-engine, supersonic fighter-bomber with heavier bombload than B-17 or B-24 (U.S. Air Force photo).

Eisenhower (USMA 1915) emphasized that in order to make effective strategic decisions he badly needed better and more timely intelligence.

As discussed in the previous chapter on the Air Force's focus on technology, General Arnold (USMA 1907) believed strongly in the power of civilian science and technology professionals collaborating with Air Force leaders to keep them on the leading edge of aerospace technology. He had tasked Dr. Theodore von Kármán in 1944 to evaluate the current state of available aerospace technology and recommend the best R&D programs for the Air Force to pursue. In 1954, President Eisenhower, facing the challenge of how to prevent a surprise Soviet nuclear attack, went to his scientific brain trust and sought their advice on the best solutions. James R. Killian, Jr., president of MIT, recommended the formation of a study group made up of top military, industrial and scientific minds to develop solutions. Eisenhower concurred and in less than a year the group produced a highly sensitive, classified report recommending the development and deployment of satellites with advanced cameras and electronic surveillance capability that would circle the globe, overfly the Soviet Union and collect the much-needed reconnaissance information. Indeed, this recommendation had previously been suggested by RAND

Corporation as the best long-term solution. As we know today, surveillance via satellites in space proved to be the future of photo, ELINT and other forms of intelligence gathering. But at the time, developing and installing reconnaissance satellites was only a concept for future development.

Since a near-term solution also was needed, the second recommendation from the group was to develop a long-range, extremely high-flying reconnaissance airplane that had been proposed by Clarence "Kelly" Johnson from Lockheed's Advanced Development Project office (nicknamed the "Skunk Works"). Both the satellite and aircraft solutions would require considerable development, but Johnson promised to have an advanced prototype reconnaissance airplane flying within eight months after signing a contract. It should be noted that, at the time, the Air Force had contracted for the development of two other less capable, high-flying airplanes. However, the president and his scientific brain trust selected Lockheed's proposal because their proposal would produce a higher flying, longer range airplane in only eight months.

The issue facing President Eisenhower was whether Johnson could deliver the prototype and thereby live up to the Skunk Work's reputation and Johnson's motto, "Be quick, be quiet, be on time." Johnson had already proven himself as one of the most innovative airplane designers through his twin-engine Lockheed P-38 fighter airplane with just over 10,000 produced and the aircraft flown by three leading aces in World War II, Richard Bong (40 kills), Thomas McGuire (38), and Charles MacDonald (36). He also had designed and developed Lockheed's F-80 Shooting Star, the country's first operational jet with more than 8,200 produced including the venerable T-33, a two-seat trainer version of the F-80 which was used to train our generation of jet pilots. The president, with Killian's support, trusted Johnson to deliver as promised, so the program, the U-2, was approved.

The P-38 figured prominently in World War II as a fighter-bomber, escort and reconnaissance aircraft and during the Normandy invasion in 1945, Lt. General Jimmy Doolittle, then commander of the 8th Air Force flew over the Normandy beachhead with Major General Partridge (USMA 1924) as his wingman in P-38s to monitor their airmen's air support of the invasion. At the same time, then Lt. Robin Olds (USMA 1943) was flying an air superiority mission ("top cover") to protect against Luftwaffe attacks which in fact never came. Olds's description of the massive invasion armada approaching from the sea and then establishing the beachhead was enthralling. In his memoirs, *Fighter Pilot*, regarding his D-Day missions, he wrote:

> we crossed the south coast of England, hugging the underside of the dark gray clouds in high winds. The turbulence was brutal. Visibility wasn't that bad, but we had to stay below 1,500 feet to avoid going completely on instruments.... Suddenly, there was a ship ahead. No, it wasn't a ship. It was an object being

towed by a large tugboat. As we hurried past, I saw that it was some kind of floating dock. What the hell was it doing out here? But then there was another and another and then, my God, there ships, tens, hundreds, thousands of ships stretching to the horizons. All headed in the same direction. There were ships loaded with tanks and trucks, destroyers and gunboats, oilers, landing craft and supply freighters—every imaginable, and some unimaginable, kind of thing that could float. It was mind boggling.... I remember chills cascading down my spine, a feeling of utter awe and the soulful realization that we were part of what would become one of history's most unforgettable events.... We had ringside seats for one of the greatest events of history.[1]

While orbiting the beachhead, Olds had thoughts of his West Point class-mates and friends in the bloody fighting below as they worked their way ashore and up the cliffs, the thought of them "in this turmoil" was sobering. With orders to fly top cover, Olds and his team had been strongly admonished not to fire at anything on the ground.

Finally, after two weeks of just observing the invasion, his squadron was shifted to the interdiction mission throughout northern and central France, strafing and bombing German airfields, truck convoys and trains. A few weeks later, he was promoted to captain, became a flight leader and in short order he was a P-38 fighter ace. After his unit received P-51s, he shot down seven more German airplanes to end World War II as a double ace.

In Korea, Captain Dolphin D. "DD" Overton III (USMA 1949) had a similar experience as Olds in World War II in that after becoming a flight leader he wasted no time in shooting down five MiGs! However, in DD's case, he pushed a little too far, crossing into Chinese airspace to destroy his last MiG, drawing swift disapproval from his superiors in Washington. Avoiding court-martial, he resigned and returned to civilian life in the U.S. This illus-trates how rapid and difficult decisions must be made by fighter pilots, par-ticularly flight leaders, in aerial combat.

Lastly, in 1979, Robin Olds came through Travis AFB on his way to give a talk to the fighter wing in the Philippines. As 22nd Air Force commander, I invited Robin to lunch at our quarters with my wife and me where we enjoyed listening to quite a few of his experiences as a fighter pilot. Later that night he gave a highly entertaining talk to a large group of our pilots.

Another story worth telling concerns Overton and his classmate, Charles G. "Chick" Cleveland (USMA 1949). Cleveland was a retired lieutenant gen-eral who had four confirmed MiG kills in Korea flying a F-86 and had a fifth kill that was not confirmed, thereby preventing him from becoming an ace. However, 55 years later after continuing to conduct research, DD Overton discovered documents from then declassified Russian Air Force materials that provided sufficient evidence to confirm Cleveland's fifth kill, thereby earning him a Silver Star and recognition as a fighter ace. This was truly a selfless act by a very determined West Point classmate.

The Lockheed U-2

Much has been written about Lockheed's U-2 Dragon Lady and we provide here only the briefest summary to describe the dramatic new capabilities of this plane and provide context for the story of those West Point graduates who played a role in the U-2 program.

At President's Eisenhower's insistence, the Central Intelligence Agency (CIA) was put in charge of the U-2 program to avoid any claim of U.S. military action against the Soviet Union. This began a long-running turf battle between the Air Force and the CIA over which agency would control the U-2 and the primary U.S. aerial reconnaissance mission.

In early 1954, and in part due to an article in *Aviation Week* regarding a new Soviet jet bomber (the Myasishchev M-4 Bison), a fear arose that the Soviet's possessed the capability to strike the U.S. with nuclear bombers and that Soviet bomber capability was superior to that of the U.S. This became known as the "bomber gap." In 1955 at Soviet Aviation Day demonstrations, 10 Bison bombers were flown past the reviewing stand multiple times, giving the impression of far greater numbers of bombers than actually existed. Western analysts extrapolated from this number to estimate that the Soviets had as many as 800 of these aircraft. This far exceeded the U.S. bomber fleet, thereby creating a perceived bomber gap with the Soviet Union.[2]

However, President Eisenhower was skeptical of the gap but lacked the hard evidence to disprove it. He therefore agreed to the development of the U-2 to conduct aerial reconnaissance over the Soviet Union to find out if a gap actually existed. Based on the highly classified photographic evidence gained from U-2 overflights of the Soviet Union in July 1956, President Eisenhower was aware that the Soviet's bomber fleet was significantly inferior to America's, but, in putting national security before politics, he did not reveal his source of information.

The requirement for a new, very high flying, long-range reconnaissance airplane was clear to many, including Kelly Johnson. Having considered for several years the concept and performance parameters of such a plane, he was convinced that he could build one, essentially a glider with an engine. The performance specifications for this new aircraft were threefold: (1) be able to fly at ultra-high altitudes that would be above all enemy defensive threats; (2) possess long-range capability such that reconnaissance of the entire Soviet Union could be conducted; and (3) be able to carry advanced cameras and electronic sensors. All other flight considerations were secondary. Johnson maintained a laser-like focus on designing an aircraft to meet these three requirements which had never been achieved before. He drove his handpicked, highly talented designers at Lockheed's Skunk Works to achieve these goals and to accomplish them as quickly as possible. He didn't accept "it can't be done." This new airplane, to be named the U-2, was specifically designed for very specific and urgent national mission. The aircraft, including its engine, fuel, oil and systems would be required to operate in a very harsh environment at 70,000 feet and minus 70 degrees Fahrenheit for long periods of time, i.e., up to 10 hours. Designed with many of the characteristics of a glider, it would have very few physical comforts for the pilot and no backup systems. To reduce its weight, the early U-2s had no ejection seat.

As if the extreme flying conditions weren't enough, the U-2 also proved to be a real challenge to fly. The design characteristics that gave the U-2 its remarkable performance also made it very difficult to fly and gave the pilot little margin for error. At maximum altitude it required very careful airspeed management to stay within the 10-knot margin between airframe buffet at maximum speed (critical mach) and minimum (stall) speed. Breaching either limit could cause airflow separation at either the wings or the tail leading to a stall that in turn might lead to loss of altitude and detection by enemy radar or even overstress and destruction of the delicate airplane. Because of this, most high-altitude missions were flown just five knots above stall speed, a condition most demanding of the pilot.

There also was difficulty with engine flameouts above 35,000 feet. My classmate Lt. General Dick Leavitt (USMA 1950) experienced a flameout at 70,000 feet on his seventh flight with no restart, forcing him to make a "dead stick" landing on a nearby dry lakebed. Landing the U-2 also posed unique challenges since the "bicycle" gear required the pilot to touch down first with the aft gear to avoid a dangerous bounce as well as careful lateral control to avoid a dangerous ground loop resulting from dragging a wing tip which was not protected by any landing gear. Though a very advanced and capable airplane, it was very demanding and unforgiving to fly. Even Tony LeVier, Lockheed's chief test pilot, had difficulty with the plane. Five planes were lost in the first two years, three including fatalities, as it was rushed into service.

In his biography, *Following the Flag*, Dick Leavitt describes in detail his 100-plus missions over a three-year period as a U-2 pilot, with many missions over enemy territory. He was in the first group of Air Force pilots to volunteer and be trained in the airplane as the operation shifted from the CIA to the USAF in 1957.

Dick described a typical nighttime U-2 flight (they were made at night to protect the airplane's secrecy): Two hours before takeoff, the face mask of his full pressure suit would be sealed and he would breathe 100 percent oxygen to prevent the bends in case pressurization was lost at high altitude. (It's interesting to note that cabin pressure of the U-2 was maintained at 28,000 feet in contrast to the 8,000 feet or lower pressurization level for commercial jetliners. A sudden drop in air pressure caused by a flameout when at 70,000 feet is extremely hazardous and would trigger inflation of the pilot's pressure suit.) Personal conditions for the long night flight was like "driving for 8 hours at high speed on an open freeway at night and never touch your face, rub your eyes, move out of your seat, stop and stretch, blow your nose, take your hands off the steering wheel, or eat anything." He noted that one Lockheed pilot who had crashed was found to have his face plate open and had died almost instantly at high altitude due to lack of oxygen—hypoxia.

When the USAF took control of the U-2 operation from the CIA in 1957, the first U-2 wing was moved from the test facilities in California to an isolated base (Laughlin) near Del Rio, Texas, and the first two wing commanders were World War II fighter aces. Because of the tight security during the CIA's watch, SAC was unaware of the poor safety record of this prototype airplane that, for good reasons, had been rushed into service. When the new wing went into operation, SAC was shocked by the high number of U-2 accidents but also the wing's accidents with the RB-57 and T-33. In 1957, Major General John McConnell (USMA 1932), the new SAC 2nd Air Force commander, visited the wing and he observed several accidents firsthand. As noted earlier, several months later, Leavitt was conducting a test flight of the wing's first U-2 with the improved high-altitude engine and experienced a flameout at 72,000 feet and performed a dead stick landing. General McConnell, who was flying nearby, took the occasion to observe this U-2 emergency. After Leavitt landed, he immediately awarded the Distinguished Flying Cross (with first oak leaf cluster) for successfully handling this hazardous flight.

A few months after this incident, the U-2 standardization chief was killed in a U-2 accident and Leavitt was assigned the job by the new wing commander, Lt. General Austin J. Russell (USMA 1940). General Russell wanted Dick to head the Standardization/Evaluation ("stan/eval") office which incidentally had just been rated unsatisfactory by SAC HQ. He also wanted him to rapidly improve the wing's very poor flying safety record. At the time, the general was just starting his U-2 training and directed Leavitt to "immediately write a flight manual that meets Air Force standards." Leavitt and his stan/eval team revised safety aspects of the limited Lockheed manual in two months and completely overhauled other training directives to gain a satisfactory rating on their next SAC inspection.

But the U-2 was a demanding and unforgiving airplane and although Leavitt and the General tightened the qualifications and standards, the accident rate was never good. As Leavitt stated in his biography: "Of 38 pilots who began USAF U-2 combat crew training during 1957–1958, eight were killed in U-2s during training or afterwards." That was a 21 percent accident rate. But the overall loss rate (including accidents and shoot downs) of all 104 U-2 aircraft flown by CIA, USAF and other countries was about the same rate. Russell later served as Air Force vice chief of staff.

In Leavitt's book, he told of many difficult and dangerous missions he experienced in the U-2. As we write this book more than 60 years after the first U-2 flight, improved models of the airplane, cameras and sensors are still flying. A remarkable, highly useful airplane operated by many dedicated pilots and support crews. As Dick wrote in summary: "It earned the reputation as the most versatile and useful reconnaissance aircraft in the history of aviation. I am proud to have been part of that long line of officers, airmen and civilians that made it possible to fly the U-2 'towards the unknown.'"

The U-2 received many accolades from senior officials within U.S. military and intelligence communities. Regarding the U-2 overflights of the Soviet Union during 1956 to May 1, 1960, when Gary Powers was shot down, Richard Helms, then Director of the CIA said that "[t]he U-2 overflights provided us with the greatest intelligence breakthrough of the twentieth century. For the first time, American policymakers had accurate, credible information on Soviet strategic assets. We could evaluate in real time the other side's strengths and weaknesses, keep current on their state of preparedness." He went on to state that "building the U-2 was absolutely the smartest decision ever made by the CIA. It was the greatest bargain and the greatest triumph of the cold war."[3]

The CIA's U-2 project officer, Richard Bissell, said that the U-2's overflights of the Soviet Union "made up the most important intelligence-gathering operation ever launched by the West." He also said, "By the Pentagon's own estimate, 90 percent of all hard data on Soviet military development came directly from the cameras on board the U-2."[4]

Although each of the U-2 flights over the Soviet Union during the 1956 through early 1960 period were tracked by Soviet radar, neither MiGs nor SAMs could reach the planes until May 1, 1960, when the Soviets fired a salvo of 14 SA-2 missiles and brought down Gary F. Powers in his U-2—together with a MiG-19, killing its unfortunate pilot—over the Soviet Union. President Eisenhower then canceled all overflights but by this time the bomber and missile gap had been disproved.

The Soviet intrusion with missiles into Cuba was identified by U-2 flights and, unfortunately, Major Rudolf Anderson was downed by a Soviet-manned SA-2 site during one of these flights. Another involvement with the U-2 by a West Pointer was in the early 1970s when Colonel Joe Guthrie (USMA 1949) was commandant of the Test Pilot School and made a local, daylight flight at Edwards AFB to evaluate the handling qualities of the U-2. As commandant, he made sure to gain experience in each of the aircraft that his students would be flying. Because of the challenging handling characteristics of the U-2, particularly its bicycle landing gear, the TPS pilots gathered at the flight line expecting to witness a less than perfect landing. However, unbeknownst to them, Joe had logged many flight hours in the B-47 which had a similar bicycle landing gear and the same tendency to float upon landing. As a result, he handled the landing with ease, just as a commandant should!

The Lockheed SR-71

Kelly Johnson of Lockheed's Advanced Development Projects, the "Skunk Works," told his engineers in 1958, two years into U-2 overflights of the Soviet Union, that a new, less vulnerable reconnaissance airplane would be needed. He proposed that they design a revolutionary Mach 3+ airplane that could fly 4,000 miles without air refueling (it ultimately reached 2,500 without refueling)[5] and overfly enemy territory at 90,000 feet—an extreme technological challenge for even Johnson's superbly innovative team. What was needed was a futuristic aircraft with powerful new engines and fuel, body and wings and systems that could operate efficiently at extremely high temperatures sometimes exceeding 1,000 degrees F. In addition, President Eisenhower's key interest was to have the plane fly undetected by the enemy. But Kelly Johnson thrived on the frontiers of aviation and Lockheed trusted and supported him with significant capital to be spent solely at his discretion. Kelly handpicked the best forward-thinking engineers for his small group and motivated them to do what most considered to be a mission impossible. The CIA and President Eisenhower pushed strongly for a new aerial reconnaissance aircraft and Johnson was competing with two other options: a hypersonic drone carried to altitude by a huge balloon and the other, the B-58 Mach 2 bomber launching a drone at high altitude and speed.

Kelly's team pushed ahead with a series of preliminary designs, but on the twelfth try he and his team produced what appeared to be a viable, buildable design with extremely high performance and considerably lower radar cross section. On August 28, 1959, their latest design, designated the A-12, was presented to the CIA project manager, Richard Bissell, Dr. Edwin Land, a presidential technical advisor from Polaroid, and CIA director Dulles. Approval was given to develop five airplanes within two years as Kelly had proposed. The Kelly Johnson U-2 business model—secret, on budget and on time—was to be followed in developing these aircraft. A key objective was to attain the lowest possible radar cross section. Kelly's team worked their way through several extremely difficult technical issues regarding engine power at extreme altitude and the heat barrier that would be encountered at hypersonic speeds. Titanium was selected for the airframe rather than stainless steel which was twice as heavy. The airplane would have two engines with an ingenious inlet spike to alter the airflow into the inlet as speed increased and essentially turned a turbo jet into a ramjet engine at the higher mach numbers and ultra-high altitudes. New aeronautical designs and radar absorbing materials (RAM) were used to reduce the radar cross section. Technological breakthroughs were required in many areas.

When the airplane was ready for flight test in April 1962, a highly experienced engineering test pilot was required. Lewis "Lou" W. Schalk, Jr. (USMA 1948), who graduated first in his class at the Test Pilot School in 1954 and, under the direction of Pete Everest and Chuck Yeager, spent three years flight-testing a variety of high-performance Century Series jet aircraft including the F-100, F-101, F-104 and F-106. By 1957 he had joined Lockheed Aircraft as an engineering test pilot and in two years was selected by Kelly Johnson as chief test pilot for Lockheed's highly classified A-12 aircraft. He helped design the cockpit and interfaced with system engineers on the refinements of the revolutionary A-12, YF-12 and finally SR-71 "Blackbirds." In 1962, Schalk made aviation history when he became the first to fly the A-12, continuing with many additional A-12 flights including the first four flights exceeding Mach 3.0, achieving a top speed of 2,287 mph above 90,000 feet. He was a pioneering test pilot who faced the daunting task of flying this dangerous experimental aircraft on a regular basis and often set new speed and altitude records. He paved the way for a greatly improved aerial reconnaissance effort to keep overflying enemy territory after Gary Powers was shot down over Russia in his U-2 in 1960 and when the U-2 had become too vulnerable for the overflight mission.

Lockheed SR-71A Blackbird. Mach 3+, high altitude strategic reconnaissance aircraft. There were 68 produced (U.S. Air Force photo).

As discussed previously, in 1965 when the Air Force took responsibility for the SR-71 program, Ben Bellis was assigned to manage the Air Force SPO for this new program with the goal of turning the CIA's A-12 photo reconnaissance aircraft into an "all aspect" data gathering aerial reconnaissance airplane with space for a reconnaissance system operator (RSO) and additional fuel and equipment to support data gathering including photography, ELINT, communications and the High Altitude Support Program (HASP) to collect nuclear debris at high altitude from the enemy's tests of nuclear weapons.

Two of the first aircraft commanders were William Campbell and Jerome O'Malley, classmates from the West Point class of 1953. They were in the program for six years and four years, respectively. O'Malley was the first SR-71 operational pilot and Campbell, who logged more than 750 hours in the SR-71, later became the SR-71 test director at Edwards AFB, remaining in that position until 1971 when he became commander of the Test Pilot School.

Campbell then went to Vietnam where he served as deputy commander for operations, 8th Tactical Fighter Wing. After returning from Southeast Asia, he was assigned to the Aeronautical Systems Division (ASD) at Wright Patterson AFB as director of development, test and evaluation for the B-1. He went on to become commander of SAC's 8th Air Force and then vice commander of SAC under General Davis.

General O'Malley commanded the 9th Strategic Reconnaissance Wing at Beale Air Force Base from 1972 to 1973. He then was named commander of the 22nd Bombardment Wing and later served as chief of staff for 15th Air Force. He went on to become the assistant deputy chief of staff for plans at SAC headquarters for one year, after which he was named deputy chief of staff for operations plans. In 1977, he moved to Washington, D.C., for duty as vice director of operations of JCS. O'Malley then served as assistant deputy chief of staff, operations, plans and readiness at USAF headquarters for a year when he became deputy chief of staff for plans and operations. He was appointed USAF vice chief of staff in 1982 and in 1983 was named commander-in-chief of the Pacific Air Forces. He assumed command of Tactical Air Command in 1984 and, though being groomed for greater responsibilities, unfortunately was killed in a T-39 accident in 1985.

Another classmate, Joe Laccetti (USMA 1950), was a highly qualified SAC bombardier/navigator in the B-47, B-52 and B-58. In 1965, Joe was assigned to SAC headquarters to manage the critical development and procurement of FB-111, B-52, and SR-71 bombing and navigation systems.

As an item of interest, when Lt. General James M. Keck (USMA 1943) was vice commander of SAC, his son Thomas J. Keck (USAFA 1969), at the time a captain, was a pilot in the U-2 and SR-71 and later, as lieutenant general, commander of the 9th Reconnaissance Wing. While he was an aircraft commander of the SR-71, his father flew with him for an orientation flight in the airplane.

With IOC in 1966 and a final flight in 1999 (by NASA), the Blackbird's 33 years of service provided the country with an important and timely intelligence capability. This included 24 years of service as a USAF reconnaissance vehicle with the remainder of its life devoted to high altitude research by NASA.

Lt. General Leavitt, as the vice commander of SAC, was sent by General Ellis to understand the SR-71 mission and capability, to fly in the aircraft and bring this information back to SAC. From this experience, he observed that the B-1 technology was outdated—lacking the stealth capability and the hypersonic speed of the SR-71.

Kelly Johnson's record with the high-flying U-2 and its successor reconnaissance aircraft, the SR-71 and its still unsurpassed speed and attitude records, sets him apart as an aeronautical genius. His protégé, Ben Rich, carried on the Skunk Works tradition with the revolutionary design and development of the F-117 Nighthawk with extreme stealth capability. When this program was in its design phase, the program was known as "Have Blue." At that time, as director of requirements at the Air Staff, two of my officers visited Lockheed's stealth laboratory and returned with a report on this new super-secret stealth technology that left us thoroughly amazed. The era of stealth aircraft, which had been attempted with the U-2, progressed with the SR-71 and was firmly established with the F-117.

In summary, while Kelly Johnson and his Skunk Works were instrumental in fulfilling our reconnaissance mission, President Eisenhower was the predominant driver of the country's aerial reconnaissance program. He recognized the absolute need for detailed reconnaissance of the Soviet Union in order to maintain U.S. superiority during the Cold War. He also tried, but failed to keep our reconnaissance capabilities secret, but he nevertheless directly contributed to our aerial reconnaissance efforts by proving with the U-2 that there was no bomber gap and established that the Soviets had a nuclear weapon. The U-2 photos also confirmed that the Soviets were moving intermediate range missiles into Cuba.

Chapter 8

Military Airlift

In early 1941, just months before Japan's attack on Pearl Harbor, the AAC had no airlift organization. However, the need for military airlift to carry personnel, equipment, and supplies in support of the war effort in Europe came into sharp focus shortly after the commencement of World War II in Europe in 1939. At the time, a number of European governments looked to the United States for military equipment, including aircraft, to combat the invading German army, but the challenge was how to deliver aircraft from the U.S. to England because of the vulnerability from German U-boat attacks of ships carrying material while crossing the Atlantic. However, the British devised a scheme to ferry aircraft across the ocean.

Despite initial skepticism about the feasibility of flying the long, over-water distance across the Atlantic, it proved to be a brilliant strategy. Aircraft were first flown from U.S. manufacturing facilities to an airport near Montreal, then flown to Royal Canadian Air Force (RCAF) Station Gander in Newfoundland to refuel for the transatlantic flight to RAF bases in Scotland. Despite the hazards of the flight, seven Lockheed Hudsons flown by civilian pilots, led by a U.S. pilot and with only one navigator for the fleet, successfully made the trip across the Atlantic. After that, the operation accelerated rapidly. Over the course of the war more than 9,000 airplanes were ferried across the Atlantic. By the end of the war, transatlantic flights had become routine.[1]

The United States was a neutral state when, on March 11, 1941, President Franklin D. Roosevelt signed the Lend-Lease Act to Promote the Defense of the United States. The program was designed to distribute food, fuel, supplies and war material, including airplanes, to the UK, free France, other European countries, China and later the Soviet Union in response to the German invasion. Lend-lease was designed to serve America's interest in thwarting Nazi Germany's aggression without actually entering the war until America was ready. The stage was set for much larger numbers of aircraft to be sent to our allies.

Just months after commencement of the lend-lease program, then Major General Hap Arnold established the Air Corps Ferrying Command organized and commanded by Brigadier General Robert Olds (Robin Olds's father). "This was the first step in the spanning of the Atlantic with an aerial supply bridge, comparable as a development in military supply to the first use of the railroad as a logistical instrument in the wars of the nineteenth century. The hazardous route across the North Atlantic constituted, however, only one segment of a long supply line that reached from the factories of southern California to the airfields of Britain."[2]

Thus began what was to become a worldwide U.S. military ferrying operation that evolved into the Military Air Transport Service (MATS, 1948–66), the Military Airlift Command (MAC, 1966–92), and then Air Mobility Command (AMC, 1992–present).

When the U.S. entered the war after the Pearl Harbor attack on December 7, 1941, re-supply of U.S. troops by airdrop or landing across Europe and later in the Pacific added hugely to the airlift requirements. Never before had the U.S. military moved so much manpower and material so quickly and to so many distant destinations. Transport by air became a key element of logistical support for military operations throughout the world.

Recognizing the benefits of existing civilian airplanes, the Air Corps purchased and modified civilian airplanes to meet the military demand. As war loomed in Europe in the early 1940s, the Air Corps began purchasing hundreds of Curtiss C-46 Commandos and more than 10,000 Douglas C-47 Skytrains to serve in the war. Indeed, after the war, General Eisenhower is said to have observed that the C-47 was one of the principal instruments of the allied victory during World War II.[3] For the long, overwater flights during the war, a number of B-24 bombers were modified as cargo planes and designated C-87s while other long-range missions were carried out by C-54s.[4]

Flying "the Hump"

In 1942 after the U.S. had entered the war, the Ferrying Command was redesignated the Air Transport Command (ATC) and Japan had closed off all land routes into China. In order to resupply the war effort against Japan and to support the AAF based in China, a remarkable airlift mission lasting 42 months was carried out. This required flying manpower, supplies and equipment from bases in India over the Himalayas into China—a daring and dangerous mission that Allied crews called "the Hump." It was a formidable 500-mile route over heavy jungle and then mountain passes at 14,000 feet flanked by peaks in excess of 16,000 ft. Flying time varied between four and six hours depending on weather conditions. Adding to the challenge was the

Douglas C-47 Skytrain. First dedicated airlift aircraft. First flight in 1941. More than 10,000 produced. Used extensively during World War II to transport troops, equipment and supplies (U.S. Air Force photo).

absence of reliable maps and navigation aids and some of the worst weather on the globe ranging from hot, tropical weather in India to freezing conditions and icing over the mountains.[5] Douglas C-47 Skytrains served as the primary aircraft during the initial phase of the mission and were supplemented in 1943 by Curtiss C-46 Commandos and later by Douglas C-54 Skymasters. Unfortunately, there were hundreds of airplane crashes along the India-China route leading some to call it "an aluminum trail of accidents."

As a major in 1941, William H. Tunner (USMA 1928) was a personnel officer for the AAF's Ferrying Command. In recognition of his demonstrated understanding of airlift challenges, Tunner was promoted to lieutenant colonel and made commander of a division of the Ferrying Command, later called the ATC. Faced with the pressing need for airlift from India to China and recognizing Turner's exemplary work in the Ferrying Command, the new commander of ATC, Major General Harold L. George, promoted Tunner to brigadier general and assigned him to lead the India-to-China airlift mission. His assignment was twofold: increase the tonnage of materials shipped over the Hump and reduce the terrible accident rate. In short order, Tunner improved the performance dramatically. In carrying out this unprecedented mission, Tunner consistently emphasized "regularity, standardization, procedure, and safety" to his troops.[6] By July 1945, the last full month of operation, 71,042 tons of supplies were delivered to bases in China, a huge increase over tonnage shipped earlier in the year.[7] Similarly, through a focus on flight safety, the accident rate declined far below what it had been at the start of the mission.

As stated by noted military historian C. V. Glines, "Besides helping to defeat Japan, the Hump operation was the proving ground for mass strategic airlift. The official Air Force history comments: 'Here, the AAF demonstrated conclusively that a vast quantity of cargo could be delivered by air, even under the most unfavorable circumstances, if only the men who controlled the aircraft, the terminals, and the needed materiel were willing to pay the price in money and in men.'"[8]

By the end of World War II and until it was discontinued in 1948, ATC had become a military airlift operation spanning the globe, in many cases flying to places where airplanes had never gone before. In its final full month of wartime operations (July 1945) with a fleet of 3,700 planes, ATC carried 275,000 passengers (50,000 domestically) and 100,000 tons of mail and cargo, most of it delivered overseas.[9]

Berlin Airlift

In 1948, shortly after the end of World War II, the Soviets blockaded all land and water routes into Berlin. This blockade, which lasted until May 1949, was one of the first international crises of the Cold War and proved to be a key milestone in the coming of age of military airlift.

To keep the city and its citizens alive, the Allies embarked upon an ambitious operation to airlift supplies into Berlin. In June 1948, General Joseph Smith (USMA 1923), previously the chief of staff for the 20th Bomber Command in India and later deputy chief of staff of the Eighth Air Force on Okinawa, was appointed as the provisional task force commander with oversight of airlift. Initially, the first C-47s carried 80 tons of cargo, including coal, food, and medicine to Berlin. In July 1948 based on successful leadership of the India-to-China operation, Tunner was assigned to the mission. By now, Tunner was recognized as "the USAF's preeminent authority on air transport," identified by Curtis LeMay as "the transportation expert to end transportation experts."[10] Now a major general, he reorganized the airlift operation and centralized control of both the USAFE and RAF operations into one Combined Air Lift Task Force (CALTF). Over the course of the airlift, aircrews from the U.S. and its Allies flew over 200,000 sorties in one year, providing coal, food, medicine and other supplies to the people of West Berlin. By early 1949, the airlift was delivering more than had previously been transported into the city by rail.

The Berlin Airlift became the first allied victory of the Cold War, in large part due to the airlift mission. One noted author wrote that the Berlin Airlift "provided the impetus for the development of purpose-built military transports such as the *Hercules* C-130.... Of more strategic importance, the

Berlin airlift once again demonstrated not only that air power could, if required, supply a huge city but also that without firing a shot it could have significant political impact."[11]

During this early era of military airlift development, three West Point graduates were commanders of MATS from 1948 to 1969 when military airlift was consolidated into the Military Airlift Command (MAC). Lt. General Laurence S. Kuter (USMA 1927) gained valuable leadership experience during the war in European, North Africa and Pacific theaters and then during the Berlin Airlift. He was eventually assigned to ATC and was responsible for developing the charter and organization of MATS before being appointed as commander.

In 1948, the airlift mission became a unified command (a military command composed of at least two military services with broad mission parameters) upon the consolidation of the U.S. Navy's Naval Air Transport Service (NATS) and the U.S. Air Force's Air Transport Command (ATC) to form MATS. This was one of the first steps in developing the most responsive military mobility capability the world had ever seen.

During World War II, Lt. General Joseph Smith (USMA 1923) served as a staff officer in a variety of positions, including with the JCS, and later became deputy chief of staff of the Eighth Air Force on Okinawa. Following the war, he had assignments with the deputy chief of staff for operations at USAF HQ and in 1951 he assumed command of MATS.

It should be noted that during this period when Tunner, Kuter, and Smith were leading efforts to operate and advance military transport operations, West Point graduates Spaatz and Vandenberg were serving as chiefs of staff of the Air Force, Spaatz (USMA 1914) during 1947 and 1948 and Vandenberg (USMA 1923) from 1948 to 1953.

Korean conflict

After North Korea and then China invaded South Korea in 1950, the most dramatic airlift operation was supporting General MacArthur's strategy to take control of Inchon Harbor and sweep across the Korean peninsula to rapidly isolate the Chinese forces. After the amphibious landing at Inchon Harbor, the UN forces advanced across the country capturing many of the invading forces. The rapid Army advancement across Korea was greatly assisted by the sustained airlift support. Immediately after the operation, General MacArthur presented General Tunner with a Distinguished Service Cross in recognition of the outstanding airlift support.

By the end of the war in Korea in 1953—50 years after the invention of the airplane and 10 years after the first army Air Corps airlift organization was formed—military airlift was well established as a critical element of modern warfare. Based on airlift's role during World War II, the Hump, the Berlin airlift and then the Korean conflict, the importance of military airlift had become well recognized by both military and political leaders faced with new global responsibilities. In addition, the early transition toward a single unified military airlift organization had begun.

Airlift Aircraft

Following the airlift demands of World War II, the Berlin Airlift and the Korean conflict, and with America's new global presence, the question of how to support the expanding worldwide airlift mission became paramount—how was this responsibility to be fulfilled? During the early years, modified commercial aircraft had helped to meet the airlift need. But after the Korean conflict, it became apparent to political, commercial and military leaders that specialized cargo aircraft capable of moving vast quantities of material were needed. Both long-range (inter-theater or strategic) and short-range (intra-theater or tactical) transport aircraft would be needed. The range and payload requirements for long-range military aircraft were similar to the requirements of various commercial aircraft in that both civil and military long-range planes needed to operate from permanent bases. But for intra-theater operations, military airlifters were required to move equipment and supplies from inter-theater, off-load air bases to austere airfields near the battle zones. Battle conditions could also require air drop delivery by transport planes to the battlefield itself.

Both short-range and long-range military aircraft would need compatible aircraft flooring and materials handling equipment for rapid on-off loading, and, in some cases, rapid air delivery without landing. It soon was realized that airlifters, freed from the restraints of roads, rails and sea, could deliver large payloads effectively to anyplace in the world. In 1979, Army Chief of Staff Edward C. Meyer (USMA 1951) summed up in a few words the critical role of airlift by stating: "to go somewhere and do something we have to be taken there."[12] In addition, another pressing requirement was the Army's need to transport—by air—heavy, outsized equipment such as tanks and other large vehicles that fit only in the C-5 and, later, the C-17.

The first operational aircraft designed for the military airlift mission were the two-engine, intra-theater Fairchild C-119 Flying Boxcar first delivered in 1947 and the four-engine, inter-theater Douglas C-124 Globemaster II delivered in 1950. The C-119 was designed to carry cargo, personnel, and a variety of vehicles and to airdrop cargo and troops by parachute. The C-124 was configured to carry a wide variety of cargo including drive-on/drive-off

Lockheed C-130E Hercules. As of 2015, more than 2,500 produced—the longest continuous military aircraft production run in history with 40 variants operating in over 60 nations (U.S. Air Force photo).

equipment. It became the primary long-range, heavy-lift transport for MATS during the 1950s and early 1960s until the Lockheed C-141 Starlifter assumed that role. These were followed in the mid–1950s by the intra-theater, turboprop Lockheed C-130 Hercules and the inter-theater Douglas C-133 Cargomaster with greater payload, range and loading capabilities.

The best example by far of the intra-theater airlift aircraft is the long-serving and frequently modified C-130 Hercules. The list of upgrades and modifications to the C-130 led to more than 40 variants of this versatile aircraft, which remains in service today both in the U.S. and many foreign countries. It remains in production because of its continued intra-theater utility and versatility and for a wide range of military and humanitarian missions.

During the late 1950s and 1960s, many innovative aircraft designs and material handling systems were proposed and flown. Some, like the C-124 and C-133 were workhorses of the time but were overtaken by specific airlift aircraft designs with jet engines. The C-135 was the first jet military airlifter but it was not designed for ease of loading. As a result, the Lockheed C-141 Starlifter and later, the Lockheed C-5 Galaxy were developed. These advanced

Top: Lockheed C-141B Stretch Starlifter cargo aircraft. There were 285 produced. Military strategic airlift aircraft in service during 1963–2006. *Above:* Lockheed C-5 Galaxy cargo aircraft. Strategic airlifter. First flown in 1968. There were 131 produced. Capacity for 36 pallets or outsized cargo (both U.S. Air Force photos).

Top: Boeing KC-135E Stratotanker refueling an F-16C Fighting Falcon. USAF's first jet-powered refueling tanker. Introduced in 1957; 803 produced. Key air refueling aircraft for more than 60 years. *Above:* McDonnell Douglas KC-10 Extender. Sixty produced. Here refueling a McDonnel Douglas F-16 Fighting Falcon, its fuel capacity nearly double that of the KC-135 (both U.S. Air Force photos).

Thirteen Boeing C-17 Globemaster III aircraft during low level tactical training in 2005. Deployed in June 1993. Carries 18 pallets with maximum payload of 170,900 pounds. Can carry outsize cargo such as primary Army battle tanks. Austere landing capability with crew of two pilots and one loadmaster (U.S. Air Force photo).

jet aircraft, including the C-141 (and its stretch and air refueling version), the C-5 (with its air refueling capability) and later, the C-17, had much greater speed, range and payload capacity. Air refueling capability provided extended range which was restricted only by crew fatigue. Additionally, these aircraft used a standard MAC materials handling system that relied upon aircraft-installed, cargo-deck rollers to move heavy palletized loads within the aircraft and loading from specialized pallet loading systems ("K-Loaders") which are now standard equipment in air transportation.

Organizational Growth of the U.S. Military Airlift

After the Japanese bombing of Pearl Harbor and America's entry into the war, the country was faced with essentially two wars: one in the Pacific against Japan and another in Europe against Germany. This placed an enormous airlift requirement on the AAF for an organization and infrastructure that could rapidly transport troops, equipment, and supplies to many overseas locations. Working closely with aircraft manufacturers and the civilian airlines, the AAF established a series of internal units to meet this need. These organizations included the Air Corps Ferrying Command (ACFC), created in 1941; the Army Air Forces Ferry Command (AAFFC) in 1942; the Army Air Forces Ferrying Command (AAFFC), established in 1942; and then the Air Transport Command (ATC), formed still later in 1942 and which operated through 1948, one year following the establishment of the USAF in 1947. When the ATC was formed in 1942, its military strength was approximately 11,000 officers and enlisted men but by 1945 as the war was ending it had reached over 209,000 military personnel with an additional 104,000 civilian personnel and a fleet of 3,700 planes.[13]

By the end of the war and after the Berlin airlift and other airlift operations, transport by air was recognized as a critical resource to not only supply troops, supplies and equipment to a war zone, but as a tool for implementing national policy and supporting humanitarian efforts. Starting from the mid–1940s, continuous long-range airlift operations were provided by U.S. air services up through today through several different organizations each of which was implemented following congressional acts:

USAAF Air Transport Command (ATC)—1942–48

USAF Military Air Transport Service (MATS)—1948–66

USAF Military Airlift Command (MAC)—1966–92

USAF Air Mobility Command (AMC)—1992–present

During 1974–75, MAC was given responsibility for both tactical airlift and strategic forces which consolidated airlift responsibilities within the U.S. and overseas. This reorganization prompted Congress, in 1977, to designate MAC as a specified command responsible directly to the JCS for contingency activities.[14] Later, in 1987, the U.S. Transportation Command was activated and charged with maintaining "a worldwide mobility system for use in contingency situations." It incorporated "the Military Airlift command, the Military Sealift Command and the Military Traffic Management Command as air, sea and land components" all under the direction of MAC's commander in chief.[15]

Prominent Airlift Missions in the '70s

The war in Vietnam, thousands of miles away from all support bases, made airlift a crucial factor in supporting the war effort. Once again, a distant military conflict cemented the need for a single airlift manager. The airlift mission also was unique in having not only to fulfill a full-time scheduled mission moving supplies, equipment and personnel around the world, but also in that airlift was required to rapidly respond to unforeseen contingencies, humanitarian crises, rescue missions, and other unanticipated crises. During the 1970s, several events highlighted the challenge of unexpected and urgent air mobility requirements.

In January 1973, the U.S. agreed to a ceasefire with North Vietnam. Included in the agreement was a provision for the release of 591 American POWs within 60 days of the withdrawal of U.S. troops. This arrangement became known as "Operation Homecoming." Mobilizing just weeks after the signing of the ceasefire agreement, the first of nearly 60 C-141s began evacuating POWs. Of the 591 POWs liberated during Operation Homecoming, "325 served in the Air Force, 138 in the Navy, 77 in the Army, 26 in the Marine Corps and 25 were civilian employees of U.S. government agencies."[16] The Operation Homecoming mission was relatively small, but a highly emotional mission. At the time, the author, as a colonel, was the assistant operations officer at MAC headquarters at Scott AFB in St. Louis and was able to observe firsthand the extremely efficient command and control over the crews and airplanes landing in Hanoi.

The rapid advance of North Vietnamese forces made immediate withdrawal and evacuation of civilians essential as well as providing support to South Vietnam's defense of Saigon. In early April 1975, MAC supplied 17 C-141s, four C-5s, and seven commercial aircraft delivering much-needed military equipment and supplies to the South Vietnamese forces. As the communists closed in on Saigon that April, the pace of MAC's airlift evacuation mission accelerated, with C-130s flying an average of more than seven missions each day. "By the time Saigon fell to the communists on 30 April 1975, MAC's airlift forces had evacuated 50,493 Vietnamese and Cambodians to staging areas in the Pacific."[17] Over the course of this airlift mission, dubbed "New Life," 375 missions had been flown including 201 C-141 missions and 174 C-130 missions.[18]

In the next phase of the evacuation, "Operation New Arrivals," MAC transported the evacuees from locations in the Pacific to resettlement centers in the United States. This was undertaken by MAC's C-141s augmented by commercial aircraft. Operating through September 1975, New Arrivals launched over 600 missions flown by C-141 and commercial carriers to transport 121,562 refugees to America.[19]

Then in April 1975, President Gerald Ford directed the evacuation of orphans from Vietnam using MAC C-5s and C-141s. Known as "Operation Babylift," more than 3,000 babies and infants were evacuated from South Vietnam for adoption by families around the world with at least 2,000 children flown to the United States and approximately 1,300 children flown to Canada, Europe and Australia.[20] Interestingly, Betty Tisdale, the wife of the author's 1950 West Point classmate, Colonel Patrick Tisdale, MD, continued the work of Dr. Tom Dooley in orphanages in Laos, Thailand, India, and South Vietnam, making scores of trips to South Vietnam during and after the war. She "worked tirelessly to raise money and supplies through lectures, articles, television and radio appearances."[21] She and her husband adopted five Vietnamese girls.

One month later, on May 12, 1975, MAC received an urgent request to support the Marines in the rescue of a 39-man crew of a U.S. merchant ship, the USS *Mayaguez*, being held captive by Khmer Rouge communists off the coast of Cambodia. Within seven hours of receiving the alert order, a C-141 departed a naval air station in the Philippines for Japan and then to Thailand followed shortly thereafter by 15 additional C-141s. Within less than 24 hours, MAC had airlifted 1,165 Marines and 121 tons of combat equipment to support the operation. MAC and Pacific Air Force helicopters also provided close-in airlift for the rescue.[22]

These unforeseen airlift missions provide good examples of the tremendous range of MAC's missions and fully confirmed the organization's responsiveness and capabilities, living up to MAC's motto: "Anything, Anywhere, Anytime!"

As the Vietnam War came to a close, MAC's commitments continued to expand. For example, in 1973 President Nixon approved the plan prepared by Air Force Chief of Staff George S. Brown (USMA 1913) and approved by Secretary of State Henry Kissinger to transport military equipment to Israel to aid in that country's war with Egypt and Syria known as the Yom Kippur War. The airlift operation (Operation Nickel Grass) took place in just over a month during which MAC shipped over 22,000 tons of tanks, artillery, ammunition, and supplies in C-141 and C-5 transports. The C-5s delivered 48 percent of the tonnage despite flying only 25 percent of the missions. The job could not have been done as quickly or effectively without the C-5s and their outsized tank carrying capability.[23] As the wing commander at Dover AFB at the time, the author can personally attest that the personnel and resources of the wing and particularly the C-5 performed admirably during this important contingency operation. This airlift helped to ensure that Israel survived the surprise attack from the Soviet-backed Arab countries.[24] After the operation, Golda Meir, Israel's prime minister, stated, "For generations to come, all will be told of the miracle of the immense planes from the United States bringing in the material that meant life to our people."[25]

During the Iranian Revolution of 1978–81, MAC provided airlift assistance to civilian personnel escaping Iran. Two C-5s and nine C-141s evacuated more than 900 dependents from Tehran to Europe or the U.S. Then, in the first months of 1979 as the demonstrations became more hostile, MAC evacuated another 4,900 dependents, 687 tons of cargo and 169 pets. After nearly all the dependents had been evacuated and Iran released the hostages in 1981, two MAC C-9s removed the hostages, airlifting them to Germany.[26]

In 1985, Congress adopted legislation mandating that MAC support humanitarian assistance programs. By September 1990, MAC had airlifted "more than three million pounds of private, humanitarian cargo to Latin America, the Philippines, Antigua, Cook Islands and the Caribbean Basin" to support humanitarian efforts.[27] Since then, MAC and later the Air Mobility Command (AMC) has continued to be involved in supporting national policies—in both peace and war—throughout the world. One historian has said that military airlift has served "as a tool for the successful execution of American foreign policy since first organized before the beginning of World War II."[28]

It is important to note that the role played by MAC (and later AMC) is unique to nearly all of the other military services in that it supports, on a daily basis, the national security interests of the U.S. both in peacetime and combat situations. As observed in *Anything, Anywhere, Anytime—An Illustrated History of the Military Airlift Command, 1941 to 1991*:

> It [MAC] has been used in every conceivable scenario across a spectrum of foreign policy options from sustaining combat forces overseas; to projecting military power to Korea, Vietnam, the Caribbean and Latin America, the Middle East, or Southwest Asia; to humanitarian airlift after disasters; to the movement of diplomats and foreign affairs advisors such as the shuttle-diplomacy missions of the early 1970s. All have been at the core of MAC's operations since the command's inception.[29]

The important role played by military airlift and air power in general in support of U.S. national security interests was summarized succinctly by Air Force historian Richard P. Hallion when describing the Air Force's *Global Reach—Global Power* plans in 1990. In that initiative it was recognized that air power "offered clear advantages unavailable to other forms of land or sea power: the ability to reach anywhere on the globe within hours with decisive military force, thanks to five unique characteristics inherent with modern air power. These were speed, range, flexibility, precision and lethality."[30]

Senior Airlift Leaders

In addition to the contributions of commanders described earlier such as Tunner, Kuter and Smith, other West Point graduates were senior leaders who advanced the development of military airlift. For example, General Joseph Kelly (USMA 1932) was the first four-star commander of MATS, serving between 1960 to 1964. He had the distinction of piloting the first jet aircraft assigned to MATS on its maiden voyage. During his tenure as MATS commander, MATS supported a number of major airlifts including Operation Deep Freeze in Antarctica, the Cuban Missile Crisis, and the Congo airlift on behalf of the UN.

General Howell M. Estes II (USMA 1936) succeeded General Kelly, serving as MATS commander from 1964 to 1969. Estes had served in the Korean War, flying combat missions over Korea in B-29s. He advanced through a series of command assignments in bomber wings and in 1954 he was assigned to several weapon system staff positions in ARDC before being transferred to HQ ARDC as assistant deputy commander for weapon systems and to HQ USAF. In 1961, he returned to AFSC and in 1962 became vice commander of AFSC. He became commander of MATS from 1964 to 1969. In reflecting on the importance of airlift in fulfilling both political and military goals, General Estes wrote, "[G]lobal military airlift has been shown, throughout the era of the cold war, to be a principal medium of achieving maximum military flexibility." By the time of the Vietnam conflict, Estes contended that MAC had become "the key element in a far-ranging change in national policy: to a strategy of multiple options for flexible, measured response to any situation in the spectrum of war."[31]

General James Allen (USMA 1944) gained his flying experience in the Philippines and South Korea where he flew P-51s and F-80C's during the Korean War followed by a tour flying F-86A fighter-interceptors in the CONUS. He was next assigned as a company TAC officer at West Point before staff duty as an executive officer to the director of plans, HQ USAFE and then HQ USAF. He commanded an F-4C fighter squadron in Vietnam and then served as deputy commander for operations. He became SAC's chief of staff in 1973 and then special assistant to the Air Force chief of staff. He was superintendent of the Air Force Academy from 1974 to 1977 before becoming the chief of staff, Supreme Headquarters Allied Powers Europe and then deputy commander in chief of the U.S. European Command in 1979. His final posting was as commander in chief of MAC in 1981, serving until 1983.

Thus, six West Point graduates served as senior airlift commanders during MAC's advancement from 1941 to 1992: Kuter, Smith, Tunner, Kelly, Estes and Allen. Four graduates became members of the Airlift/Tanker Association Hall of Fame. As a result of Tunner's outstanding contributions to the Air Force's airlift heritage, the Airlift/Tanker Association (A/TA) in 1989 selected Tunner as the first inductee into the association's Hall of Fame and recognized him as the "Father of the Military Airlift Command." Other West Point inductees in the Hall of Fame include Laurence S. Kuter (USMA 1927), Joseph Smith (USMA 1923), and Carl A. Spaatz (USMA 1914).

It also is noteworthy that another inductee into the Hall of Fame is Nancy

Harkness Love. A qualified pilot in her own right, in 1942 Ms. Love worked for Tunner in the ATC Ferrying Division and recognized the potential for women ferrying pilots. She convinced Tunner to employ experienced women pilots in the ferrying mission. With Tunner's support, in 1942 she helped establish the Women's Auxiliary Ferrying Squadron (WAFS), which began operations under ATC's 2d Ferrying Group.

In 1989, General Hanford T. Johnson (USAFA 1959) became the first USAFA graduate to become commander of MAC/AMC. In 1992, General Ronald Fogleman (USAFA 1963) became the second USAFA grad to become the military airlift commander and the first airlift commander to become CSAF. As an interesting final note, in June 1993 when AMC was established, U.S. air refueling resources were consolidated with airlift to make AMC a much larger and more complex organization thereby creating far greater responsibilities for these two Air Force Academy graduates.

Chapter 9

ICBMs

In a 1946 RAND study regarding the feasibility of developing a reconnaissance satellite, an observation was made that later would prove prescient: "the development of a satellite will be directly applicable to the development of an intercontinental rocket missile."[1] This was for the simple reason that both ICBMs and satellites required rocket engines sufficiently powerful to launch payloads into space. At the time, it was becoming clear to some within the scientific and military communities that the best way to conduct reconnaissance of the Soviet Union was by orbiting satellites rather than overflights by aircraft. Less than 10 years later, in October 1954 and after much study and analysis, the "ICBM Scientific Advisory Group" recognized the interaction of satellite and other missile proposals with the ICBM efforts underway, assigning the task to the Air Force.[2]

As was the case with the Wright brothers' breakthrough into aerodynamic flight based on the engine designed by mechanic Charlie Taylor, a unique and powerful engine was needed to provide the thrust necessary to gain entry to space, whether to launch a satellite into orbit or to launch an ICBM at an enemy. The progress being made in the late 1950s and early 1960s in the development of Atlas, Thor and Titan rockets for ICBMs proved to be the solution for both missions.

Equally important, the development of ICBMs for wartime use provided the basis for the U.S. space program, with Atlas and Titan missiles sending the first astronauts into space. And many technologies developed for these missile programs such as digitized computers, miniaturized electronics, guidance systems, new "space age" materials and advanced telecommunication systems are in use today in modified form providing the foundation for entirely new industries.

Air Force officers from West Point classes of the 1940s and 1950s served at a time of tremendous technological growth, witnessing the invention or advancement of thermonuclear weapons, rocket propulsion, guidance systems, integrated circuits and computers, and other technologies that led to operational ballistic missiles and space systems. The Cold War, with the U.S. and Soviet Union armed with 30-minute time-to-target nuclear warheads, made warning time of utmost importance. This warning came from constant surveillance and accurate knowledge of enemy capabilities and status of forces. The result was a high priority race for improved ICBMs and reconnaissance capabilities. The Air Force was assigned the long-range ballistic missile development and operational mission, but space missions and control of the requirements and budget was not. Over this period, huge budgets were provided for these two critical missions. The internal struggle between government agencies, scientists, engineers, industries, politicians and the military services was fierce.

In 1947 when the Air Force was established, there was no focused effort on ballistic missile development except at the Army's Redstone arsenal. However, as the Cold War escalated, USAF missile R&D increased and in 1951 the initial phases of the Atlas project were started. In 1953 under the leadership of Professor John von Neumann, the Strategic Missiles Evaluation Committee (code-named the "Teapot Committee") conducted an evaluation to determine the feasibility of developing an ICBM as a weapon system. The committee recognized that the U.S. was as much as five years behind the Soviets in the development of a thermonuclear bomb, so there was an urgent need to counter the Soviet threat. By 1954, the committee had concluded that an ICBM could be developed and deployed if sufficient funds and talent were applied to the challenge. They also recommended that the existing five-engine Atlas be redesigned as a smaller missile to take advantage of a smaller thermonuclear warhead.[3]

Based on the findings and recommendations of the committee, in 1954 the secretary of the Air Force and Air Force chief of staff, General Nathan F. Twining (USMA 1918), commissioned the work to plan and organize a "massive ballistic missile development program."[4] After 1954, the ballistic missile program became the highest priority within the Air Force.

With responsibility for the task of developing our ICBM forces settled, the Air Force established the Western Development Division (WDD) of ARDC. It was led by Brigadier General Bernard Schriever. WDD was located in Los Angeles close to the major aerospace contractors that would build the missiles and also to provide some separation from the Air Force's strategic bombing emphasis at Wright Field near Wright-Patterson AFB in Ohio.[5] This new division had responsibility for developing the first American ICBM, the Atlas, described by at least one authority "as the most complex technological juggling act in history."[6] While initially deployed on launch pads at Vandenberg AFB in California, Atlas D, E and then F versions were later deployed to other locations in the U.S. By 1965, approximately 350 Atlas missiles of all versions had been built with a peak deployment of 129 missiles in silos at various locations in the U.S. The Atlas later was replaced by the Minuteman missile which first became operational in 1963 although the Atlas continued to be used as a launch vehicle for some of the Mercury program launches.

By 1955, WDD commenced concurrent development of a backup two-stage ICBM, the Titan, in Titan I and Titan II variants, which first flew in 1959 and became operational by 1963, being dispersed to six states throughout the U.S. In total, approximately 135 Titan II missiles were built. Though replaced by the Minuteman, the Titan's reliability made it the choice of rockets for NASA's Gemini space program and the Air Force continued to use it as a space launch vehicle.[7]

Among the team that Brigadier General Schriever assembled in the early days of the Air Force's missile development program were three West Point grads:

Atlas missile launch, 1958. First flight in 1957. Family of liquid propellant ICBMs with more than 500 launches. Launched four astronauts in the Mercury program (U.S. Air Force photo).

• Colonel Harold W. Norton (USMA 1941)—Colonel Norton served as a missile test wing commander and became Schriever's assistant for technical operations.

• Lt. General John B. Hudson (USMA June 1943)—Lt. General Hudson became one of the early members of WDD in 1954. After other assignments at HQ USAF he returned to the ballistic missile and space program in Los Angeles, where he became assistant deputy for engineering and later deputy for launch vehicles, Space Systems Division. As part of his duties he directed launch vehicle activities of the Air Force and NASA space programs

An LGM-25C Titan II missile is launched at Vandenberg Air Force Base, California, in 1975. More than three hundred Titans were launched, including all Gemini flights (U.S. Dept. of Defense photo).

including the Scout, Thor, Atlas, Titan II, Gemini, and Agena launch vehicles.

• Colonel Norman J. Keefer (USMA June 1943)—Colonel Keefer, a B-29 and B-47 pilot and AFIT graduate, held various posts in ARDC. In 1960, he was transferred to the Ballistic Missile Division to work in the Minuteman program. He held numerous key positions related to missile development including vice commander of the 6595th Aerospace Test Wing and his final career assignment as chief of staff at the Space and Missile Center at Vandenberg Air Force Base.[8]

Recall that in 1957 the Soviet Union launched Sputnik into orbit. This event (the "ultimate bell ringer" for the U.S. as observed by General Thomas Moorman, Jr.)[9] sent shock waves through the nation as well as within the ranks of the Department of Defense. It triggered the start of what came to be known as the "space race." President Eisenhower's science advisor, Dr. James Killian, referred to the event as "a crisis of confidence that swept the country like a wind-blown forest fire."[10] Sputnik was followed shortly that same year by Sputnik II carrying a dog ("Laika") in orbit, and then in 1961 Russian Yuri Alekseyevich Gagarin became the first man launched into orbit.[11] With these significant breakthroughs by the Soviet Union in space technology, it is no wonder that American insecurities were heightened.

In response, the Air Force was given greater responsibility to accelerate the development of both ICBMs and reconnaissance satellites. In the same year that Sputnik was launched, 1957, WDD was redesignated the Ballistic Missile Division (BMD). "Sputnik also galvanized Air force efforts and gave 'Bennie' Schriever the attention and priority he required to develop our military space and missile systems."[12] Later that year, the first successful launch and short-range flight of the Atlas took place, followed by Titan launches. By this time, advances in solid propellants, inertial guidance systems, and in-silo launch capability for the Titan II were in process. Importantly, development of the Minuteman ICBM was initiated in 1958, with a first launch only three years later in 1961.

In 1961, the Air Force realigned its organizations, creating AFSC and the Air Force Logistics Command (AFLC) from the former ARDC and AMC. As part of this reorganization, the resources of the Ballistic Missile Division were split between two new commands—Ballistic Systems Division (BSD) and Space Systems Division (SSD). Both new organizations were placed under a deputy commander for Aerospace Systems (DCAS). After additional organizational changes in the mid–'60s, the Space and Missile Systems Organization (SAMSO) of AFSC was activated in 1967.

The Minuteman Program

Building on the lessons learned from the liquid-propelled Atlas and Titan programs, BMD continued research into solid-fuel ballistic missiles

Minuteman III missile (solid propellant ICBM) test launched from Vandenberg AFB headed to Kwajalein Missile Range in the Marshall Islands, 4,200 miles away in 20 minutes. 1994 (U.S. Air Force photo).

due to the problems inherent in liquid-fueled systems. These efforts led to the development of the Minuteman I missile system in 1957. The Minuteman I was distinguished from the Atlas and Titan missile systems not only by its propellant, but by its smaller size, its three-stage design, its lower cost and ease of maintenance as well as its basing in dispersed silos all electronically linked to underground launch control centers (LCCs) located in the middle of the U.S. Starting with the first deployment of a Minuteman squadron of 10 missiles in 1962, some 800 Minuteman I missiles were in place by 1965.[13]

Throughout the 1960s, advances in the Minuteman program continued. The Minuteman II was a significant improvement over its predecessor with a new second stage motor and increased range up to 7,000 miles. By 1969, the Air Force had installed 500 operational Minuteman IIs together with 500 Minuteman I's. Development of the final phase of the Minuteman series, the Minuteman III, began in 1964 with first deployment in 1970. It was distinguished from the Minuteman I missile largely by an improved third-stage booster, increased range to over 8,000 miles, increased payload capacity and, most significantly, three multiple independently targetable reentry vehicles (warheads) or MIRVs each of which could be programmed to hit a different target. Though these thermonuclear warheads at 170 kilotons each were smaller than the earlier Minuteman I and II warheads with a yield of 1.2 megatons, their greatly enhanced guidance systems coupled with warhead clustering at designated targets yielded much more destructive power and vastly compounded the challenge for an enemy's anti-ballistic defenses. The first squadron of Minuteman IIIs became operational by 1971. Within four years, the Air Force had 450 Minuteman IIs and 550 Minuteman IIIs placed in silos in bases throughout the central plains of the U.S. Minuteman missiles were dispersed in hardened silos and managed by underground launch control centers through a system of hardened cables. Two-officer launch crews remained on alert around the clock. The Air Force continued to upgrade the Minuteman force throughout the coming decades.[14]

As clearly summarized in Mark Berhow's book, *U.S. Strategic and Defensive Missile Systems, 1950–2004*:

> The Cold War produced sweeping changes in the United States military establishment, American technological development, and American society at large. For more than 40 years, the United States prepared to defend itself against a massive nuclear attack that never came. The United States reversed its long-standing policy against maintaining a large peacetime military establishment and utilized the nation's industrial might and scientific genius to fashion the ultimate weapons of war and a means to defend against them. High technology became the ultimate arbitrator of military power, culminating in the nation's guided missile programs. Armed with nuclear warheads, the guided missiles became the defining weapons of the Cold War.

Cold War Realities

The first use of nuclear weapons against Japan at Hiroshima and Nagasaki to end World War II, coupled with the rapid development of thermonuclear bombs of far greater destructive power, had fundamentally changed the face of warfare. In a very short period, strategic bombardment became capable of delivering more destructive power with one aircraft with one thermonuclear bomb than even the huge fleets of bombers with conventional bombs launched during World War II. The threat of massive retaliatory response by the U.S. or the Soviet Union avoided total war between adversaries possessing nuclear weapons—a standoff that has existed to this day. The ability to rapidly deploy nuclear weapons provided a strong incentive for any enemy to engage only in limited war that avoided use of nuclear weapons. This condition of nuclear "mutual assured destruction" (MAD) became the new reality of the Cold War. It was in this era that new West Point graduates began their Air Force careers.

The command structure of the country's military nuclear forces was established under the centralized control of the President of the United States as Commander-in-Chief of the Armed Forces. This structure was developed under the Single Integrated Operational Plan (SIOP) that was first established in 1961. SIOP, probably the most highly classified document in the government, gave the president a range of targeting options and set forth launch procedures for our nuclear forces. SIOP integrated the capabilities of the nuclear triad of strategic bombers, ICBMs, and submarine-launched ballistic missiles (SLBM).[15] Classmate Ken Moll (USMA 1950) was a staff officer for SAC HQ, AF HQ and JCS during the development and operation of the SIOP.

Among the most critical challenges facing the country's nuclear response were those of prelaunch survivability and penetration of enemy defenses. When an enemy could launch a first-strike nuclear assault on the United States in a matter of minutes rather than days or weeks, it was of utmost importance that the TRIAD of nuclear forces be able to survive such a strike. This required lightning-fast command and control of these forces with well-trained crews ready to respond immediately to orders issued by the National Command Authority (the president and secretary of defense).

All legs of the TRIAD were designed for survivability, each with its own unique strengths and weaknesses. Bombers rely on rapid launch response after warning while SLBM forces are particularly durable due to their movement and concealment. ICBMs are located in well-dispersed, hardened underground silos that help ensure survivability in the event of a nuclear attack.[16] Regarding the challenge of penetrating enemy defenses, standoff technologies such as SRAMs, AGM-28 air-launched "Hound Dog" cruise missiles and successively advanced models of air-launched cruise missiles such as the AGM-86 have

Operation Castle Romeo nuclear test (yield 11 megatons) on Bikini Atoll, March 27, 1954 (U.S. Dept. of Energy photo sourced from National Nuclear Security Administration, Nevada Site Office Photo Library).

enhanced the probability of defeating enemy defenses and delivering bombs to target.

Advances in command, control and communication systems effectively allowed the National Command Authority to convey orders directly to officers in the field thereby greatly concentrating control at the highest levels of command. This centralization of control was to migrate from control of the country's nuclear forces to more limited military engagements.

The Air Force's Strategic Air Command (SAC) was given top priority for full-scale development of a large strategic bomber force armed with nuclear weapons as well as ICBMs. SAC Commander General Curtis LeMay developed a well-disciplined, closely controlled bomber and ICBM force designed to survive an enemy first strike and then deliver an even more devastating retaliation. SAC's official motto became "Peace is Our Profession" but sometimes it was translated to "War is Our Business."

This nuclear stalemate created the reality of limited warfare with an ever-present concern for avoiding any chance of escalation into nuclear conflict. The first examples of such "limited" wars followed quickly with the conflicts in Korea and then in Vietnam.

Another by-product of the Cold War was the intense rivalry between the Air Force and Navy for control of the nuclear mission and its related budgets. Debate raged as to which leg of the TRIAD was most effective. Budgets for each service's nuclear arsenal ran into the billions, so the economic impact of a decision to buy, expand or cancel a given program had huge political consequences. The era was characterized by heated competition between the services, and their respective congressional supporters, for weapon system selection and related budgets.

The Strategic Air Command with a fleet of bombers and ICBMs became the priority command and created no small degree of rivalry between SAC pilots and air crew with other pilots throughout the Air Force. SAC's favored position was manifested in spot promotions awarded to SAC aircrews and the many advantages its officers and crewmen enjoyed as well as placement of SAC officers in many senior leadership positions. For example, nine out of the first ten chiefs of staff had extensive bomber experience and it wasn't until 1982 that the first career fighter pilot, General Charles Gabriel (USMA 1950), became the Air Force chief of staff. In addition, General LeMay kept his SAC crewmembers on alert in the U.S. rather than send them to the "limited" Korean War that was being fought, to a large degree, by Air Force Reserve and Air National Guard crewmembers, most of whom had served in World War II. This policy was changed for the war in Vietnam.

MX program

In 1971 after the last Minuteman III had been deployed, SAC began planning for a more technologically advanced ICBM with increased range and better accuracy. This next generation of ICBM was identified as the LGM-118 Peacekeeper, also known as the MX (for "missile experimental"). The MX was a four-stage missile capable of carrying up to ten MIRVs with greater accuracy than its predecessor Minuteman missiles.

By 1975 when I was assigned to HQ USAF DCS R&D Requirements, one of the main issues surrounding the MX concerned its pre-launch survivability from an increasingly accurate Soviet ICBM attack. (Coincidentally, at that same time my son [co-author] was serving at F. E. Warren AFB in Wyoming as a missile launch control officer.) One of the early basing modes called for deploying the MX on a mobile transporter system (train rails) to make it a more difficult target for the Soviets to hit. After considering more than 40 basing alternatives, in 1979 President Carter approved the development and deployment of a mobile MX. However, this basing plan triggered a public outcry in the western United States and, after extensive and acrimonious political debate, the next administration under President Reagan decided to place the MX in preexisting but strengthened Minuteman silos. The president had appointed a commission (headed by then Lt. General Brent Scowcroft (USMA 1947) to evaluate basing options), finally recommending immediate deployment of one hundred Peacekeepers in existing Minuteman silos at F.E. Warren AFB. Ultimately, 50 Minuteman IIIs were placed in Minuteman silos at F.E. Warren AFB. Initial operational capability was attained in 1986 while full operational capability occurred by 1988 when the 50th Peacekeeper missile was installed. The MX missiles were retired in 2005 after nearly two decades of service.

Several West Point graduates who played key roles in the history of the Air Force's ballistic missile programs are listed below. It is important to note that due to the highly classified nature of the Air Force's space and ICBM programs, gaining information on details surrounding the exact roles and responsibilities of these officers often proved challenging. Furthermore, through the rotation of assignments, many of these grads worked, sometimes concurrently, in different units supporting a variety of missile and space system applications.

HQ USAF–R&D Directorate

While I was assigned to HQ USAF as the deputy chief of staff (DCS) for R&D Requirements, two very capable officers (colonels at the time), one from West Point, James Dalton, the other from Annapolis, Monroe Hatch, worked directly with me on a number of ICBM and related programs, including the MX program. Through progressively more responsible assignments, each advanced in their careers to the rank of general.

- General James Dalton (USMA 1954)—Early in his career, General Dalton was a project officer in the guidance and control directorate of the Ballistic Systems Division in Los Angeles responsible for the development of targeting programs for the inertially guided Atlas, Titan and Minuteman ICBMs. He later became a project officer in the missile division, Office of the Deputy for Strategic Forces for R&D at HQ USAF. Thereafter he became the program element monitor for the Advanced ICBM program and then deputy director of concepts in the Office of the Deputy Chief of Staff, Plans and Operations at HQ USAF. In 1977, General Dalton was assigned to the organization of the Joint Chiefs of Staff and served as deputy director for force development and strategic plans in the plans and policy directorate. His final assignment was chief of staff, Supreme Headquarters, Allied Powers, Europe in Belgium.

• General Monroe Hatch (USNA 1955)—After flight training and flying experience in the B-47 and B-52, General Hatch became a special projects officer and later program officer in the Advanced Technical Division, Headquarters SAC, later serving as an operations staff officer in the astronautics technology and applications office under the deputy chief of staff for plans. In 1970, he was assigned to OSD in Washington, D.C., where he served as military assistant for strategic analysis in the Office of the Deputy Director for Strategic and Space Systems. After graduating from the National War College, General Hatch was assigned to the Aircraft Division, Directorate of Operational Requirements and Development at HQ USAF. After serving as deputy division chief, he became chief of the division in 1976, advancing in 1978 as deputy director for strategic forces, DCS R&D. He went on to become SAC's chief of staff and inspector general of the Air Force. In 1987, he became vice chief of staff of the Air Force.

Space Systems Division (SSD)

• Lt. General Howell M. Estes, Jr. (USMA 1936)—General Estes became the director of weapon systems operations at ARDC in 1954. He was transferred to HQ USAF as the assistant chief of staff, Air Defense Systems in 1957 and in 1961 became AFSC's deputy commander for aerospace systems in Los Angeles, later becoming vice commander of AFSC and commander of MAC in 1962.

• Major General Robert E. Greer (USMA 1939)—General Greer was the deputy assistant, chief of staff for guided missiles at HQ USAF until 1959 when he became the vice commander for satellite systems at BMD. He then became vice commander, Space Systems Division in Los Angeles and director of the Satellite and Missile Observation System (SAMOS) Project.

• Major General John E. Kulpa (USMA 1950)—with an MS in aeronautical engineering from AFIT and a background in navigation and reconnaissance, General Kulpa was assigned as a project engineer for propulsion and flight test in the Snark Weapon System Project Office and then operational manager in the AGM (air-to-ground)-77 Hound Dog Project Office. (Coincidentally, as a test pilot at the Flight Test Center at Edwards AFB, I performed the B-52 AGM-77 flight tests.) In 1963, General Kulpa joined the Space Systems Division in Los Angeles as a project manager responsible for the development of a research satellite, later becoming a SPO director for a classified Air Force satellite program. He became commander of the Air Force Avionics Laboratory and then deputy for engineering at ASD. He then was assigned to the Office of the Secretary of the Air Force as deputy director for programs, Office of Space Systems, becoming the director in 1973. From 1975 to 1983 he served as the Director of the Secretary of the Air Force Special Projects unit (SAFSP), a unique and highly classified organization within the Air Force that gave birth to the Air Force satellite reconnaissance mission, interfacing regularly with the Central Intelligence Agency (CIA).

• Colonel Toby Gandy (USMA 1947)—Colonel Gandy played key roles with the Manned Orbital Laboratory (MOL) and Atlas programs while at SAMSO during 1965–69. He later became vice commander of SSD.

Ballistic Missile Division (BMD)

• Major General John L. McCoy (USMA 1939)—A former B-29 pilot and commander, in 1959 General McCoy was transferred to BMD, becoming the deputy for ballistic missiles in 1960. He was named program director for the Titan ICBM in 1961 and in 1966 he became the program director for the Minuteman program responsible for its development, production and turnover to SAC.

• Major General Donald R. Ostrander (USMA 1937)—General Ostrander's career in missiles began when he was appointed assistant for guided missiles production with the NATO international staff in Paris returning to the United States in 1959 as deputy director of ARPA (Advanced Research Projects Agency) at the Pentagon. From 1959 to 1961 he served as director of the Office of Launch Vehicles at NASA and in 1961 he became vice commander of the Ballistic Systems Division in Los Angeles. In 1962, he assumed command of the Office of Aerospace Research in Washington, D.C.

• Lt. General John G. Albert (USMA 1949)—General Albert's career spanned a wide variety of assignments devoted to the development of ICBM and space systems. With a master's degree in aeronautical engineering from the University of Michigan, he first served at the Air Force Missile Test Center where long-range missile testing capability was being established. He taught at West Point for three years as an assistant professor for guided missiles and atomic weapons and went on to assignments at BMD where he served as project officer for the operational propellant loading system of the Atlas ICBM, development of an operational communications satellite, and finally as director for the Mariner launch vehicle. He went on to be chief of the Gemini Launch Division and launch director for all 12 of the Gemini launches. In 1968, General Albert was assigned to HQ USAF in the Directorate of Space, where he served successively as chief, Program Development Division and chief, Policy and Plans Group until 1970, when he was named the director of space. He held this position until July 1972, when he was assigned to SAMSO as the deputy for space defense systems. He finished his career as commander, Air Force Acquisition Logistics Division, Air Force Logistics Command.

Space and Missile System Organization (SAMSO)

• Lt. General Dick Henry (USMA 1949)—General Henry became one of the key figures in the Air Force's space and satellite programs. He gained his early experience while assigned to HQ USAF in 1960 as a requirements officer in the Directorate of Operational Requirements working with the military space programs. In 1962, he joined the Office of Manned Space Flight at NASA and was named chief, Apollo Navigation/Guidance and Lunar Module Development programs. From 1963 to 1964, he served as director of Gemini program control. He then transferred to the Manned Spacecraft Center, Houston, as manager of the Gemini program until 1966. After a tour of duty in Vietnam as vice commander of the 37th Tactical Fighter Wing at Phu Cat Air Base, he returned to the 33rd Tactical Fighter Wing at Eglin Air Force Base in Florida, becoming wing commander in 1970. In 1974, he was named vice commander of SAMSO and then served as director of development and acquisition at DCS R&D in 1976 until 1978 when he was named commander of SAMSO. The organization's name was changed to the Space Division in October 1979.

• Major General Jessup D. Lowe (USMA 1943)—Early in his career, Lowe was assigned to the Directorate of R&D, Headquarters USAF, where he worked with the missile development programs for four years. He then was transferred to BMD as chief of the Space Systems Division and later to AFSC as assistant deputy commander for space and in 1967 he became director of space systems. He later was assigned as commander of the Air Force Satellite Control Facility and finally as commander of the Space and Missile Test Center.

• Major General Gerald K. Hendricks (USMA 1951)—With a Master of Science degree in nuclear engineering from AFIT and assignments with

SAC and TAC, much of General Hendricks's experience was in the defense R&D area. He was assigned to the Atomic Energy Commission's Nuclear Propulsion Office and later served with Headquarters Research and Technology Division at Bolling Air Force Base. He became the commander of AFSC's command liaison detachment in Vietnam where he also served as a fighter and transport pilot in a variety of aircraft. He went on to several positions in AFSC including feasibility assessment of a precision standoff modular glide weapon, a remotely piloted vehicle, and other guided weapon technologies. He later became commander of the Air Force Armament Laboratory at Eglin Air Force Base where he was responsible for directing the development of all non-nuclear munitions, air-launched weapons, missiles, guns, ammunitions, targets and related hardware for use throughout the Air Force. After other assignments within AFSC, he became the vice commander of SAMSO.

• Colonel William K. Kincaid (USMA 1938)—Trained as a combat pilot, Colonel Kincaid became the commander of the Naha, Okinawa, Air Base and the wing commander of its two fighter squadrons during the Korean War. He later became wing commander of the Satellite Test Wing, SSD. Following his retirement from the Air Force, Kincaid continued to work as the operations director for the MOL (Manned Orbiting Laboratory) program at General Electric Space Systems.

• Brigadier General Lewis S. Norman (USMA 1944)—With a master's degree in electrical engineering from the University of Michigan, Norman spent much of his early career in communications and engineering units eventually becoming chief of the communications division at WDD. He later became program director of an important satellite program at SSD and then chief of the Special Engineering Division at HQ USAF. He went on to become commander of the Air Force Satellite Control Facility and then deputy director for programs, Defense Communications Agency (DCA).

• Colonel John J. Schmitt, Jr. (USMA 1946)—Colonel Schmitt worked at the Air Force Satellite Control Facility and later at BMD and the SecDef's office.

• Colonel Joe E. Sanders (USMA 1956)—Colonel Sanders worked at the Air Force Satellite Control Facility, at the Space Test Wing, and later at DCS R&D at the Air Staff.

Chapter 10

Space

General Arnold had the foresight after the technological surprises of World War II from German jet aircraft and rocket-propelled V-2s to attempt to forecast what technologies were most promising for the future Air Force. Dr. von Kármán, director of the SAG, later named SAB, and RAND Corporation concluded that large rockets launching satellites into earth's orbit were feasible. Then, in 1954, RAND, after an extensive eight-year study ("Project Feedback," as in feeding back data from space to the earth), reported that photo coverage of great intelligence value could be obtained from satellite overflight of the Soviet Union. Based on recommendations and designs from RAND, the Air Force initiated a program known as Weapon System (WS) 117L, Advanced Reconnaissance System, and assigned the project to Brigadier General Schriever who, as we saw in the previous chapter, also was responsible for development and production of intercontinental missiles. The same rocket engines would be employed to launch nuclear warheads or satellites. At this time, the Cold War was very active, and President Eisenhower urgently needed to look behind the Iron Curtain and assess the actual Soviet military capability in order to avoid a possible Pearl Harbor–type of surprise attack.

America's space activity accelerated dramatically after the Soviet launch of Sputnik into orbit in 1957 followed by putting a man (Yuri Gagarin) in orbit in 1961 and then, in 1965, launching three men into orbit in a capsule, including a 10-minute space walk and a new rocket three times as powerful as the Gemini program's Titan II rocket. The U.S. was fearful of Soviet technological advances and was playing catchup when Lockheed's Kelly Johnson promised the president that Lockheed would deliver—in five months—a high-flying reconnaissance aircraft which would be invulnerable to Soviet defenses while overflying Soviet territory. The president accepted his offer as a near-term solution while keeping the satellite program under development. Kelly fulfilled his motto of "be quick, be quiet and be on time" and the U-2 met the

Lockheed U-2 Dragon Lady. There were 104 produced. A high altitude reconnaissance aircraft, with its first flight in 1955. Upgrades continued through 2012 with the U-2S (U.S. Air Force photo).

schedule and successfully overflew the Soviet Union from 1956 to 1960 when Soviet SA-2 missiles shot down Gary Power's U-2. As previously discussed in the Aerial Reconnaissance chapter, for this period the U-2 cameras provided 90 percent of all hard data of Soviet military capability.

In 1955, ICBMs were the nation's top military priority in the Cold War but the space threat commencing with the launch of Sputnik in 1957 initiated a critical period through the early '60s for U.S. military space missions. Accordingly, President Eisenhower established a high priority national space program. The president's desire for a policy of "space for peace" with "open skies" led to his establishment of NASA in 1958. NASA would be responsible for civilian space activity while all military activity would be conducted by the DOD and CIA on a super-secret basis, managed by the newly established ARPA (Advanced Research Projects Agency) serving as a centralized agency for all DOD space research and development activities.[1] A third sector, that of intelligence gathering through reconnaissance satellites, was established leading to the creation in 1961 of the highly classified National Reconnaissance Office (NRO).

As noted in the monograph commemorating NRO's 50th Anniversary, "it seems remarkable that even as the United States was achieving its goal of putting a man on the moon, there was an equally ambitious and technologically challenging American space program proceeding along a parallel path—but in strictest secrecy. Indeed, it was not until 1978 that a President acknowledged the basic fact that the United States carried out reconnaissance from space, and not until 1992 that the government acknowledged the NRO's existence.... Originally the NRO and its mission were totally unacknowledged, first to protect the source and method; and second, in deference to the sensitivity that some countries might have to U.S. satellites orbiting over their territory"[2]

During this tumultuous period, implementation of the space program was in constant flux as the government grappled with how best to organize and manage the major space functions with their not-yet-fully-defined missions and rapidly expanding budgets. In his presentation at the "U.S. Air Force in Space—1945 to the 21st Century" symposium in September 1995 (hereinafter the "1995 Space Symposium")[3] David M. Spires provided extensive detail on the many pressures and changes occurring within these organizations at the time. He noted that "despite the apparent logic in assuming that NASA would be responsible for civilian space activities and DOD would handle military interests, the demarcation line between civilian and military space concerns often proved artificial and unattainable. Moreover, NASA, like ARPA, represented another space agency that challenged the Air Force for space responsibilities and program funding."[4]

As described earlier, in 1961 the Air Force established the Air Force Systems Command (AFSC), with responsibility for all development and acquisition of aerospace and missile systems. One of its four subordinate organizations would be a new Space Systems Division, later consolidated into the Space and Missile Systems Organization (SAMSO). No longer combined with ICBM responsibilities, space development received its own organization to better prepare the service for the expanded space role it expected to acquire. General Bernard Schriever became the first AFSC commander upon promotion to four-star rank.

Satellite Missile Observation System (SAMOS)

General Robert E. Greer (USMA 1939) was the first director of the Air Force's Satellite Missile Observation System (SAMOS) project operating as a field extension of the Office of the Secretary of the Air Force for Special Projects (SAFSP).[5] SAMOS was a unique program started as part of the WS-117L satellite reconnaissance program in 1956 and operating in the early 1960s under extreme secrecy and with access to the highest levels of government including the secretary of defense and the president. SAMOS was patterned after the ongoing CIA/Air Force satellite program. The first SAMOS launch was in 1960 from Vandenberg AFB. Unlike the CORONA satellite developed by the CIA[6] which took photographs and returned them to Earth in a film capsule, SAMOS satellites electronically scanned photographic film and sent images down to earth via radio link.

These satellite systems, together with the CIA's A-12 and the Air Force's U-2 and SR-71 reconnaissance aircraft programs, provided the building blocks of what would become the NRO, a classified agency within the Department of Defense. However, the NRO, CIA, Air Force and Navy "often worked together, drawing on common technology and support infrastructure."[7] Today, the director of the NRO reports to both the director of national intelligence and the secretary of defense and serves in an additional capacity as assistant secretary of the Air Force (Intelligence Space Technology).[8]

Under General Greer's initial leadership within SAFSP, tremendous strides were made during the early 1960s in the buildup of the country's satellite capabilities, including replacement of ICBM boosters with more powerful and reliable launch vehicles and refined satellite reconnaissance systems, improvements which continued in the decades to come.

Global Positioning System (GPS)

A landmark turning point in the evolution of military space applications was the NAVSTAR (for "Navigation System Using Timing and Ranging") Global Positioning System, GPS. The Pentagon first proposed a global positioning satellite system in 1973 for the purpose of delivering weapons precisely on target. The first group ("Block I") of 10 GPS satellites starting with NAVSTAR I were launched from Vandenberg AFB in 1978 using Atlas rockets that were converted ICBMs. This first block of satellites was used to validate the system's concept at various stages of development. The first of the nine satellites in Block II representing the first operational satellites were launched shortly thereafter during 1989–90. By 1993 with the placement of a full constellation of 24 satellites, GPS attained initial operational capability (IOC). Full Operational Capability (FOC) was attained in 1995, signifying full availability of the military's secure Precise Positioning Service (PPS). In 1996, in recognition of the importance of GPS to civilian users as well as military users, U.S. President Bill Clinton issued a policy directive declaring GPS a

Artist's conception of GPS Block II-F satellite in orbit. GPS, reconnaissance, communications and weather support satellite systems are in earth orbit today (NASA illustration).

dual-use system and established the Interagency GPS Executive Board to manage it as a national asset.[9]

As noted by General Moorman in his briefing at the 1995 Space Symposium:

> This military space system has had enormous ramifications for warfare, transportation, surveying/mapping, and even science of the atmosphere on and above the Earth's surface. This space system had multiple weapon system applications, including the aiming of precision guided munitions (PGMs), ballistic and cruise missiles, and artillery fire. It can guide ships, tanks and people precisely to a destination across featureless oceans or deserts. It has revolutionized aviation command, control and communications (C^3).... Altogether, the effect of GPS was so profound and such a warfighting enabler that it ensured that the military would hereafter be highly dependent on space systems.[10]

As will be seen in the coming pages, many West Point grads in senior positions of responsibility played important roles in the development and operation of GPS.

Man-in-Space

Meanwhile, out at Edwards AFB in the early 1960s we were involved in the early preparations for entry into space. The first manned flights into space were accomplished by the X-15 launched from a B-52 carrying the X-15 under its wing up to an altitude of about 45,000 feet at which point the X-15 was released for acceleration by rocket to record-breaking speeds and altitudes. On several flights the X-15 climbed out of the earth's atmosphere, defined as 50 miles above the earth's surface. After completing a very successful test program of 199 flights, the X-15 was retired in 1968.

On one record-breaking flight piloted by then Major Bob White (later a major general and commander of the Flight Test Center), the X-15 was launched from a B-52 flown by two West Point and Test Pilot School graduates, Frank Cole (USMA 1946) and myself (USMA 1950). Major General Joe Engle, who flew the X-15 16 times and later commanded the space shuttle on two flights, credits the X-15, which has similar flight characteristics to the shuttle, with laying the foundation for the shuttle design and piloting techniques such as the capability to reenter the atmosphere and glide with no power to a precision landing using first reaction control jets for flight control in space and then a smooth transition to conventional controls in the atmosphere for approach and landing. Joe officially became an astronaut three times when he flew the X-15 to the fringes of space before he twice took the shuttle into space.

Two Air Force man-in-space programs, the Dyna-Soar and the Manned Orbiting Laboratory (MOL), were also started in the 1960s at Edwards AFB. At that time the Test Pilot School was preparing to train astronauts and renamed the school the Aerospace Research Pilot School (ARPS), with the first class starting in 1961. The Dyna-Soar crews had been selected from test pilots at Edwards since the vehicle, when reentering the atmosphere, would be piloted much like an airplane, with maneuverability and precise landing capability. A few years later after further development this concept evolved into the space shuttle. While working with contractor engineers, the program was cancelled due to its costs and its questionable utility relative to landing capsules in the ocean.

These two space programs were viewed as a duplication of mission with NASA efforts and were cancelled at about the same time that NASA was launching astronauts in space. As mentioned earlier, two of the test pilots, Neil Armstrong and Pete Knight, went on to fly the X-15 and fame as flight record setters. The Air Force's space-related efforts at Edwards AFB were terminated upon the transfer of astronaut training responsibilities to NASA. Only Frank Borman (USMA 1950) and Jim McDivitt, who had helped to develop the astronaut training program at ARPS, and four of the students in training for the MOL program went on to become NASA astronauts.

The path to becoming an astronaut was long, demanding and extremely competitive with hundreds of other well-qualified candidates and many physical, mental, and psychological examinations to be completed. The earlier test pilot criteria of demonstrated courage, drive and outstanding hand-eye coordination and flying skills had changed. Now the emphasis shifted to higher technical education and the ability to manage complicated systems and teamwork in a small capsule traveling in the harsh, unforgiving environment of space. Those selected had the modern version of "the right stuff."

As chief of bomber flight test at Wright-Patterson AFB, I had the pleasure of writing letters of recommendation for several of my test pilots applying for astronaut positions with NASA. Gordon Fullerton, an outstanding pilot who wrote high quality test reports and had graduated from Caltech with engineering degrees and who had been in training for the MOL program stood out in my group. He was selected for the astronaut program and began a long career with NASA, first as one of the pilots flying tests of the shuttle approach and landing characteristics after being launched from the top of a uniquely modified Boeing 747. (Not coincidentally, the pilot of the 747 for each of these flights had been my well-respected boss at Edwards AFB, Fitz Fulton.) Gordon went on to pilot two shuttle space flights. He later stayed with NASA as an experimental test pilot until he retired after having flown 135 different types of aircraft and accumulating 16,000 flying hours. He loved to fly and was an expert at evaluating and reporting on aircraft characteristics and capabilities.

As a prelude to this chapter about West Point graduates' contributions to the space mission, it should be clear that we have only scratched the surface of the fascinating story of man's trip to the moon through the ambitious efforts of the Mercury, Gemini and Apollo programs. Our slice of the story focuses on West Point grads who played a role in these programs. For those wishing to learn more, we recommend a visit to NASA's website, to the Smithsonian's many fine publications regarding spaceflight, and to a few books that we've referenced in writing this chapter: Gene Kranz's *Failure is Not an Option*; *Apollo: The Epic Journey to the Moon* by David W. Reynolds, Mike Collins's *Carrying the Fire*, and Robert Kurson's recent *Rocket Men* about Apollo 8 and man's first journey to the moon. These and other books provide far greater detail regarding the events surrounding NASA's man-in-space programs.

As this chapter has emphasized, many West Point grads were instrumental in the development and support of the Air Force's missions in space and, later, many of NASA's missions. These grads played many different roles in the development of the space mission, whether for peace or wartime. As noted in an article in AOG's Fall 2016 *West Point* magazine, "West Point and America's Space Program," quoting astronaut R. Shane Kimbrough (USMA

1989): "Space magnifies West Point value. Negotiating extreme conditions, taking care of people, working with diverse teams, and knowing when to be a leader and when to be a follower are all lessons I learned at West Point."[11]

Some of the more prominent players in this fascinating story are identified in the following table. In the early days of the space mission, many of these individuals worked in both military (Air Force) and peacetime (NASA) space systems.

West Point Grads Who Played Key Roles in the Space Mission

Name	Rank	USMA Class	Key Role in Space
Early Visionaries			
Henry H. "Hap" Arnold	General	1907	Instituted high tech in the Air Force
Dwight D. Eisenhower	President	1915	Spearheaded NASA and freedom of space
Nathan F. Twining	General	1918	CSAF, 1953–57
Thomas D. White	General	1920	CSAF, 1957–61; Oversight of AF leadership in space
Military and NASA Support			
Robert E. Greer	General	1939	SecAF-SP; VCmdr., Space Systems
Edmund O'Connor	Lt. General	1943	Manager of Saturn launch vehicles
Rocco Petrone	Director	1946	Redstone missile development, Apollo Program Director
David D. Bradburn	Major General	1946	Director Special Projects, OSAF; Chaired 1975 study on space systems
John G. Albert	Lt. General	1949	Gemini Launch Director
John E. Kulpa, Jr.	Major General	1950	Director of Special Projects, OSAF
Organizers of AF Space Command			
Lew Allen, Jr.	General	1946	CSAF, 1978–1982; Oversight of AF Space Command
Robert T. Marsh	General	1949	Cmdr. AFSC and Space Systems; 1981–1984

Name	Rank	USMA Class	Key Role in Space
Jerome O'Malley	General	1953	Promoted AF Space operational command
Bennie L. Davis	General	1950	CINC—Strategic Air Command
Charles A. Gabriel	General	1950	CSAF, 1982–86; Supervised Space Cmd.
Men in Space			
Edward H. White II	Lt. Colonel	1952	Astronaut—Gemini IV; Apollo 1
Frank F. Borman	Colonel	1950	Astronaut—Gemini VII, Apollo 8
Buzz Aldrin	Colonel	1951	Astronaut—Gemini XII, Apollo 11
Michael Collins	Major General	1952	Astronaut—Gemini X, Apollo 11
David R. Scott	Colonel	1954	Astronaut—Apollo 9, 15
Alfred M. Worden	Colonel	1955	Astronaut—Apollo 15
11 West Point grads	Colonels	1955–89	STS 6 through STS 126
5 West Point grads	Colonels	Various	Commanders of International Space Station (ISS)
Space Applications in Support of War			
James V. Hartinger	General	1949	Cmdr., Space Cmd., NORAD—1982–84
Richard C. Henry	Lt. General	1949	Cmdr., SAMSO
Donald Kutyna	General	1957	Cmdr., Space Cmd., NORAD
H. Norman Schwartzkopf, Jr.	General	1956	CINC Desert Storm— Army's validation of space support

Mercury Program

On May 25, 1961, President John F. Kennedy announced the ambitious goal of sending an American to the moon before the end of the decade. He was under great pressure for the U.S. to catch up and overtake the Soviet Union in the space race. Just three years earlier, in 1958, the first manned space flight program, Project Mercury, had been started, providing President Kennedy with a reasonable, but extremely ambitious, basis for setting this goal.

There was tremendous public enthusiasm and publicity for the Mercury astronauts.[12] They were heroes, but the U.S. was still behind the Soviets in the race to the moon.

Mercury's objectives were threefold:

- Place a manned spacecraft in orbital flight around the earth.
- Investigate man's performance capabilities and his ability to function in the environment of space.
- Recover the man and the spacecraft safely.[13]

Mercury's first preliminary steps into space used existing technologies and off-the-shelf equipment to ensure reliability and control costs. For example, the first launch, a suborbital flight, was by an operational Army Redstone missile. Subsequent launches would take place using modified rockets from Air Force ballistic missiles such as the Atlas D. A modified Atlas D rocket launched astronaut John Glenn into orbit in 1962, making him the first American to orbit the earth.

The Mercury capsules allowed for the pilot to manually operate the system for launch escape ejection and control of the capsule attitude. On May 15, 1963, during the final Mercury mission, astronaut L. Gordon Cooper successfully used the manual attitude control for reentry when the automatic system failed, using his view of the earth and stars through the capsule's window to orient the spacecraft for reentry. During the six years of the Mercury program (1958–63), 20 unmanned and six manned flights took place, four of which orbited the earth.

Gemini Program

Project Gemini was NASA's second human spaceflight program. It started in 1961, two years prior to the completion of the Mercury program, and concluded in 1966. Unlike the Mercury launches, which carried individual astronauts, Gemini spacecraft carried a two-astronaut crew. During the 1965–66 period, 10 Gemini crews flew low earth orbit (LEO) missions, significantly advancing the U.S. in the space race against the Soviet Union.

Gemini's primary objective was to develop space travel techniques that would support the subsequent Apollo mission to put astronauts on the Moon. Gemini had four main goals:

- Test an astronaut's ability to fly long-duration missions (up to two weeks in space).
- Understand how spacecraft could rendezvous and dock in orbit around the Earth and the moon.

Mission	Command Pilot	Pilot	Year	Highlights
Gemini 3	Virgil I. "Gus" Grissom	John W. Young	1965	First flight with three orbits
Gemini IV	James A. McDivitt	Edward H. White (USMA 1952)	1965	First EVA
Gemini V	L. Gordon Cooper, Jr.	Charles Conrad, Jr.	1965	120 orbits in a week
Gemini VII	Frank F. Borman (USMA 1950)	James A. Lovell, Jr.	1965	Two-week mission
Gemini VI-A	Walter M. Schirra	Thomas P. Stafford	1965	First rendezvous in space
Gemini VIII	Neil A. Armstrong	David R. Scott (USMA 1954)	1966	First docking with another space vehicle
Gemini IX-A	Thomas P. Stafford	Eugene A. Cernan	1966	Three types of rendezvous; two hours EVA; 44 orbits
Gemini X	John W. Young	Michael Collins (USMA 1952)	1966	First use of Agena propulsion system and rendezvous with target vehicle from Gemini VIII
Gemini XI	Charles Conrad, Jr.	Richard F. Gordon, Jr.	1966	Record altitude of 739 miles; first orbit rendezvous and docking; 44 orbits
Gemini XII	James A. Lovell, Jr.	Edwin E. "Buzz" Aldrin (USMA 1951)	1966	Rendezvous and docking manually; EVA of 5.5 hours; 59 orbits

- Perfect reentry and landing methods
- Further understand the effects of longer space flights on astronauts.[14]

Like the rockets used in the Mercury program, Gemini relied upon modified ICBMs, two-stage Titan II rockets, for launches into space. The first Gemini launch was launched without pilots to test its reliability and safety.

Three of Gemini's astronauts, Cooper, Grissom and Schirra, were drawn from the "Mercury Seven." To take full advantage of the experience gained during the Gemini program, 15 Gemini astronauts continued on to the Apollo mission: Edward White, Gus Grissom, Wally Schirra, John Young, Jim McDivitt, Charles Conrad, Frank Borman, Jim Lovell, Tom Stafford, Neal Armstrong, Dave Scott, Eugene Cernan, Mike Collins, Richard Gordon, and Buzz Aldrin went on to the Apollo program. The preceding table (page 186) lists the Gemini astronauts.

Apollo Program

The six manned Mercury flights and 10 manned Gemini missions worked at the frontiers of space and demonstrated that man could get into space, orbit the earth, walk and work in the unforgiving environment of space and safely return to earth. The technology and engineering knowledge, launch facilities, and communication systems had been developed providing a good foundation for the Apollo race to the moon. But still, no man had gone beyond a few hundred miles from earth and the moon was 240,000 miles away; how to reenter and safely return to earth were still unknowns. There was much more to do with known and unknown risks and a demanding time schedule of two years to get it done by the end of the 1960s. The astronauts well understood the dangers involved. In fact, Gus Grissom made a time-honored statement about "mission before self" when he said, "If we die, we want people to accept it. We hope that if anything happens to us it will not delay the program. The conquest of space is worth the risk of life."[15]

When Apollo I was in a full-scale countdown exercise with the entire team from the Houston command center to the Cape launch pad and with Gus Grissom, Ed White and Roger Chaffee sealed in their command module atop the Saturn 1B launch rocket, a horrendous fire broke out in the module. The astronauts were dead in seconds and the Apollo program was forever changed.

What happened, how it happened and why it happened were the questions to be answered as they always are after an accident. Frank Borman (USMA 1950) was the astronaut on the investigation team. He was a capsule expert, tireless investigator and determined to discover (a) what killed these astronauts, including his and his family's close friend Ed White and then (b) how to prevent it from happening again. The conditions that led to the fire were obvious—the capsule was pressurized with pure oxygen (as were the capsules in the Mercury and Gemini programs) and many materials in the capsule were combustible. While no single ignition source of the fire was conclusively identified, electrical arcs in the wiring likely provided the spark.[16] Frank was sent to Congress to testify regarding the accident and convinced Congress and the general public that NASA management and engineering staff were competent and that the Apollo program should continue.

Frank also was fully involved in the capsule redesign effort which produced more than 1,300 design changes and the safest command module (CM) ever built. During one contentious CM redesign meeting, Frank sternly directed, "Enough—let's get on with the job. It's time to fly."[17] This was to happen sooner than he expected. In October 1968, 10 months after the fire, Apollo 2 and 3 were cancelled and unmanned Apollo 4, 5, and 6 were launched followed by the first successful manned flight of the program, Apollo 7, on October 11, 1968.

Two key risky decisions were made after the Apollo 1 fire in an effort to make up lost time and attempt to meet the moon landing goal in the 1960s. George Mueller, senior NASA administrator for manned space flight, over the objections of rocket expert Wernher von Braun's incremental test plan for Saturn V directed an "all-up" Saturn V test for Apollo 4.[18] Mueller had high confidence in von Braun's team and considered the risk acceptable in order to reach the Apollo mission's goals. The successful unmanned launch of Apollo 4 in November 1967 with a complex three-stage rocket engine put the U.S. back in the race to the moon.

The second key decision to be made involved the lunar module (LM) which was planned to be tested by Apollo 8 in low-earth orbit but was not ready at the time. George Low, Apollo program manager, saw an opportunity to shift the Apollo 8 mission to the Apollo 10 moon mission but without the LM. It was a high-risk change to the orderly, step-by-step NASA procedure— but if successful, it would make it possible to accomplish the major goal of reaching the moon before the end of the decade. A huge program acceleration would be required to launch in four months, but as Borman had said, "it's time to fly." In fact, when NASA administrator James E. Webb was told of the plan he said, "are you out of your mind?"[19]

Apollo 8

Apollo 8 was the second manned spaceflight mission in the Apollo program. It was launched on December 21, 1968, and was to set numerous records. Its three-astronaut crew—commander Frank Borman, command module pilot

James Lovell, and lunar module pilot William Anders—became the first humans to travel beyond low Earth orbit, to orbit another celestial body (the moon), to escape the gravity of the moon, to reenter the earth's gravity and to return safely to earth. The rocket powering Apollo 8 to the moon was the Saturn V. It was that rocket's third flight but first launch carrying a crew.

It is important to recognize that while many challenges awaited the Apollo 8 crew, the three that posed the greatest risks to the crews' lives—the launch, the trans-lunar injection (TLI) and reentry—were tested for the first time by Apollo 8. The Saturn V rocket had previously been used for unmanned launches—this would be its first launch with a crew of astronauts aboard. Furthermore, in its previous launch the rocket had suffered a number of problems including first-stage oscillation, second stage engine failure and third-stage ignition problems. However, teams from the Marshall Space Flight Center worked around the clock making corrections right up until the day of launch. Second, escaping the earth's gravity on the way to the moon, something that had never been attempted by man, required further acceleration using the Saturn's third stage during the TLI maneuver to launch the craft toward orbit of the moon. Third, after completion of the moon orbits and to return to earth, the crew would initiate a trans-earth injection (TEI), the critical burn of the return trip which would be executed on the far side of the moon out of the reach of communication with the earth. Failure of the propulsion system to ignite and burn for the specified time would condemn the crew to a lunar orbit with little chance of rescue. This, coupled with the inherently risky aspects of reentry to the earth's atmosphere, were of major concern and none of these maneuvers had been done before.

After a rapid and intensive review by all of the team leaders, the decision was made to change Apollo 8 to a moon mission with 10 orbits of the moon and with a launch scheduled in four months using the Saturn V rocket, an engine that had suffered a number of problems in its prior flight. "It was the most daring proposal NASA had ever seriously considered. No one had ever flown on a Saturn V, and we were proposing to send the first manned team of astronauts all the way to the moon."[20] Long hours and seven-days-a-week work schedules were required by several thousand workers to prepare for this highly complex trip into unknown hazardous territory with many new engineering issues still to be resolved. Preparation and training for space flight in previous missions within earth's gravity had taken a year or more, so providing only four months until launch was a radical compression of the schedule. After the Apollo 1 disaster, flight director Gene Kranz had issued a new creed to his teams: "Failure is not an Option."[21] So the overall objective for this risky experimental mission was in fact defined as "go fast, go safe."

Four months later, on December 21, 1968, the three astronauts took the elevator up 363 feet to the Apollo 8 capsule. Their friend, Günter Wendt, a former German Luftwaffe mechanic affectionately called "der Führer of der Launch Pad" helped them into their capsule seats, wished them well and closed the hatch. It's interesting to note that Wendt, an émigré from Germany, was the last in a string of individuals of German descent, including Bernard Schriever, born in Germany and the leader of the U.S. ICBM effort and Wernher von Braun, the German inventor of the V-2 rocket, to have participated in the race to beat the Soviets to the moon. In a sense the Germans still had a hand in fighting the Soviets, but this time with the U.S. in a race to the moon!

The significance of this first launch out of the earth's gravity and to the moon was clearly recognized as a historic event by one of the earliest pioneers of flight, Charles Lindbergh, who met with the astronauts the day before the launch and observed the flight the next day.[22]

After a perfect launch and after all systems had been checked out during three earth orbits, flight director Kranz authorized the CAPCOM (capsule communicator), astronaut Mike Collins, to transmit to Borman, his fellow West Pointer: "Apollo 8, you are GO for TLI."[23] For the first time, man would trigger a rocket burn accelerating Apollo 8 from 17,000 mph to 24,000 mph that would send man beyond the earth's gravity.[24] And in setting another of many records, the 24,000 escape velocity was faster than any man had gone before.

After reaching the moon and during ten orbits, several interesting events occurred which portrayed the human reaction to this historic event. During the Apollo 8 mission, the astronauts communicated as a standard procedure with the CAPCOM at the Houston Control Center. CAPCOMs for Apollo 8 were Mike Collins (USMA 1950), Ken Mattingly (a naval officer and graduate of the Air Force Research Pilot School who later flew on Apollo 16 and STS 4), and Gerald P. Carr (a Marine Corps officer who later flew on SkyLab 4). Collins, as CAPCOM, and Borman as capsule commander—the two West Point grads with the Apollo 8 mission—talked during many eight-hour shifts, sometimes at distances of up to 240,000 miles—surely a distance record for West Point grads' communications! During one shift, Mattingly observed, "There's a beautiful moon out there tonight." Frank responded, "There's a beautiful earth out there."[25] And on Christmas eve while orbiting the moon, the astronauts read from Chapter 1 of the Book of Genesis regarding God's creation of the earth—a message heard around the world. Also during the mission, Bill Anders took what became perhaps the most famous photograph of the earth shining beyond the moon's horizon.

But now they had to get home. At least two critical events were still to come: the rocket burn and exit from the moon gravity and, secondly, the

Apollo 8 crew at Kennedy Space Center simulator. From left to right are James A. Lovell, Jr., William A. Anders, and mission commander Frank Borman (USMA 1950). Borman was the first of six West Point grads in the Apollo program (NASA photo).

return trip and reentry back to earth. The return trip involved a treacherous deceleration from over 24,000 mph and capsule shield temperatures of up to 5,000°F down to the much more tolerable conditions floating in a raft in the Pacific Ocean. As we all know after the fact, it went well.

Borman later turned down the offer of another trip to the moon, stating that his goal to beat the Soviets to the moon had been satisfied. Fellow travelers to the moon Neil Armstrong and Mike Collins considered Apollo 8 to be a critical Apollo milestone because of the many first-time barriers in space travel to be overcome. As a result of this successful mission, Borman and his crew were invited to brief a joint session of Congress.

As the springboard mission for putting man on the moon, the Apollo 8 mission accomplished its goal with flying colors. Many have commented on the important role Apollo 8 played in this endeavor, but comments from astronauts and others who followed Apollo 8 are most telling:

- Neil Armstrong called Apollo 8 "an enormously bold decision that catapulted the American space program forward."

- Harrison Schmitt (Apollo 17) stated "It was probably the most remarkable effort that the NASA team down here ever put together."

- Mike Collins, when asked to compare Apollo 8 to his historic Apollo 11 flight said, "I think Apollo 8 was about leaving and Apollo 11 was about arriving, leaving Earth and arriving at the Moon. As you look back one hundred years from now, which is more important? I'm not sure, but I think probably you would say Apollo 8 was of more significance than Apollo 11."

- From Chris Kraft, flight director for all of the Mercury and many of the Gemini missions and who directed the design of mission control at the Johnson Space Center: "It took more courage to make the decision to do Apollo 8 than anything we ever did in the space program."[26]

The next critical systems needed to reach and safely return from the moon—the surface and lunar modules—were tested in space during the Apollo 9 and 10 missions. All systems for the final push to the moon were tested and ready. In fact, the CM and LM pilots of the next three missions— Apollo 9, 10, and 11—were test pilots with EVA, rendezvous and docking experience in space gained from the Gemini program. NASA was prepared for the worst but planning for success.

The U.S. mission in space and to the moon was a proud era in U.S. history and West Point grads made a significant contribution to this national effort.

The following is a listing of the Apollo missions and crews:

Mission	Launched	Crew	Highlights
Apollo 1	Feb. 21, 1967	Virgil "Gus" Grissom Ed White (USMA 1952) Roger B. Chaffee	Not flown; all crew members died in a cabin fire on the launch pad on January 27, 1967.
Apollo 7	Oct. 11, 1968	Wally Schirra Walt Cunningham Donn Eisele	First mission in the Apollo program to carry a crew into space. First mission to carry a live TV broadcast from the spacecraft. Made 163 orbits.
Apollo 8	Dec. 21, 1968	Frank Borman (USMA 1950) James Lovell William Anders	First manned flight to leave earth orbit, reach the moon, conduct 10 orbits of the moon in 20 hours and return safely to Earth. Paved the way for Apollo 11's moon landing.
Apollo 9	Mar. 3, 1969	James McDivitt David Scott (USMA 1954) Russell Schweickart	First manned flight of Command/Service Module (CSM) and Lunar Module (LM) in Earth orbit; demonstrated Portable Life Support System to be used on the lunar surface. 10 days in earth orbit.
Apollo 10	May 18, 1969	Thomas Stafford John Young Eugene Cernan	Used as a "dress rehearsal" for Apollo 11's moon landing. LM descended to 8.4 miles above moon's surface before returning to dock with the CSM.
Apollo 11	Jul. 16, 1969	Neil Armstrong Michael Collins (USMA 1952) Edwin "Buzz" Aldrin (USMA 1951)	First manned landing on the moon (Armstrong and Aldrin) and return to the CSM (piloted by Collins) and earth.
Apollo 12	Nov. 14, 1969	C. "Pete" Conrad Richard Gordon Alan Bean	Second landing on the moon near the site of the unmanned probe, Surveyor 3.
Apollo 13	Apr. 11, 1970	James Lovell Jack Swigert Fred Haise	Third landing attempt aborted near the moon after an oxygen tank exploded, crippling the SM. Crew used LM as a lifeboat to return to Earth.

Mission	Launched	Crew	Highlights
Apollo 14	Jan. 31, 1971	Alan Shepard Stuart Roosa Edgar Mitchell	Third landing on the moon. Spent 33.5 hours on the moon with 9.5 hours of EVA.
Apollo 15	Jul. 26, 1971	David Scott (USMA 1954) Alfred Worden (USMA 1955) James Irwin	Fourth landing on the moon. Lunar Roving Vehicle used for first time. Three days spent on the moon with 18.5 hours of EVA.
Apollo 16	Apr. 16, 1972	John Young T. Kenneth Mattingly Charles Duke	Fifth landing on the moon. Three days spent on the moon moon with 20 hours of EVA. Subsatellite released from SM.
Apollo 17	Dec. 7, 1972	Eugene Cernan Ronald Evans Harrison Schmitt	Final manned moon landing. Three days on lunar surface, use of Rover and extensive moonwalks and scientific measurements. First visit by geologist.

Creation of Air Force Space Command

In the 1960s and 1970s, Air Force programs in space were R&D projects assigned to AFSC and NRO with the primary objective being reconnaissance of enemy territory. As satellite capability expanded into navigation, early warning, weapons delivery, communications and weather, the question of how and who would manage space assets became a serious and complicated issue. In 1974, General David Jones, CSAF, asked his major commanders (MAJCOMS) in writing—should there be an operational space organization and, if so, to which MAJCOM should it be assigned? There were no conclusive responses and many studies followed by ADCOM, SAC, TAC, AFSC and the Air Staff. Brigadier General David Bradburn (USMA 1946) chaired the first study by SAFSP while at the Aerospace Defense Command (ADCOM), Major General Bill Burroughs (USMA 1948) led the ADCOM effort. Burroughs, General Chappie James and others were critical of the SAFSP study, advocating an operational space organization as part of ADCOM.[27] After additional studies, in 1979 a final decision to deactivate ADCOM was reached and its assets and mission were assigned to SAC and TAC.

Shortly after this realignment, there were two false alarms of missile attacks on the U.S., one in 1979 and the next in 1980.[28] It was obvious to all that missile early warning was a critical high priority mission. In 1980, the Air

Force Scientific Advisory Board reviewed Air Force space operations and concluded that the Air Force was "inadequately organized for operational exploitation of space."[29] As a result, AFSC assigned Major General Jack Kulpa (USMA 1950) as deputy commander for space operations. At that time, Kulpa was also director of SAFSP and deputy commander of SAMSO. Later, Kulpa headed a study which resulted in 1981 with a Consolidated Space Operation Center (CSOC) in Colorado. At that time, General Jerry O'Malley (USMA 1953) was DCS, plans and operations on the Air Staff. He supported the concept of a separate space command.

Discussions concerning space issues were being held between Generals Hartinger (USMA 1949) at NORAD, Marsh (USMA 1949) at AFSC, Bennie Davis (USMA 1950) at SAC and O'Malley (USMA 1953) at DCS Plans and Ops. CSAF Lew Allen (USMA 1946) was concerned that the space issue was in disarray. Undersecretary of the Air Force Pete Aldridge spoke of creating a space command and secretary of the Air Force Verne Orr accepted that a space command might be advisable. Then in January 1982, the GAO criticized the DOD for poor management of space systems and recommended withholding funds until DOD developed an overall plan for military exploitation of space.[30] MAJCOM studies went on and General Allen directed generals Hartinger and Marsh to make recommendations by April 1982. There were too many contentious issues to mention here, but a rough plan was submitted in April to the air staff for review.[31] In 1982, General Charles Gabriel (USMA 1950) became CSAF with O'Malley as vice chief, who led the way for a separate and unified space command which was activated on September 1, 1982. As these events make clear, West Pointers were pivotal players in the establishment of the U.S. Air Force space command.

It should be emphasized that the investment in satellite-based early warning, reconnaissance, navigation, communication, weather, mapping and other systems have been fully validated in recent years. For example, during the Gulf War, which sometimes has been called "the first space war" because of the extensive and highly successful use of space-based high-tech assets to command and control military forces on the battlefield including the use of GPS by ground troops, marked its first major test in combat. When asked how all the high-tech equipment worked during Desert Storm, General Norman Schwarzkopf (USMA 1956) stated: "Beyond our wildest expectations."[32] And in a Department of Defense report to Congress: "NAVSTAR GPS played a key role and has many applications in all functional war-fighting areas. Land navigation was the biggest beneficiary, giving Coalition forces a major advantage over the Iraqis."[33]

The evolution of military space operations separate from those of NASA (formed in 1958) and the NRO (1961) has been a long and tortuous path and, to some degree remains unresolved to today. But the story of U.S. policy and activity in space is probably far from over. In June 2018, President Trump ordered the creation of a new military branch, the "Space Force," which would be a separate military branch added to the Army, Navy, Marines, Air Force, and Coast Guard. "A Joint Chiefs of Staff official said 'space is a warfighting domain' and that the Joint Chiefs of Staff will work with the Pentagon, Congress, and other stakeholders to follow the president's guidance."[34] As perhaps expected, senior officials at the Air Force, which had been responsible for military space operations, expressed reservations to Congress about the creation of a separate space force. Nonetheless, on December 20, 2019, the U.S. Space Command (SPACECOM) was established as a separate military service. We note that eighty-six cadets from the 2020 graduating class at the Air Force Academy entered the Space Force following graduation.

But as this chapter has revealed, many West Point grads played an important role in leading the development of space technologies that will set the stage for years to come.

Chapter 11

U.S. Air Force Academy

One of the most enduring legacies of West Point grads upon the U.S. Air Force is the role they played in the formation and development of the U.S. Air Force Academy (USAFA). West Point graduates such as Generals Eisenhower, Arnold, Spaatz and Harmon recognized the need for a dedicated air academy and were at the forefront of the drive for the U.S. Air Force Academy. But unlike the Army and Navy with centuries of history to mold their academies, the Air Force was a new armed service, founded just in 1947, and based on a technology—the airplane—that was less than 50 years old at that time.

Even before plans for the academy were established, many questions and challenges faced those who were responsible for creating it. While programs and curricula at West Point (in particular) and Annapolis provided a useful guide, including that of an honor code that was integral to the cadet experience, those who planned and developed the Air Force Academy sought a new military institution oriented toward aeronautics that would produce highly qualified, trained and motivated young officers of character to meet the needs of this new military service. This new academy would have an enduring impact on the Air Force, much as West Point does upon the Army and Annapolis upon the Navy.

In addition to the influence of senior Air Force officers who had graduated from West Point many years earlier, West Point grads from the '40s and '50s also had a big impact on the academy. For example, when as young lieutenants, they served as surrogate upperclassman (air training officers or ATOs). These West Point grads had direct, day-to-day contact with the new Air Force Academy cadets, a responsibility given to upperclassmen at the other academies. Other West Point grads, now captains or majors, served as air officers commanding (AOCs) for the early USAFA classes.

It should be noted that the history of the founding of the Air Force Academy is thoroughly and vividly brought to life in two excellent texts: George V. Fagan's 1988 book, *The Air Force Academy—An Illustrated History*, and later in Phillip S. Meilinger's 2009 book, *Hubert R. Harmon—Airman, Officer, Father of the Air Force Academy*. Brigadier General Fagan (USAF, Ret.) was an original faculty member at the academy, serving as a professor of history and library director until his retirement from the Air Force in 1969. His development of the academy library was critical for the academy's accreditation before graduating its first class in 1959. Meilinger is a 1970 graduate of the Air Force Academy, a retired Air Force colonel and a PhD in history from University of Michigan. These well-researched books provide a rich resource of the history of the Air Force Academy for those interested in learning more. However, our focus here is upon the many contributions to the academy made by West Point graduates.

The Air Force Academy was officially established on April 1, 1954, although that date was actually the culmination of many years of debate and analysis about the need for another military academy. Of course, at that time, West Point and Annapolis served as the primary institutions for providing trained and motivated young officers to the Army, including the Army Air Corps and the Navy. But the seeds of the idea for a separate air academy go back to the earliest days of flight and to World War I where an Army Air Service officer, Lt. Colonel Arthur J. Hanlon (USMA 1908) wrote in a November 26, 1918, letter: "As the Military and Naval Academies are the backbone of the Army and Navy, so must the Aeronautical Academy be the backbone of the Air Service. No service can flourish without some such institution to inculcate into its embryonic officers' love of country, proper conception of duty and highest regard for honor."[1]

In the months to follow, others, including Brigadier General Billy Mitchell, issued supporting memos of the concept of an air academy modeled after that of West Point and Annapolis but with additional thoughts about the purpose and curriculum of an academy to prepare young pilots for careers in the air forces. In a study entitled "Quest for an Air Force Academy," by M. Hamlin Cannon and Henry S. Fellerman, Mitchell testified before Congress on January 31, 1925, that it was "most essential ... to have an air academy to form a basis for the permanent backbone of your air service and to attend to the ... organizational part of it, very much in the same way that West Point does for the Army, or the Naval Academy for the Navy."[2]

The proponents of a new air academy received a huge boost in momentum when the Air Force was established as a separate military service in 1947. It stood to reason that if the Army and Navy each had their dedicated service academies, the Air Force should have the same. But despite this very positive development, the notion of a separate academy took time to become a priority. After the bombing of Pearl Harbor on December 7, 1941, West Point was authorized to commission up to 60 percent of its graduating class in the Air Corps. The Class of 1943 that graduated early in January saw 164 of its 410 graduates (40 percent) earn their wings, while 206 of 514 (40 percent) from the Class of 1944 became pilots. The Class of 1945 graduated 294 pilots out of a total class of 852 (35 percent). By 1948, 36 percent of the class elected to enter the Air Force and in 1949, 42 percent elected to become pilots. Thereafter, an interim solution was negotiated between the military secretaries whereby volunteers for the West Point and Annapolis graduating classes from 1954 to 1958 would provide up to 25 percent of each class to the Air Force. This operated until 1959 with the first graduating class of the Air Force Academy. In total, during the period 1947 through 1958, approximately 1,600 West Point graduates elected to enter the Air Force.[3]

It is interesting to note that as early as 1923, West Point graduates could elect to enter the Army Air Service (the predecessor organization of the USAF in operation between 1918 and 1926) directly upon graduation rather than first entering the Army and transferring at a later date. One such graduate, General Hoyt S. Vandenberg (USMA 1923), discussed below, chose the Air Service upon graduating from West Point in 1923.[4]

Recognizing that the provision of officers from West Point and Annapolis was only a temporary solution, in 1948 the Air Force's first secretary, W. Stuart Symington, appointed a board to study the military academies and to make recommendations regarding junior officer education and training. The board was co-chaired by Colorado University President Dr. Robert L. Stearns and retired Army General Dwight Eisenhower (USMA 1915), then president of Columbia University (hence the name of the board, the "Stearns-Eisenhower Board"). Assisting the board was a small group of five civilians and three military officers: the superintendents of West Point and Annapolis and Major General David M. Schlatter (USMA 1923). The board issued its final report less than a year later, recommending "that an Air Force Academy should be established without delay and that appropriate legislation to accomplish this purpose, including the authorization of interim plans, should be obtained."[5]

In 1948, the Air Force chief of staff, General Hoyt Vandenberg, convened a board chaired by his vice chief of staff, General Muir S. Fairchild (later becoming the namesake of the academy's academic building). After extensive analysis and debate, particularly regarding the question of whether the academy curriculum should include flight training, the board recommended that the academy include a four-year course of instruction similar to that of the two other service academies and that it would not include pilot training. Vandenberg next directed the Air University to establish the Air Force Academy Planning Board to thoroughly examine the goals and objectives of an air force academy. The makeup of the planning board was impressive, including many distinguished military and civilian academicians and advisors, several of whom came from the West Point faculty. The results of the planning board's study would have a crucial impact upon the mission, structure, organization, and staffing of the Academy. Ultimately, most of their recommendations were fulfilled in the planning and development of the academy.

The planning board produced an extensive report in January 1949 setting forth the academy's mission statement which included such goals as to prepare officers with a thorough grounding in Air Force principles, with a broad-based education and with a sense of loyalty, duty and service.[6] They recommended that the academy be based on three main pillars, not unlike that of the other service academies: (1) academic instruction headed by a dean of the faculty; (2) military training under a commandant of cadets; and (3) athletic training and intercollegiate sports under a director of athletics, all of whom would report to a superintendent. As explained in his book about Harmon and based on his detailed study of the planning board's findings and recommendations, Meilinger noted:

> The Planning Board looked to the West Point model and used it extensively.... As at West Point, there would be no electives and no academic majors. There was, seemingly, a bit more emphasis given to the humanities and social sciences in this proposal, but not enough to shift the overall preponderance of academic focus from mathematics, science and engineering—39 percent of the curriculum would be mathematics/science bases, and 34 percent of the curriculum would cover humanities and social sciences. The remainder would be military studies. To indicate a modicum of change, courses in aerodynamics would be substituted for "bridge-building." As for other aspects of cadet life, once again the similarities to West Point were more remarkable than the differences. Classes would be conducted six days per week; athletics, drill, and tactical training would occupy a cadet's after-class time. Commissioned officers, termed tactical officers as at West Point, would be assigned to each air cadet squadron. An Honor Code would be imposed on cadets to inculcate the proper aspects of ethical conduct.[7]

Hubert R. Harmon, Father of the Air Force Academy

In 1953, at the request of the President of the United States, Dwight D. Eisenhower (USMA 1915), retired Lt. General Hubert R. Harmon (also USMA 1915) was called back to active duty to become special assistant to the chief of staff for Air Academy Matters. On August 14, 1954, General Harmon became the first superintendent of the United States Air Force Academy at its temporary home in Lowry Air Force Base, Colorado. He held that office from 1954 to 1956 as a lieutenant general, the rank held by nearly all academy superintendents. Harmon later became the namesake of the academy's administration building.

Harmon's role in the successful establishment of the Air Force Academy cannot be over emphasized. As an officer well known for his honesty and integrity, and when needed, candor, Harmon was involved in nearly every aspect of the planning, development and operation of the Air Force Academy from its earliest days. For example, even in 1949, Harmon served on the academy's Site Selection Board, chaired by retired General Carl Spaatz (USMA 1914) and including members such as Major General George F. Schlatter, Major General Laurence C. Craigie (USMA 1923), and Dr. Bruce Hopper from Harvard University.[8] Harmon later was appointed as special assistant for air academy matters. He even had a hand in the early drafting of the legislation enacting the academy. And

Lt. General Hubert Harmon (USMA 1915). Developed plans for the Air Force Academy and was its first superintendent (U.S. Air Force photo).

most importantly, Harmon was instrumental in setting the guidelines for the type of education and training that cadets should receive at the new academy to qualify them to serve as air officers. As highlighted in Meilinger's biography of Harmon, he recognized the need for academy graduates who would be educated citizens as well as effective military officers. The academy's curriculum would provide a good general education in the humanities and social sciences that were as essential for the future air officers as for the future citizen. Faced with the looming Cold War, Harmon recognized that "you cannot produce air officers by merely 'training' boys to fly and shoot: we need educated officers who can help prevent war, as well as to insure winning a war after shooting begins."[9] Much of the eventual academic curriculum was influenced by Harmon's views on just how a cadet should be trained to be an effective Air Force officer.

When the academy celebrated its 50th anniversary in 2004, Harmon was officially named as the "Father of the Air Force Academy," honoring the pivotal role he played in its planning and establishment. Following his death in 1957 and in accord with his wishes, he was cremated and his ashes preserved until 1958 when he was interred at the new Air Force Academy cemetery.

On April 1, 1954, President Eisenhower signed the legislation establishing the Air Force Academy.

On July 11, 1955, the same year that construction activity began for the new campus outside of Colorado Springs, the first class of 306 men was sworn in at a temporary site, Lowry Air Force Base, near Denver. At the dedication ceremony held on a runway adjacent to the academy, more than four thousand seats were arranged for attendees, with many more in attendance. Fittingly, among those in attendance was none other than retired Major General Benjamin D. Foulois who had learned to fly with Orville Wright in the first military airplane in 1909.[10]

At the dedication ceremony on July 11, 1955, at USAFA's temporary quarters at Lowry AFB, the secretary of the Air Force, Harold Talbott, conveyed a message from the President of the United States, Dwight D. Eisenhower (ailing at the time and unable to attend) that provided a fitting launch of the new academy[11]:

Dear Mr. Secretary,

Please convey my greetings to those who are present with you at the foundation ceremony of the United States Air Force Academy. In taking its place beside West Point and Annapolis, the Air Force Academy joins a proud company. The honored histories of the two older institutions provide a peerless standard against which, in future years, the excellence of the new Academy will be measured and found worthy. The American people, I know, wish the Air Force Academy brilliant success.

Sincerely,
Dwight D. Eisenhower

And Secretary Talbott's remarks served to emphasize the role that airpower and the graduates of this new military academy would play in keeping world peace[12]:

At last, the uncertainties, the turmoil of the past have given way to a great national institution dedicated to the leadership of United States airpower. Yes, the Air Force Academy is built upon a proud foundation and so it should be. For the Academy is a bridge to the future, gleaming with promise of peace in a stable, sane world.... Our airpower has kept the peace ... it is keeping the peace, God willing, it will keep on doing so. This Academy we are founding today will carry forward that great effort.

From these inspiring words it is easy to understand the academy's stated mission: "to educate, train, and inspire men and women to become leaders of character, motivated to lead the United States Air Force in service to our nation."[13] As of 2020, more than 50 years after the first class began its instruction, the academy had graduated more than 52,000 young officers intent on serving their country.[14]

Superintendents

As listed below, 10 of the first 11 superintendents at the Air Force Academy were USMA graduates. As the senior officer at the Academy, these West Point graduates wielded tremendous influence on the development and operation of the academy.

One of these graduates from the class of 1950 was Lt. General Winfield W. "Skip" Scott, who served as the ninth West Pointer to become superintendent of the Air Force Academy. He was ideally suited for the position. Skip came from a long line of Army families—his father, a battalion commander in Bataan during World War II, fought and died while a prisoner of war. Skip also was a fine football and track and field athlete at West Point. He backed up three-time All-American halfback Glenn Davis for one year on the national championship football team and then became a star himself on the football field. In track and field, he set an academy record in the broad jump. After an RF-51 combat tour in Korea, he went on to win fighter pilot competitions first in the F-100 and then the F-4 and 108 combat missions in the F-4 in Vietnam. He has been commander of a pilot training wing, an air division in Korea, the Alaskan Air Command, and deputy commander of U.S. forces in Korea before becoming superintendent of the Air Force Academy in 1983. He commented in an interview that as a commander he learned the importance of integrity and honesty, "so you can depend on what people are telling you is true."

Interestingly, when Skip served as USAFA Superintendent from 1983 to 1987, two of his sons had already graduated from the Air Force Academy and two other sons were cadets, one at West Point and one at the Air Force Academy. While superintendent, he completed the full cadet parachute training course and qualified along with the cadets as the oldest and highest-ranking officer at the academy to receive jump wings. From these experiences and accomplishments, it's clear that Skip is committed to do the very best at all times. He has shown himself to be a leader, a competitor and a winner and both Skip and his wonderful wife, Sally, were fully prepared for this important assignment.

In a 2003 interview sponsored by The Friends of the Air Force Academy Library and the Association of Graduates of the U.S. Air Force Academy, Skip stated the following when asked if his West Point experiences influenced him at the academy:

> Yes, as you well know, almost all of the tradition, if you will, of West Point at that particular time, and I'm speaking now of when this Academy [USAFA] started, was transferred out here. Primarily because it was really West Pointers who came out here at the helm of the Air Force Academy.... I realize that my roots are there at West Point although I also feel very strongly that this is my

Academy. But certainly I learned things about loyalty, commitment, duty and most important about integrity and honesty as a cadet at West Point.[15]

When asked in his interview about the importance of heritage to cadets and graduates of the Air Force Academy especially in contrast to the centuries of heritage at West Point and Annapolis, he remarked:

I think heritage is important. We are reaching a position where we do have heritage. Now obviously some of our so-called heroes, aviation heroes, came along during the earlier years and most of them were West Point grad[s] as a matter of fact, not all of them. Jimmie Doolittle, I don't think, went to West Point. Arnold did, and Eaker did,[16] and some of those. We have heroes, and we have heritage. Some of the heritage was transplanted, and it has grown. Now our own are coming of age and providing that heritage.[17]

Like General Scott's experience, many leaders who played important roles in planning and developing USAFA's academic curriculums, military and athletic training programs, and intercollegiate athletic teams received their own training and sense of commitment, honesty and duty from their years at West Point.

Harmon, as the first superintendent during the critical first years of the academy, was succeeded by Lt. General James E. Briggs (USMA 1928). Briggs, on August 29, 1958, supervised the move of the cadet wing of 1,145 cadets from Denver to its permanent site. Less than a year later, the academy received academic accreditation and graduated its first class of 207 cadets on June 3, 1959. By 1964, the authorized strength of the cadet wing was increased to 4,417. The present authorized strength is 4,000.[18]

First 11 USAFA Superintendents[19]

#	Start	End	Name	Class Year
1	1954	1956	Hubert R. Harmon	USMA 1915
2	1956	1959	James E. Briggs	USMA 1928
3	1959	1962	William S. Stone	USMA 1934
4	1962	1965	Robert H. Warren	USMA 1940
5	1965	1970	Thomas S. Moorman	USMA 1933
6	1970	1974	Albert P. Clark	USMA 1936
7	1974	1977	James R. Allen	USMA 1948
8	1977	1981	Kenneth L. Tallman	USMA 1946
9	1981	1983	Robert E. Kelley	AFROTC 1956
10	1983	1987	Winfield W. Scott, Jr.	USMA 1950
11	1987	1991	Charles R. Hamm	USMA 1956

From this brief recap of the history of the academy, it is clear that West Point graduates had a tremendous influence on the Air Force Academy, particularly as compared to the influence of West Point graduates of this era on the Air Force as a whole. As noted earlier, 10 of the first 11 superintendents from 1954 through 1991 were USMA graduates. The first 10 commandants of cadets were West Point graduates and three of the first four deans also hailed from West Point, including General Robert F. McDermott who served as dean for 12 years (1956 to 1968) and established USAFA's academic curricula and standards for many years to come.

Deans of the Faculty

The first academic dean of the faculty was General Don Z. Zimmerman (USMA 1929) with a master's degree in meteorology from Cal Tech. Zimmerman also had been an outstanding athlete at West Point, lettering in football, basketball and baseball.[20] His vice dean, to become dean within two years, was Colonel Robert F. McDermott, also a West Point graduate, Class of 1943, with a master's degree in business administration from Harvard and teaching experience at West Point.[21] In selecting faculty for the new academy, the criteria for selection was that "graduates of the two service academies (West Point and Annapolis) and military colleges (such as Virginia Military Institute and the Citadel) should be well represented" and "Whenever possible, the Academy should draw from the rosters of West Point and Air Force Institute of Technology graduates who had demonstrated instructor potential."[22]

Following is a list of USAFA deans during the period 1954 through 1983, by which time the first USAFA graduate became dean. Three of these five deans were USMA grads.[23]

Start	End	Name	Class Year
1954	1955	Don Z. Zimmerman	USMA 1929
1956	1968	Robert F. McDermott	USMA 1943
1968	1978	William Woodyard	Missouri 1950
1978	1983	William A. Orth	USMA 1954
1983	1986	Ervin Rokke	USAFA 1962

It would not be an overstatement to classify Brigadier General McDermott as among those West Point graduates with the longest lasting influence upon the Air Force Academy and, in turn, the Air Force. As a USMA graduate in 1943, combat experience as a P-38 pilot in World War II, an MBA from Harvard in 1950 and teaching experience at West Point, he was appointed by President Eisenhower as the first permanent professor of the academy in 1957 and as the first permanent dean of the faculty in 1959. His promotion to brigadier general that accompanied his appointment as dean made him the youngest general on active duty at that time. As one author put it referring to McDermott's position at the Pentagon prior to his Academy days, he "was a one-man dynamo in a one-man office developing college degree programs in civilian institutions for Air Force officers. He also had the job of selecting the officers who would be given the opportunity to attend the new Air Force professional schools—the Air War College and the Air Command and Staff College."[24]

McDermott stepped into the role of Dean of this new institution based on a template drawn from the traditions of West Point and Annapolis. While this served as a solid launching pad, as history would reveal, McDermott was not content with an academic curriculum at the Air Force Academy simply mirroring that of its predecessor academies. He sought the creation of an academic institution equaling that of the finest universities in the country with the added dimensions of superior military and athletic training of its cadets. When he became dean, the academy was not yet an accredited university, something he sought to attain before the first class graduated in 1959. A formidable undertaking indeed for a new university, yet one that he spearheaded to fulfillment, gaining him appointment by the president as permanent dean of faculty.

McDermott's contributions to the academy are too numerous to list here, but a few are worth noting. Above all, he developed curriculums that served to meet the academy's mission of developing career Air Force officers. While supporting a core academic curriculum made up of science, math and engineering subjects, in the early '60s he launched an ambitious "curriculum enrichment program" that allowed cadets to develop their own special interests and talents through the establishment of academic majors, unique among the military academies. This broadened the courses available to the cadets including the arts, humanities, foreign languages and philosophy. He also created cooperative master's degree programs with leading universities throughout the country including UCLA, Georgetown, Indiana, Ohio State and Purdue. And he was a staunch advocate of having an all-military faculty at the academy since these officers/teachers brought their military experiences into the classroom and served as good role models for these future Air Force officers. These instructors, with advanced degrees in the subjects they taught, also were to be active teaching members of the faculty. He also successfully advanced the employment of "permanent professors" to provide academic continuity to the curriculum. A number of these professors were USMA graduates such as Brigadier General Philip J. Erdle (USMA 1952) with a master's degree from Michigan in engineering mechanics and a PhD from Colorado,[25] Lt. Colonel Anthony J. Mione (USMA 1949) with a PhD in nuclear engineering who would head up the physics department and Lt. Colonel Jesse D. Gatlin, Jr. (USMA 1945) with an M.A. in English who would lead the english department.[26]

It should be noted that McDermott's accomplishments at the Air Force Academy are wonderfully chronicled in the 2006 book, *Battling Tradition— Robert F. McDermott and Shaping the U.S. Air Force Academy* by retired Air Force colonel, Paul T. Ringenbach, PhD. Those interested in learning more about McDermott's contributions should refer to this informative text.

Commandants

In the role of the Academy's first commandant of cadets, Harmon appointed Colonel Robert M. "Moose" Stillman (USMA 1935). Stillman had been an All-American football player at West Point and served as a line coach under the legendary coach Colonel Earl "Red" Blaik (USMA 1920). He had been the commanding officer of a B-26 bomber group in 1943 when he was shot down by the Germans and taken prisoner until he was freed in 1945. While working at the Pentagon under the deputy chief of staff for personnel, General Emmett "Rosie" O'Donnell (USMA 1928), Stillman contributed to some of the early planning for the academy. In that capacity, Stillman believed in adhering to the military academy pattern, later recalling that "I think the West Point mold was a good one to start with.... It was a good foundation ... and it certainly had the approval of the Air Staff at the time."[27] Because of this, as commandant, Stillman filled positions at the new academy with West Point graduates as often as possible. His deputy was Colonel Benjamin B. Cassiday, Jr. (USMA 1943) while other cadet training positions were filled by other 1943 classmates, Colonels Henry L. Hogan and A. W. Holderness.[28]

One of Stillman's subordinates was Colonel Robin Olds (USMA 1943), also an All-American football player from West Point and renowned fighter ace. As noted in Meilinger's book, "Olds would later relate that he made a deliberate attempt to place as many athletes on the new Academy staff as possible. He defended this policy by stating simply that he believed collegiate athletics gave officers a sense of teamwork, discipline and aggressiveness that was unmatched. He thought it wise that the Air Force Academy benefit from such qualities."[29]

Sensing a close relationship between West Point athletes and later career success, Harmon later asked West Point if it had any data on this. After studying the matter, West Point responded that there was a strong connection in that participation in college athletics helped produce a "dynamic character" and that fully 63 percent of all graduates who became general officers had either lettered while at the academy (USMA) or at least participated in intercollegiate athletics.[30]

All commandants at the academy during its first 24 years of existence were USMA graduates. Similarly, every senior officer assigned to the commandant's office and many of the air officers commanding (AOCs) were USMA graduates. It wasn't until the school year commencing 1981 that a USAFA graduate from the first graduating class of the Air Force Academy in 1959 became commandant of cadets (Robert D. Beckel). It is worth noting that Lt. General Beckel was an excellent basketball player at USAFA, being named to the Helms All-American basketball team in 1959 and later the U.S. Air Forces in Europe and all–Air Force basketball teams in 1961.

The list of USMA graduates serving as commandant of cadets during the period includes[31]:

#	Start	End	Name	Class Year
1	1954	1958	Robert M Stillman	USMA 1935
2	1958	1961	Henry R. Sullivan	USMA 1939
3	1961	1963	William T. Seawell	USMA 1941
4	1963	1965	Robert W. Strong, Jr.	USMA 1940
5	1965	1967	Lois T. Seith	USMA 1943
6	1967	1971	Robin Olds	USMA 1943
7	1971	1973	Walter T. Galligan	USMA 1945
8	1973	1975	Hoyt S. Vandenberg, Jr.	USMA 1951
9	1975	1978	Stanley C. Beck	USMA 1954

Other West Point graduates served at the academy at different stages of their careers to share their experience and training with the cadets. Three examples mentioned in an earlier chapter include Lt. General Brent Scowcroft (USMA 1947), Lt. General Robert E. Pursley (USMA 1949) and Colonel Frank Zagorski (USMA 1950).

Scowcroft, after pilot training and serving in a variety of operational and administrative positions, earned an MA in 1953 and later earned a PhD in international relations in 1967, both from Columbia University. Based on this academic training and operational experience, he spent time at the academy as a member of the faculty. Later in his career, Lt. General Scowcroft went on to be a national security advisor for two presidents and military advisor to two other presidents.

Pursley, after gaining a master's degree in business administration from the Harvard School of Business in 1957 under the AFIT program, transferred to USAFA for an extended period of time as an instructor eventually becoming an associate professor in the Department of Economics. He later went on to be the military assistant to three secretaries of defense.

Zagorski attended graduate school at the University of Pittsburgh and received his master's degree in international relations. His next assignment was as a Russian instructor for the foreign language department at USAFA and he was later appointed a tenured professor. Following his academy assignments, he served a tour of duty in Vietnam from 1970 to 1971 as a staff officer.

The influence of West Point grads went from junior officers to the senior ranks of leadership. As a new military academy patterned in many ways after West Point, the question arose as to how the new cadets would receive their early military training. While there was discussion of importing upperclassmen from West Point, it was decided that Air Force officers recently graduated from flight training would serve as surrogate upperclassmen.[32] These air training officers, or ATOs, were to be on the front lines of training and supervising the cadet wing until the Class of 1959 completed its third year. As noted in Meilinger's book, "Of the sixty-six ATOs in the initial cadre, eight were Annapolis graduates, eleven were West Point graduates, twenty-three had been commissioned from ROTC, and twenty-four had been through the Aviation Cadet program."

An air officer commanding (AOC) at the rank of captain or major would have supervision over the ATO assigned to each cadet squadron. AOCs would "fulfill the functions of the tactical officers (Tacs) at West Point."[33] As mentioned previously, many of the AOCs were West Point graduates and many had been jet fighter pilots during the Korean War. Most AOCs went on to very successful Air Force careers such as Kenneth L. Tallman (USMA 1946) who later became USAFA's eighth superintendent in 1977. Although the vast majority of AOCs at the academy were Air Force officers, a small number came from other military branches. One such example was Stewart Wood (USMA 1950) who served as an Army instructor at USAFA in the mid–1960s.[34] Stewart provided an impressive guidepost for what it meant to be an Army officer and West Point graduate for the young USAFA cadets. He devoted himself tirelessly to all aspects of cadet life—academics, military training, the honor code and athletics.

In a letter to the author, Zagorski noted that "there were countless West Pointers who served in lower echelon positions as faculty members; air officers commanding; directors of admissions and registrars; athletic coaches, etc. and were responsible for motivating cadets as well as educating them. With such a concentration of West Point grads in key positions at the AFA, it was inevitable that their impact on the growth and development of the AFA would be was indeed significant.... In toto, however, there can be little doubt of the legacy of West Pointers on the AFA, particularly in the first three decades of its operation."[35]

Zagorski recalled the following members of the Class of 1950 who played roles at one time or another at the Air Force Academy (in alphabetic order):

Clark Allison	Michael DeArmond	Jack Magee	Mal Ryan
Joe Anderson	Charlie Gabriel	"Real" McCoy	"Skip" Scott
Frank Bonano	Chuck Hammond	Pete Nibley	Ralph Stevenson
Bolo Brunson	Bob Hoover	John Pennecamp	Ty Tandler
Bob Clement	Lou Leiser	Pete Pettigrew	Stu Wood
Monty Coffin	Pat MacGill	Harvey Prosser	Frank Zagorski

It is noteworthy that many of this group attained prominent positions in their careers, including General Gabriel who became chief of staff of the Air Force, General O'Malley, a four-star prospective chief of staff, Lt. General Scott, became superintendent of the Air Force Academy, Major General Robert Clement, retired as commander of USAFE 16th Air Force after 34 years of distinguished service and Brigadier General Michael DeArmond, a Korean War POW flew total of 268 combat sorties in Korea and Vietnam. When he retired, he was the commander of the Defense Contract Administrative Services Region, assuring the quality and timely delivery of government-purchased equipment.

The first director of athletics and head football coach was Colonel Robert V. Whitlow (USMA 1943). His assistant was Major Frank Merritt, an All-American football player at West Point, later to become athletic director from 1967 to 1974. Whitlow had lettered in three sports at West Point (football, basketball and track) and was an avid golfer whose partners included Harmon, O'Donnell and Talbott and even President Eisenhower when he came to Denver![36] A listing of the first five athletic directors follows:

Start	End	Name	Class Year
1954	1957	Robert V. Whitlow	USMA 1943
1957	1960	George B. Simler	Maryland 1940
1960	1963	Maurice L. Martin	USMA 1943
1963	1967	Edmund A. Rafalko	USMA 1945
1967	1975	Francis E. Merritt	USMA 1944

In addition, there were many other West Point graduates involved in athletic programs at the Air Force Academy such as Frank Fischl (USMA 1951) who had been an outstanding halfback at West Point and Brigadier General Michael DeArmond (USMA 1950) and later a Korean War POW who had been a fine athlete in three sports at West Point.

The Academy's Honor Code

As cited earlier in Lt. General Scott's oral history, the Air Force Academy's honor code and honor system initially were taken from West Point, although they were slightly modified over time. The honor code is the cornerstone of a cadet's professional training and development at the Academy, setting the standard of ethical conduct that cadets expect of themselves and their fellow cadets. As explained on the academy's website, its wording is as follows:

> *We will not lie, steal or cheat, nor tolerate among us anyone who does.*
>
> To set the tone for all cadets to come after them, the first graduating class at the Academy, the Class of 1959, wrote and adopted the Honor Code—a cadet owned system. Being honorable implies much more than a person who doesn't lie, cheat, steal or tolerate, and our Honor Education lessons expand on what it really means to be an honorable person. Cadets are expected to report themselves for any violation. In addition, they must confront any other cadet they believe may have violated the Honor Code and report the incident if the situation is not resolved. This creates an atmosphere of trust that is absolutely essential for future military service.[37]

As with any exacting honor system, violations occur, some with greater impact than others. Most have been dealt with successfully by the cadets themselves while others have required intervention by senior officers. For example, shortly after assuming responsibilities as superintendent, General Scott was confronted with an honor incident stemming from cadets collaborating on a physics exam which led to a far-reaching examination of the honor system. As described in his oral history, General Scott personally led an in-depth investigation of not only this honor violation but the workings of the honor system as a whole based on his initial findings of the system's operation. His investigation led him to conclude that the extent of the problem was much deeper than initially thought. By the summer of 1984 and in coordination with the dean, the commandant, the athletic director and dean of admissions, 19 cadets had been suspended. A three-month amnesty program was put in place and an honor assessment committee was established. Remarkably, General Scott personally interviewed "every one of them [the 19 cadets] at least four times … to get a handle on the magnitude of the problem I had."[38] His direct involvement included meetings with cadets in leadership positions encouraging them to "exert some leadership and get your group to come forward and start admitting what has happened."[39]

When he was commandant, Olds commented that one of his biggest challenges revolved around the honor system. As he said: "Honor, to me, is a simple do or don't. USAFA had gone through some recent cheating scandals, which threw a sharp focus on the system of dealing with honor violations and demoralized the wing. At the academy our honor system seemed bogged down by specifics and nuances of meaning. It was treated like a court of law, which shocked me."[40]

As a consequence of the extent of problems discovered by Scott, for a period of time the management of the honor system was taken away from the cadets, something that had never before been done, with honor violations being resolved through court-martial type of proceedings with Article 15's issued to some violators.[41] By January 1985 a revised honor system was developed and Scott personally briefed each cadet class on the revised system. He briefed or had his senior staff members brief AOG chapters throughout the world to explain the honor code violations that had occurred and the corrective action taken. He also kept the secretary of the Air Force and chief of staff of the Air Force fully informed of these actions. General Scott's constant follow-up and leadership with the commandant, dean, athletic director, dean of admissions and the cadet wing during this troubled period made honorable conduct in all aspects of cadet life of paramount importance.

Both Robin Olds as commandant in the late 1960s and Skip Scott as superintendent in the 1980s had concluded that the academy's honor system focused too much on the mechanics and punishments of the system rather than the spirit and essential nature of the honor code. Scott undertook a major effort to understand the depth and scope of the problem and even sought the advice of Frank Borman who had led the investigation of honor violations at West Point in 1976. Both concluded that the honor system violations were much greater than the individual scandals. Scott's personal involvement and focused leadership at the academy certainly inspired a more workable and durable honor system and promoted honorable conduct in all aspects of cadet life.

Balancing Acts at USAFA—Academics, Athletics, and Military Training

Among the biggest challenges at the Air Force Academy was how to develop a program of cadet training that balanced the three primary dimensions of that training—academics, athletics and military training. After all, there were only 24 hours in a day and the cadets faced one of the most grueling undergraduate schedules of any university in the country. Finding that balance was a challenge faced by every superintendent throughout the school's history. This issue struck at the very core of what the academy was all about—an institution of higher learning with the purpose of producing educated, honorable, physically fit and militarily trained Air Force officers. But how much training in each aspect was enough? Each had its champion, with the dean emphasizing academics, the commandant emphasizing military training, and the athletic director emphasizing athletics and physical fitness. And none of these individuals were shrinking violets! This balancing act was described to General Albert P. Clark (USMA 1936), the incoming superintendent in 1970, by General George Simler who had been the second director of athletics during 1957 to 1960. He explained that "the biggest job of the Superintendent is to orchestrate the three big competitors of cadet time—the Dean, the Commandant and the Director of Athletics."[42]

Brigadier General McDermott became the dean in 1956 and was later afforded a "permanent" position in 1959 similar to that of a tenured professor at a university. He was dean for 12 years, very unlike the position of super-intendent and commandant with officer rotations every two, three or four years. This provided a continuity of academic instruction that was critically important in the early years of this new institution of higher learning. But, rightly or wrongly, this tenure also contributed to the dean's 12 years of insti-tutional influence and, in some cases, friction between the departments, par-ticularly with new superintendents or commandants who felt differently about the balance between academics, military training and athletics.

This tension was vividly described by Robin Olds when he assumed the role of Commandant in 1967:

> Ted [referring to Brigadier General Ted Seith (USMA 1943) and fellow West Point varsity football player, the outgoing commandant] tried to impress upon me what a bunch of bastards were in the faculty. His predecessors, Sewell, Strong, Stillman and Sullivan … had fought an ongoing battle with the dean of faculty, Brigadier General Robert F. McDermott. Old McD had been in place since the establishment of the Academy in 1954. He became a permanent Dean of Faculty in 1959. As head of all academic programs he had the military equivalent of tenure, which offered him absolute power to challenge traditions in military education. He had introduced about thirty academic majors to the Air Force Academy and brought a degree of flexibility to curriculum requirements, but his lock on the place created contention among the three domains of academics, commandant and athletics. The goals of the three different branches were not exactly mutually supportive, particularly considering the egos involved. Life on the various staffs had devolved into a possessive fight for time in the individual cadet's daily schedule. Each section of the triumvirate was trying to do its best to fulfill what it knew for a certainty was the most important phase in the devel-opment of these future officers. It was a mess.[43]

But despite this history, Olds struck a cooperative working relationship with the dean and "we never had any problems." It's also interesting to note Old's initial impressions of the military training at USAFA:

> Despite the internal staff battle, it was immediately apparent that USAFA's mil-itary training was far superior to my cadet training at West Point. Hell, West Point in the 1940s was like a summer camp in comparison! Oh yes, we'd gone on forced marches, fallen over rocks at night, crawled through some mud, shot Springfields loaded with blanks at one another, learned to drink beer, and had a wonderful time, but it bore no resemblance to the great training at the academy. What was the fuss all about?[44]

Notwithstanding the challenges of balancing academics, athletics and military training, it should be noted that the academy has experienced a stellar reputation as a first-class academic institution and one that has produced many fine military officers. For example, by 1992, six chiefs of staff of the Air Force (CSAF) had been USAFA graduates: General John M. Loh (USAFA 1960, who served as acting CSAF when General Dugan was incapacitated by an accident), General Ronald R. Fogleman (USAFA 1963), General Michael E. Ryan (USAFA 1965), General Norton A. Schwartz (USAFA 1973), General Mark A. Welsh III (USAFA 1976), and General David L Goldfein (USAFA 1983).[45] As of 2016, 549 USAFA graduates have become general officers. The academy has graduated 37 Rhodes Scholar recipients, 14 Marshall Scholarship recipients, and 16 Truman Scholarship recipients. According to *U.S. News & World Report*'s "America's Best Colleges 2015," the United States Air Force Academy was ranked:

- #2 in Aerospace/Aeronautical/Astronautical Engineering, for the 13th consecutive year
- Tied for #5 in Undergraduate Engineering with the U.S. Naval Academy
- #4 in Electrical, Electronic and Communications Engineering
- #5 in Mechanical Engineering

High school counselors ranked the Air Force Academy third-best liberal arts college in the nation.[46]

Legacy

During the first 40 formative years of the Air Force Academy, West Point graduates, whether serving as statesmen, senior officers or surrogate upperclassman had a profound influence on the new air academy. They played a central role in developing the organization, procedures, ethos and basic credibility of the academy. This resulted in the graduation of academically and physically fit young military officers of character oriented toward military activity in air and space. By the late 1980s, West Point grads had left their enduring legacy to the Air Force.

Based on this foundation of excellence, the Air Force Academy has produced not only many fine Air Force officers since its first graduating class in 1959, but also many other USAFA graduates who have used their training and expertise gained at the academy and in the Air Force in unique ways. For example, Air Force Colonel (Ret.) Karol Bobko from the Class of 1959 was the first USAFA graduate in space, piloting the space shuttle *Challenger*

More than 1,300 basic cadets during their first reveille formation at the U.S. Air Force Academy in Colorado Springs, 2009 (U.S. Air Force photo).

in April 1983. Lt. General (Ret.) Susan J. Helms, Class of 1980, as a major was the first female graduate to fly in space as a mission specialist aboard *Endeavor* in 1993. She flew on numerous space shuttle flights and served aboard the International Space Station as a member of the Expedition 2 crew in 2001. To date, 39 Academy graduates have become astronauts for NASA.

Another example is Chesley B. "Sully" Sullenberger III (USAFA 1973, squadron mate of the co-author and former F-16 pilot) who was piloting U.S. Airways Flight 1549 (an Airbus A320) out of LaGuardia Airport on January 15, 2009, when his plane struck a flock of geese and suffered a double engine failure. Unable to reach a nearby airport, he made a quick decision and expertly ditched in the Hudson River off midtown Manhattan. All 155 passengers and crew were rescued by nearby boats.[47]

Many other USAFA graduates have used their USAFA and USAF training and experience, albeit far less dramatically than Sullenberger's experience! For example, as a partner with the CPA and consulting firm of Price Waterhouse (now PricewaterhouseCoopers), during 1992–93 I (co-author) led a team of accountants and database analysts in collaboration with lawyers from an international law firm in a project in Kuwait on behalf of the Kuwait government. The purpose of the project was to quantify Kuwait's war losses and submit claims to the United Nations stemming from Iraq's occupation of

Kuwait during the 1991 Gulf War and Operation Desert Storm. Among the many losses quantified during the project were the damages to the reinforced bunkers housing Kuwait's aircraft that resulted from the USAF and coalition aerial bombing campaign to drive Iraqi forces from Kuwait. We observed first-hand the deadly accuracy of the Air Force's precision-guided ordnance on hardened aircraft shelters. And, with a knowledge of military hardware and munitions, we documented and claimed losses of military assets measured in the hundreds of millions of dollars. In a later project on behalf of the International Advisory and Monitoring Board, I conducted an evaluation of the settlement between the U.S. Army Corps of Engineers and a major U.S. engineering and construction firm related to the task force for the restoration of Iraq's oil infrastructure. As these and many other examples illustrate, the lessons learned by cadets at the Air Force Academy and later in their careers in the Air Force, no matter the duration, provided an invaluable foundation for future service, whether in the Air Force or private sector.

Chapter 12

Leadership

Leadership is a much discussed, debated and written-about subject in both the military and business world. My active involvement with military leadership extends from the '40s to the '80s with duty as a Marine private to Air Force major general. I was indoctrinated in the fundamentals of leadership at West Point, the Navy Command and Staff School and the Air War College. During this time, stern discipline was initially the leadership style, but it changed with the cultural shift in the '60s and '70s to a more persuasive style to justify and explain why certain actions were needed. The war in Vietnam caused a significant weakening of trust in military and political leaders.

In trying to characterize the leadership traits that were so prominently displayed by those described in this brief slice of Air Force history, we have examined what others had to say about the subject. Among these were notable leaders that succinctly defined the requirements for effective leadership:

- Winston Churchill, who said that "the price of greatness is responsibility," and "courage is the finest of human qualities because it guarantees all the others."[1]

- Similarly, General Curtis LeMay defined his leadership priority as "a sense of responsibility. I would forgive a mistake if somebody did something in a crisis and did the wrong thing, but I couldn't forgive the guy that sat there and did nothing."[2]

- Dwight Eisenhower's (USMA 1915) definition was that "the supreme quality for leadership is unquestionable integrity. Without it, no real success is possible."[3]

- At West Point, character, with emphasis upon honor, and mission and country before self were consistently emphasized.

To take General LeMay's statement a little further, responsibility includes the acceptance of responsibility for all actions taken within a leader's command. A good leader would not accept finger pointing or ducking the blame.

One additional bit of leadership advice that I particularly liked was given by General Spaatz to Robin Olds, then a major, at the end of World War II in Europe. The two were old friends from Robin's youth when his father, Major General Robert Olds, and his Air Corps buddies such as Arnold, Spaatz, Eaker, Rickenbacker and other well-respected aviators from World War I were gathered. (Incidentally, General Arnold pinned on Robin Olds's pilot wings.) General Spaatz's personal advice was: "Your most difficult problem will be the people in the military—they mostly divide themselves into four major categories. There are the 'me firsters,' the 'me too'ers,' the 'dead wood,' and the 'dedicated.' You are among the minority, the dedicated. Stick with them, search them out and work hard to be worthy of their company. You won't be popular with a lot of your bosses who act dedicated but really aren't and they can make life difficult. You don't want yes man around you but you can't always avoid them."[4] General Spaatz well knew from experience that to be an effective leader you also needed effective followers.

General Spaatz, along with other key military World War II leaders, was a dedicated reader, primarily biographies and military history. His and their motivation for reading was a firm belief that you either learn from history or you are doomed to repeat it. In his well-researched book, *American Generalship*, Edgar F. Puryear, Jr., describes many of these highly successful leaders who were avid readers.[5] They all deliberately set aside private time in their demanding schedules to read, sometimes at very early hours of the day when they had time to read and reflect. Examples include Generals Eisenhower, Marshall, Bradley, MacArthur, Patton as well as Spaatz. They each sought to broaden their intellectual knowledge and understanding of how other leaders had reacted to the challenge of making critical decisions. Senior generals of my era such as Jones, Meyer, and White likewise sought to broaden their knowledge by reading extensively. General Jones summed it up nicely by stating, "I have an insatiable appetite for information. Life is one of constant learning."[6]

The idea of using air and space as an environment for military conflict, including support for land and sea combat from the air, was an entirely new concept following the invention of the airplane. And even then, it wasn't until the establishment of the Air Force in 1947 that the integration of high technology applications to weapon systems really took off. Not surprisingly, the impact of these advances, including inter-service budgetary competition, was not always well received or understood by the military establishment. How military leaders dealt with these changes in terms of organizing and managing people and resources was a big challenge that required entirely new ways of approaching leadership.

If we step back and compare the pre–1947 Army Air Forces to the post–1947 Air Force era which has been the focus of our book, there are a number of tectonic shifts in technology which occurred that forever changed what it meant to be a leader in the Air Force. These included:

1. The introduction of high technology applications to weapon "systems" arising from advancements in a variety of scientific and engineering disciplines (e.g., propulsion, computers, electronics, materials, aircraft design, etc.);

2. The collaboration of civilian scientists, engineers and contractors with military leaders in the development of new weapon systems;

3. The reality of constant advancements in technology required organizational flexibility and adaption to new weapon systems and considerable centralization of command;

4. The increased importance of advanced education, particularly in STEM subjects, for R&D and operation of new weapon systems and career advancement;

5. The integration of a more racially and gender diverse work force.

Adapting to these changes was seldom easy. But as was repeatedly learned, sometimes the hard way, adapting was a prerequisite to becoming an effective leader. Those Air Force officers who recognized and even embraced these changes developed leadership traits and styles to effectively lead in this new era.

In this chapter we've sought to emphasize some of the West Point grads serving in the Air Force who best demonstrated strong leadership in this new Air Force. Unlike the previous era where excellence in operations and combat were the prerequisites for success and career advancement, a new set of skills was needed to operate in the post–1947 period subject to the changes mentioned above. Furthermore, these leaders were extraordinarily diverse—they include military officers who were pilots, system operators, R&D managers, civilian scientists, civilian contractors and educators.

Selecting the individuals who best represented leadership traits in various categories proved quite challenging. Above all, it was a subjective exercise as there were so many others, including civilian scientists and contractors as well as Air Force leaders from other universities and colleges, who also demonstrated outstanding leadership. As this is a book about West Point grads, we've kept the focus on them.

Examples of superior leadership can be found in many officers who served in the U.S Army Air Forces and later in the U.S. Air Force. Many of these leaders were West Point graduates whom we elected to divide between those serving in the U.S. Army Air Forces prior to the establishment of the

U.S. Air Force in 1947 and those graduates from the classes of 1948–58 who entered the Air Force directly upon graduation from West Point.

Nine of the first eleven chiefs of staff of the Air Force were West Point graduates, eight having been World War II pilots. However, with the increasing role that science and technology was having upon the Air Force, General George S. Brown and General Lew Allen (who had a PhD in science), both of whom served as commanders of AFSC, became chiefs of staff. As a consequence of the combat role played by fighter aircraft in Korea and Vietnam, subsequent chiefs of staff, starting with General Charlie Gabriel (USMA 1950) were career fighter pilots or in several cases had airlift experience.

In addition to those chiefs of staff, many other West Point grads as well as other civilian scientists, engineers and designers demand recognition as exemplars of fine leadership in the high-tech U.S. Air Force. We have identified just a few standouts whose influence on the Air Force had a lasting impact, many of whom I had the opportunity to work with. It is striking to note how diverse were both their backgrounds and their contributions to the Air Force. In their own unique ways, they were developers of entirely new weapon systems, the new Air Force Academy and AFIT, and leaders of a well-educated and integrated Air Force to operate these systems.

Unfortunately, there were other very highly qualified general officers and contemporaries who did not attain their highest levels of responsibility because they were killed in aircraft accidents. These include General Jerry O'Malley, killed in a T-39 accident while serving as commander of TAC; Lt. General George B. Simler, killed in a T-38 accident while serving as ATC commander; Lt. General Robert Bond, killed in an experimental flight in a captured Soviet MiG-23 while serving as vice commander, Air Force Systems Command[7]; and Major General Irving L. Branch, commander of Edwards AFB, killed in a T-38 accident while serving as the commander of the Flight Test Center.

Billy Mitchell and Benjamin Foulois were the early leaders and strongest advocates of airplanes as a new weapon of war. General Arnold (USMA 1907) fully agreed with them and carried this concept forward. Arnold was taught to fly by the Wright brothers, but he also recognized the total logistical and manpower requirements to make air power a reality. He led the Army Air Service expansion in World War II from a few hundred people to more than 2.3 million personnel, supervised steady air power advocacy and advised allied military and political leaders on air combat strategy during the war. General Eisenhower (USMA 1915) supported Arnold's advocacy of unified command of air forces throughout the war and later as president. General Arnold had the vision and stature to lead the development of the foundation for an independent Air Force. In addition, Arnold learned from World War II technology breakthroughs—jet aircraft, V-2 rockets and the atomic bomb—of the critical need for developing new technology. In 1944, he directed Dr.

von Kármán, director of the AAF's SAG, to conduct a thorough review of the technology the new Air Force should pursue to stay in the forefront of modern weaponry. A year later, a 12-volume report, *Science the Key to Air Supremacy*, served as a guide for the new high-tech U.S. Air Force R&D effort.

Following General Arnold, the Air Force had two of the most significant R&D leaders, Benjamin Schriever and Wernher von Braun. They moved the military weapons of war into space and provided the foundation for NASA's man-in-space program. General Schriever, as a colonel, was assigned by General Arnold to be chief of the AAF Scientific Liaison Office, which interfaced with companies throughout the aerospace industry. From the many lessons he learned in this position, he continued throughout his career to work closely with industry to the great benefit of the Air Force. Along with von Braun and his German engineering team, he led the development of rocket launchers for both ICBMs, satellites and later, astronauts into space. General Schriever significantly improved the AFSC development and acquisition process and finally, in 1963, directed Project Forecast, a comprehensive long-range assessment of military science and technology.

An interesting aspect of Air Force space projects, which included NRO projects, was that many, if not most of them, were highly classified, compartmentalized "black" satellite programs reporting to the undersecretary of the Air Force. Four West Point grads were directors of this special projects office. General Allen, with a PhD in nuclear physics and experience with atomic testing and with the CIA, and as director of NSA later became commander of AFSC and CSAF from 1978 to 1982. In addition, Generals Greer (USMA 1939), Bradburn (USMA 1946), and Kulpa (USMA 1950) held this position. Major General Kulpa was the last West Point grad to be director of Special Projects office (SAFSP) and at the same time he served as the deputy commander at SAMSO and as deputy commander for space at AFSC HQ.[8]

As noted previously, when they were undersecretaries of the Air Force for special projects and later secretaries of the Air Force, John McLucas and Hans Mark both had PhDs in physics. This underscores the highly educated nature of the organizational leaders of programs to develop these complex and sensitive systems on the frontiers of space.

In the early 1970s, SecDef Melvin Laird asked SecAF John McLucas to identify some successful Air Force aircraft programs in order to respond to pressure he was receiving from Congress. McLucas identified four programs that were examples of well-run aircraft development and acquisition programs. These four programs, each managed by a West Point grad, included the F-15 program managed by Ben Bellis (USMA 1946) and then Robert Mathis (USMA 1948), the AWACS program managed by Ken Russell (USMA 1945), the A-10 program managed by Thomas H. McMullen (USMA 1951), and the B-1 program managed by Abe Martin (USMA 1949). In addition, two of the

AFSC commanders during this period were also West Point grads—Lew Allen, Jr. (USMA 1946) and Robert Marsh (USMA 1949). As you can see, during this critical phase of aircraft development, West Point grads at different levels played a leading role in the effort to integrate advanced technology into a wide variety of military aircraft. Over the years, AFSC had seven West Point grads serving as commanders—Major General David M. Schlatter (USMA 19230), Lt. General Earl E. Partridge (USMA 1924), Lt. General Samuel E. Anderson (USMA 1928), General George S. Brown (USMA 1941), General William J. Evans (USMA 1946), General Lew Allen, Jr. (USMA 1946), and General Robert T. Marsh (USMA 1949).

The Air Force Logistics Command (AFLC), was responsible for the maintenance and modification of all Air Force airplanes. Nine West Point grads served as commanders of AFLC: General Nathan F. Twining (USMA 1918), General Joseph T. McNarney (USMA 1915), General Benjamin W. Chidlaw (USMA 1922), Lt. General William F. McKee (USMA 1929), General Samuel E. Anderson (USMA 1928), General Mark E. Bradley, Jr. (USMA 1930), General Kenneth B. Hobson (USMA 1932), General Jack G. Merrell (USMA 1939), and General Bryce Poe II (USMA 1946).

The Strategic Air Command was responsible for command and control of two of the three components of the U.S. military's strategic nuclear strike forces: the land-based strategic bomber aircraft and ICBMs. It first should be noted that General Curtis LeMay formalized the idea of strategic bombing that Spaatz had instigated during World War II and made it into the major U.S. strategic nuclear force. Among the commanders of SAC were the following West Point grads: General John D. Ryan (USMA 1938), General Joseph J. Nazzaro (USMA 1936), General Bruce K. Holloway (USMA 1937), General Bennie L. Davis (USMA 1950), and General George L. Butler (USAFA 1961). SAC was deactivated in 1972 and redesignated as the U.S. Air Force Global Strike Command.

The Tactical Air Command (TAC), another MAJCOM first activated in 1946 as part of the AAF, was responsible for providing primarily tactical (fighter) aircraft in support of air defense, tactical air and air reserve forces of the Air Force. Among the commanders of TAC were the following West Point grads: Major General Robert M. Lee (USMA 1931), General Frank F. Everest (USMA 1928), Major General Walter C. Sweeney, Jr. (USMA 1930), General Gabriel P. Disosway (USMA 1933), and General Jerome F. O'Malley (USMA 1953).

The Military Airlift Command (MAC) was the primary strategic airlift organization of the Air Force until 1974 when tactical airlift units were merged into MAC to create a unified airlift organization. Among the commanders of MAC were the following West Point grads: Lt. General Lawrence S. Kuter (USMA 1927), Lt. General Joseph Smith (USMA 1923), Lt. General William

H. Tunner (USMA 1928), General Joe W. Kelly (USMA 1932), General Howell M. Estes, Jr. (USMA 1936) and General James R. Allen (USMA 1948).

Aerospace Defense Command (ADC, previously Air Defense Command) provided air defense for the continental United States (CONUS) which included radar systems for continental defense as well as missile warning and space surveillance systems. Among its commanders were the following West Point grads: Lt. General George E. Stratemeyer (USMA 1915), General Benjamin W. Chidlaw (USMA 1926), General Earl E. Partridge (USMA 1924), Lt. General Robert M. Lee (USMA 1931), General Lucas D. Clay, Jr. (USMA 1942), and General James V. Hartinger (USMA 1949).

These MAJCOMS received equipment developed and acquired by AFSC which then were under the direction of their commanders for leading, training and motivating their personnel. Finally, the CSAFs provided oversight to these MAJCOMS. West Point grads serving as CSAFs included General Carl A. Spaatz (USMA 1914), General Hoyt S. Vandenberg (USMA 1923), General Nathan F. Twining (USMA 1918), General Thomas D. White (USMA 1920), General John P. McConnell (USMA 1932), General John D. Ryan (USMA 1938), General George S. Brown (USMA 1941), General Lew Allen, Jr. (USMA 1946), General Charles A. Gabriel (USMA 1950), and General Michael J. Dugan (USMA 1958). Twining and Brown went on to be chairmen of the Joint Chiefs of Staff.

With respect to the man-in-space programs, Frank Borman (USMA 1950) was a unique astronaut leader in investigating the Apollo 1 fire, assisting in the redesign of the command module and as the mission commander in Apollo 8, and taking many of the critical first steps toward putting a man on the moon. In addition, Borman was the astronaut spokesman to Congress regarding the investigation of Apollo 1 fire and ultimately helped to convince Congress to continue with the Apollo program.

Generals Benjamin O. Davis (USMA 1936) and Chappie James (Tuskegee Institute 1942) led the Air Force in breaking the military racial barrier. General Davis established his courage, determination and leadership very early on by gaining the respect of his fellow cadets after four years of discrimination at West Point. He went on to an outstanding career as combat commander of black airmen in World War II and ended his career as a lieutenant general in command of the racially integrated Thirteenth Air Force. General James, with combat missions in Korea and Vietnam was a highly respected public speaker to both military and civilian audiences. He focused on patriotism, racial justice, and a commitment to serving the Air Force.

Within the field of education and training, those who were responsible for the founding and development of the U.S. Air Force Academy also deserve special mention as they led the professional development of future Air Force officers. General Hubert R. Harmon (USMA 1915), the "Father of the Air Force

Academy," served as the school's first superintendent. He not only helped draft the legislation signed by President Eisenhower establishing the academy, but he played a key role in leading the development of the curriculum and training that cadets were to receive there. He recognized the need to provide a well-rounded education for future officers who could lead not only in war but in peacetime.

Brigadier General Robert McDermott (USMA 1943) served as the academy's dean of faculty for an unprecedented 12 years (1956 to 1968), giving him the opportunity to shape the school's curriculum. Though he maintained a core academic curriculum of science, math and engineering, he promoted what was, at the time, a unique curriculum enrichment program allowing cadets to pursue academic majors. His leadership in the establishment of a cooperative master's degree program with universities around the country provided academy graduates an opportunity to develop specialized areas of interest, primarily in the aeronautical engineering area, but in many other disciplines as well. This was to be of tremendous value to future officers as they entered a technologically advanced Air Force. Through these and other initiatives, McDermott's contributions to the academy had a long-lasting impact on academy graduates that resonated throughout the Air Force for many years to come.

As noted previously, West Point graduates had a tremendous influence on the Air Force Academy, particularly at the senior ranks providing leadership for future Air Force officers. For example, 10 of the first 11 superintendents from 1954 through 1991 were USMA graduates. Interestingly, the class of 1936 from West Point produced two West Point superintendents and one Air Force Academy superintendent, Albert P. Clark. That class also was the first class to have produced seven four-star generals, three of whom were Air Force generals: Howell M. Estes, Joseph J. Nazzaro and Benjamin O. Davis. The first 10 commandants of cadets were West Point graduates and three of the first four deans were also graduates. The ninth academy superintendent, serving from 1983 to 1987, Lt. General Winfield W. "Skip" Scott (USMA 1950), had a prominent impact on the cadet honor code. In addition to his many other leadership duties at the academy, Scott undertook a major initiative to evaluate and revise the cadet honor system that permeated all aspects of cadet life both during his tenure and for years to come. His personal involvement and focused leadership at the academy following the investigation of honor code violations inspired a more workable honor system that was to endure not only at the academy but in the future professional lives of its graduates.

Another West Point grad, Brigadier General Robin Olds (USMA 1943), left a prominent imprint on many academy grads when he served as commandant from 1967 to 1971. A former All-American football player and fighter ace with combat experience flying P-38's and P-51's during World War II and later in Vietnam as an F-4 pilot and wing commander and said by some to be the country's greatest aerial warrior, he provided an inspiring role model for young cadets. He, like Superintendent Scott, addressed honor code issues and was instrumental in restoring cadet morale to the academy.

West Point has maintained a steady purpose over several centuries to produce military leaders of character. Over the years, the superintendents, the Congress and even the president have debated about the correct balance between academics, athletics and military training in the busy and disciplined life of the cadets. However, the qualities sought in a graduate have remained character, competence and country before self. In the early years, West Pointers led the country especially as civil engineers and military leaders. General MacArthur and later Maxwell Taylor as superintendents adapted the curriculum to keep up with the changes in the country's culture. President Eisenhower considered the main focus at West Point to be honor. At the West Point centennial in 1903, aviation emerged and began the great wave of technological progress that West Pointers experienced in the next 90 years in the Army Air Forces and U.S. Air Force. The fact that West Pointers have exceeded in achieving high level leadership positions is not surprising because the academy is a unique university with the prime objective of producing military officers of character, confidence and leadership ability.

Epilogue

West Point graduates have a long and distinguished tradition of outstanding service to the United States. West Point graduates in the Army air services and Air Force continued the West Point tradition of exemplary service. These graduates served at a time when the world's greatest wave of technological advancement occurred: airplanes, nuclear weapons, rocketry, ICBMs, satellite systems in inner space and finally man in outer space to the moon. In addition, all these systems were tested and validated in six major wars—World War I, World War II, Cold War, Korea, Vietnam and the Middle East. These officers served at a challenging time of revolutionary change in technology and they contributed to or led this revolution.

The technological advances made during West Points grads' Air Force service have been nothing short of astounding. The most dramatic new weapon systems such as thermonuclear bombs, ICBMs, space systems, stealthy aircraft, standoff air-to-air and air-to-ground missiles with amazing accuracy occurred after the establishment of the Air Force in 1947. General Arnold (USMA 1907) envisioned and implemented a unique collaboration of civilian scientists and engineers together with Air Force officers to effect these advances. From our perspective today, decades after the nearly 100 years of West Point grads' service in the Air Force has ended, many of the weapon systems that they helped develop and operate are still operational today with numerous upgrades, modifications and changes in mission. Examples of this legacy include airplanes with more than 60 years' service such as the B-52, the C-130, the U-2 and the KC-135 and fighters with more than 40 years' service such as the A-10, F-15 and F-16. Similarly, the Minuteman missiles have been in service for more than five decades.

These advances were all the more dramatic considering the severe military demobilization and budget cutbacks of the Army Air Forces after World War II in addition to the growing pains the new USAF faced with the Cold

War buildup, the Berlin airlift and the war in Korea. Nevertheless, the advances in aerospace power fundamentally changed the nature of warfare and moved the Air Force to the forefront of military influence. The more senior West Pointers led the way during these difficult times while younger grads directly experienced air warfare and the new dual track of nuclear war alert in addition to conventional war with strong air support.

In World War I, aerial reconnaissance was the primary mission for the Army's air forces. However, fighter aircraft protecting reconnaissance balloons and airplanes became an integral part of the mission and control of the air became critical to all military missions. Colonel Billy Mitchell commanded strong air support for Army General Pershing (USMA 1886) and their combined forces defeated the Germans at Saint-Mihiel. During World War II, General Eisenhower (USMA 1915) fully recognized the importance of General Arnold's air offensive and air support in winning the war. As president, Eisenhower supported an independent air force and establishment of the U.S. Air Force Academy. After World War II, air warfare was carefully constrained to avoid the threat of escalation into nuclear warfare. As a result, two major conventional wars followed with a standoff at the 38th parallel in Korea and a long, drawn-out U.S. defeat in Vietnam. In both wars, air power was severely restricted to avoid any risk of nuclear exchange.

During this period of West Point grads' service in the air forces, warfare changed from a methodical, slow-moving endeavor on the battlefield as witnessed in World War I trench warfare to massive strategic bombing of the enemy's weapons facilities, industries and civilian populations in World War II, to the Cold War with the Soviet Union when nuclear survivability was critical. The threat of devastating nuclear warfare which was unacceptable to both nations caused the stalemate known as mutual assured destruction (MAD). In this era when ICBMs could hit their targets halfway around the globe in under half an hour, survivability was critical and a first strike had to be considered an option. The duality of nuclear and conventional war missions placed an enormous responsibility on the U.S. military and particularly upon the Air Force which had the primary nuclear mission as well as a conventional war obligation.

Regarding the impact that technology has had upon warfare, no one said it better than Dr. Donald R. Baucom, PhD and former historian of the Ballistic Missile Defense Organization: "When the Cold War started in the wake of World War II, one could scarcely have imagined that the decisive theater in this conflict would be space. Nevertheless, by 1961 at the end of the 'formative years,' space technology had opened up an entirely new domain for military activities. This technological revolution was as significant as that produced by the application of the airplane to warfare." He went on to state that "technology indeed can make policy obsolete."[1]

In the 1980s, Generals Charlie Gabriel (USMA 1950, Air Force chief of staff) and John Wickstrom (USMA 1950, Army chief of staff) collaborated to enhance joint combat force effectiveness. In 1991 during the Iraqi Gulf War, the country's investment in the Air Force's technology-based warfighting capability including satellite-based reconnaissance, navigation, and communication systems were fully validated through joint cooperation of Air Force and Army units during Desert Shield and Desert Storm commanded by Army General Schwarzkopf (USMA 1956). The warfighting capability of space assets as advocated years earlier by Lt. General Henry (USMA 1949) when he was commander of SAMSO and later the Space Division and then as managed by General Kutyna (USMA 1957) as commander of the Space Command led to rapid victory on the battlefield.

Regarding the success of airpower during Desert Shield and Desert Storm, it is important to note it was not widely anticipated in the days leading up to the war that aerospace technology in all its facets (including stealth, standoff cruise missiles, unheard-of accuracy of munitions and satellite-based navigation, reconnaissance and communication) would play such a decisive role. As noted in Richard Hallion's in-depth book about the war, *Storm over Iraq—Air Power in the Gulf War*, Defense Secretary Dick Cheney stated when asked why the war went as it did, "It [Iraqi forces] was crushed, I think by the air campaign, and the way in which we went about the [air] campaign meant that when we finally did have to move our ground forces in, and we sort of kicked in the door, they collapsed fairly rapidly." Cheney went on to add "They [the Iraqis] didn't fight back because the air war turned out to be absolutely devastating."[2] As summarized succinctly by Admiral Arthur Radford of the U.S. Navy: "Today air power is the dominant factor in war. It may not win a war by itself alone, but without it no major war can be won."[3]

I am particularly proud of four of my 1950 West Point classmates, Charlie Gabriel, who became chief of staff of the U.S. Air Force, Bennie Davis, commander-in-chief of the Strategic Air Command, Skip Scott, superintendent of the Air Force Academy and Frank Borman, commander of the first crew to enter outer space, orbit the moon and safely return to earth.

When the last West Pointers serving in the Air Force retired, General Ward in 1991 from the Class of 1950 and General Kutyna in 1992 from the Class of 1957, it brought to an end the era of West Point's contributions to the development of the Air Force. By that time, the Air Force had grown from a fledgling startup to a well-established military service and the world's strongest aerospace power. All West Pointers should be proud of their graduates' contributions to the formation of the U.S. Air Force.

Chronology of Key Events

This chronology is sourced largely from the 2003 publication *One Hundred Years of Flight—USAF Chronology of Significant Air and Space Events, 1903–2002*, by Daniel L. Haulman and the Air Force History and Museums Program in association with the Air University Press at Maxwell Air Force Base and supplemented with events cited in the text.

December 17, 1903—Orville and Wilbur Wright piloted a powered, heavier-than-air aircraft for the first time near Kitty Hawk, North Carolina.

August 1, 1907—The Army's Signal Corps established a new Aeronautical Division under Capt. Charles deForest Chandler to take charge of military ballooning and air machines.

December 23, 1907—Brig. Gen. James Allen (USMA 1872), chief signal officer, issued the first specification for a military airplane. It called for an aircraft that could carry two people, fly at a minimum speed of 40 miles per hour, go 125 miles without stopping, be controllable for flight in any direction, and land at its takeoff point without damage.

September 17, 1908—Lt. Thomas E. Selfridge (USMA 1903) of the Army became the first U.S. military member to die in an airplane accident when he crashed with pilot Orville Wright during a flight test at Fort Myer, Virginia.

July 30, 1909—Cross-country speed test at Fort Myer, Virginia, piloted by Orville Wright with Lt. Benjamin D. Foulois as his observer.

August 2, 1909—The Army accepted its first airplane from the Wright brothers after the aircraft met or surpassed all specifications in flight tests at Fort Myer, Virginia. The Army paid the Wrights the contract price of $25,000 plus $5,000 for speed in excess of 40 miles per hour.

January 19, 1910—The Army's Lt. Paul W. Beck, flying with Louis Paulhan in a Farman airplane, dropped three two-pound sandbags over a target at an air meet in Los Angeles, testing the feasibility of using aircraft for bombing.

March 2, 1910—Lt. Benjamin D. Foulois made his first solo flight at Fort Sam Houston, Texas. At the time, he was the only pilot assigned to the Aeronautical Division of the Army Signal Corps and, thus, the only one with flying duty.

March 3, 1911—Congress passed the first direct appropriation for U.S. military aviation, devoting "not more than $125,000 ... for the purchase, maintenance, operation and repair of aeroplanes and other aerial machines" for fiscal year 1912.

July 3, 1911—The Army Signal Corps designated the flying field at College Park, Maryland, as the Signal Corps Aviation School. The War Department appointed Capt. Charles deForest Chandler as the school's commander. Among the school's instructors were 2d Lt. Henry H. "Hap" Arnold (USMA 1907) and 2nd Lieutenant Thomas D. Milling who had just learned to fly at the Wright school in Dayton, Ohio.

February 23, 1912—War Department Bulletin No. 2 for 1912 established the rating "military aviator."

July 5, 1912—Capt. Charles deForest Chandler, 2nd Lt. Thomas D. Milling, and 2nd Lt. Henry H. Arnold became the first Army pilots to qualify as military aviators.

March 2, 1913—Congress approved flight pay of 35 percent over base pay to reward officers who volunteered for aviation duty.

July 7, 1914—The U.S. government issued a patent to Dr. Robert H. Goddard for a multistage rocket design. On July 14, the government issued another patent to Goddard for a liquid-fueled rocket design. These designs laid the foundation for future spaceflights.

May 20, 1915—The Army accepted its first Curtiss JN-2 aircraft for use by the 1st Aero Squadron. This craft was the first mass-produced U.S. airplane.

March 15, 1916—The 1st Aero Squadron, under Capt. Benjamin D. Foulois, became the first U.S. aviation unit to engage in field operations when it joined Brig. Gen. John J. Pershing's punitive expedition against Mexican revolutionary leader Pancho Villa.

May 20, 1916—Lt. Col. George O. Squier (USMA 1887) assumed command of the Signal Corps' Aviation Section, replacing Lt. Col. Samuel Reber (USMA 1882).

April 6, 1917—President Woodrow Wilson signed a congressional declaration of war against Germany, by which the United States entered World War I.

July 24, 1917—Congress appropriated $640 million for Army aviation and authorized the Aviation Section to expand to 9,989 officers and 87,083 enlisted men.

September 3, 1917—Brig. Gen. William L. Kenly (USMA 1889) was appointed first chief of the Air Service, American Expeditionary Forces, thus becoming the first single head of all U.S. air activities in-theater.

November 27, 1917—Brig. Gen. Benjamin D. Foulois replaced Brig. Gen. William L. Kenly as chief of the Air Service, American Expeditionary Forces.

May 15, 1918—Army pilots began flying the government's first permanent airmail route—Washington, D.C., to New York.

May 24, 1918—U.S. Army Air Service is established as first independent air force organization.

May 29, 1918—Brig. Gen. Mason M. Patrick (USMA 1886) becomes chief of Air Service.

September 12, 1918—Brig. Gen. William "Billy" Mitchell commanded the largest air armada ever assembled—1,481 Allied airplanes—during the first major American offensive of the war at Saint-Mihiel, France. General Pershing (USMA 1886) was the commander of the first major offensive of the war.

October 2, 1918—The United States successfully flight-tested a pilotless aircraft called the Kettering "Bug" at Dayton, Ohio.

November 6, 1918—At Aberdeen Proving Ground, Maryland, Dr. Robert H. Goddard demonstrated tube-launched, solid-propellant rockets, forerunners of the bazooka—an antitank weapon of World War II.

January 2, 1919—Maj. Gen. Charles T. Menoher (USMA 1886) became director of the Army Air Service.

June 4, 1920—Congress passed the National Defense Act to establish the Air Service on a permanent basis as a combatant arm of the Army, making it the equivalent of the infantry, cavalry, and artillery. Congress also created the rating of "airplane pilot" and authorized flying pay of 50 percent above base pay.

July 21, 1921—Under the leadership of Brig. Gen. William "Billy" Mitchell, Martin and Handley Page bombers from the Army's 1st Provisional Air Brigade bombed and sank the captured German battleship *Ostfriesland* in Chesapeake Bay. The tests proved General Mitchell's contention that airplanes could sink the largest and most powerful naval vessels.

October 5, 1921—Maj. Gen. Mason M. Patrick (USMA 1886) replaced Maj. Gen. Charles T. Menoher (USMA 1886) as chief of the Air Service.

March 27, 1923—A War Department board headed by Maj. Gen. William Lassiter recommended legislation to reorganize and expand the Air Service, including a suggestion to provide aviation forces that could operate under a general headquarters to accomplish strategic missions independent of surface forces.

September 5, 1925—Billy Mitchell charged that the loss of a Navy airplane on a flight from California to Hawaii and the loss of the Navy dirigible *Shenandoah* in Ohio resulted from "incompetency," "criminal negligence," and "almost treasonable administration" by the Navy and War Departments. As a result, President Calvin Coolidge ordered Mitchell's court-martial.

November 30, 1925—A board appointed by President Calvin Coolidge and headed by Dwight W. Morrow released a report recommending conservative reorganization of the Air Service and its redesignation as the Air Corps, rather than establishment of an independent air force coequal with the Army and Navy.

December 17, 1925—After a seven-week trial, the Army convicted Billy Mitchell of violating the 96th article of war by having made "insubordinate" statements. Sentenced to five years' suspension of rank, pay, and command, he resigned from the Army shortly thereafter.

March 16, 1926—At Auburn, Massachusetts, Dr. Robert H. Goddard successfully launched the world's first liquid-fueled rocket.

July 2, 1926—The Air Corps Act redesignated the Army Air Service as the Army Air Corps and created an assistant secretary of war for air, as recommended by the Morrow Board in November 1925. On the same day, Maj. Gen. Mason M. Patrick (USMA 1886), chief of the Air Service, became chief of the Air Corps.

May 21, 1927—In his airplane Spirit of St. Louis, Charles A. Lindbergh, a captain in the Missouri National Guard's 110th Observation Squadron, completed the first solo nonstop flight across the Atlantic Ocean, from New York to Paris, a distance of 3,610 miles, in 33 hours and 39 minutes. By act of Congress, Lindbergh received the Medal of Honor for this flight.

January 7, 1929—Maj. Carl Spaatz (USMA 1914), Capt. Ira C. Eaker, 1st Lt. Harry A. Halverson, 2nd Lt. Elwood R. Quesada, and SSgt. Roy W. Hooe set an endurance record for a refueled airplane in flight, having flown for 150 hours, 40 minutes, and 15 seconds since January 1 in the *Question Mark*, a Fokker C-2 Trimotor airplane. Refueling 37 times in the air, they demonstrated the practicality of aerial refueling.

September 24, 1929—Lt. James H. "Jimmy" Doolittle made the first instruments only flight, from takeoff to landing. He flew over Mitchel Field, New York, in a Consolidated NY-2 airplane with a completely covered cockpit, accompanied by a check pilot who monitored the flight.

June 20, 1930—The Air Corps established Randolph Field at San Antonio, Texas, for primary and basic pilot training. Known as the "West Point of the Air," the field eventually became headquarters of Air Education and Training Command.

January 9, 1931—Gen. Douglas MacArthur (USMA 1903), Army chief of staff, and Admiral William V. Pratt, chief of naval operations, came to a verbal agreement that the Army Air Corps would have primary responsibility for coastal defense.

May 21, 1931—Brig. Gen. Benjamin D. Foulois, assistant to the chief of the Air Corps, commanded a provisional division in the largest Air Corps maneuvers to date, involving 667 airplanes and 1,400 men in flights over several northeastern and midwestern states.

December 20, 1931—Maj. Gen. Benjamin D. Foulois succeeded Maj. Gen. James E. Fechet as chief of the Air Corps.

October 11, 1933—Secretary of War George H. Dern approved the report of an Army board chaired by Maj. Gen. Hugh A. Drum, which recommended establishment of a General Headquarters Air Force.

November 27, 1933—The Army accepted delivery of its first production-model Martin B-10, the nation's first all-metal monoplane bomber produced in quantity. The twin-engine airplane featured an internal bomb bay, retractable landing gear, rotating gun turret, and enclosed cockpit.

March 10, 1934—The Army Air Corps suspended domestic airmail deliveries temporarily because of nine crash fatalities. Lack of instruments in Army aircraft for night and bad-weather flying contributed to the accidents.

August 20, 1934—Lt. Col. Henry H. Arnold (USMA 1907) and 10 Martin B-10 bomber crews completed a month-long air trip of more than 7,000 miles from Bolling Field, Washington, D.C., to Fairbanks, Alaska, and back.

March 1, 1935—The War Department activated the General Headquarters Air Force under Brig. Gen. Frank M. Andrews (USMA 1906) at Langley Field, Virginia, to manage tactical air units in the United States, with the exception of observation squadrons allotted to ground forces. This action largely fulfilled the recommendations of the Drum and Baker Boards of 1933 and 1934.

December 17, 1935—First flight of the Douglas Sleeper Transport, the first of 10,654 DC-3s and derivatives Douglas will build between 1935 and 1947. The U.S. military uses C-4s in three wars, and some "Gooney Birds" are still in use today. The DC-3 is one of the most famous airplanes of all time.

December 22, 1935—Brig. Gen. Oscar Westover (USMA 1906) succeeded Maj. Gen. Benjamin D. Foulois as chief of the Air Corps.

June 7, 1936—Flying from New York to Los Angeles entirely on instruments, Maj. Ira C. Eaker completed the first transcontinental "blind" flight.

September 29, 1938—Maj. Gen. Henry H. Arnold (USMA 1907) became chief of the Army Air Corps, formally taking the place of Maj. Gen. Oscar Westover (USMA 1906), who died in an airplane crash at Burbank, California, on September 21.

April 3, 1939—President Franklin D. Roosevelt signed the National Defense Act of 1940, which provided the Army Air Corps with more than 48,000 personnel, a $300 million budget, and 6,000 airplanes. It also authorized the Air Corps to train black pilots.

September 1, 1939—Germany invaded Poland, precipitating World War II. Two days later, Great Britain and France declared war on Germany.

April 15, 1940—The War Department issued a new field manual, FM 1-5, on the employment of Army aviation. It advocated the centralized use of air power against strategic and interdiction targets and mentioned that airplanes could be used to support tactical commanders on the battlefield.

May 16, 1940—President Franklin D. Roosevelt called for the production of 50,000 airplanes per year.

September 16, 1940—Congress passed the Selective Service Act, which not only instituted a peacetime draft, but also required all arms and services to enlist blacks.

March 11, 1941—President Franklin D. Roosevelt signed the Lend-Lease Act, which authorized the lending of war materiel, including aircraft, to any nation whose defense he considered vital to that of the United States.

March 22, 1941—The 99th Pursuit Squadron, the first black flying unit, was activated at Chanute Field, Illinois, under the command of Capt. Harold R. Maddux.

June 16, 1941—The Consolidated B-24 Liberator, a four-engine bomber that could fly faster and farther than the similarly sized B-17, entered the Air Corps inventory. More than 18,000 B-24s were produced during World War II, a greater number than any other U.S. aircraft.

June 20, 1941—The War Department established the Army Air Forces under Maj. Gen. Henry H. Arnold (USMA 1907). It encompassed both the Office of the Chief of the Air Corps under Maj. Gen. George Brett, who was responsible for research, development, supply, and maintenance, and Air Force Combat Command (formerly General Headquarters Air Force) under Lt. Gen. Delos C. Emmons (USMA 1909), who was responsible for doctrine and operational training. (He later replaced General Andrews as Commander of GHQ.)

July 19, 1941—Capt. Benjamin O. Davis, Jr. (USMA 1936), whose father had been the first black graduate of the U.S. Military Academy, reported to Tuskegee Institute in Alabama with 12 aviation cadets to begin flight training as the first class of black pilot candidates in the U.S. military.

December 7, 1941—Japanese torpedo bombers, dive bombers, and fighters from six aircraft carriers attacked naval and air installations around Pearl Harbor, Hawaii, crippling the U.S. Pacific Fleet. In two waves, the Japanese airplanes sank four U.S. battleships and damaged nine other major warships. The surprise attack, which killed some 2,390 personnel, propelled the United States into World War II.

December 10, 1941—The 93d Bombardment Squadron of the 19th Bombardment Group used five B-17s to carry out the first heavy bomb mission of World War II, attacking a Japanese convoy as it landed troops on the northern coast of Luzon.

December 20, 1941—Under the leadership of Claire Chennault, the American Volunteer Group, also called the "Flying Tigers," flew its first mission against the Japanese in China. The Flying Tigers, consisting of U.S. volunteer pilots, flew P-40 airplanes in the service of the Chinese government of Premier Chiang Kai-shek.

March 6, 1942—The Army Air School at Tuskegee, Alabama, graduated the first five black military pilots, including Capt. Benjamin O. Davis, Jr. (USMA 1936). By the end of the war, the "Tuskegee Airmen" would number 950 pilots and open the door to the armed forces for other African Americans.

March 9, 1942—By executive order, the War Department reorganized into three autonomous sections: Army Air Forces, Army Ground Forces, and Services of Supply. The Air Corps continued to exist as a combatant arm of the Army.

April 8, 1942—First flight of military transport aircraft from India to China ("Over the Hump") to resupply the Chinese war effort and units of the U.S. Army Air Forces in China.

April 18, 1942—Col. James H. "Jimmy" Doolittle led 16 B-25s from the aircraft carrier *Hornet* to bomb Tokyo and other sites in the first U.S. air raid on Japan. Because of the range, the raiders had to crash-land in China. Although the raid caused little destruction, it raised U.S. morale and damaged that of the Japanese, reversing what had seemed to be an endless stream of Japanese victories. For leading this mission, Doolittle earned the Medal of Honor.

June 4, 1942—The Japanese attempt to take the island of Midway in the mid–Pacific failed in a major battle—the most important turning point in the war in the Pacific. Having broken the Japanese code, U.S. forces were ready for the invaders. As a result of the Battle of Midway, fought primarily by carrier aircraft but also by some Army Air Forces aircraft from Midway, the Japanese lost four aircraft carriers, a heavy cruiser, 322 aircraft, and some 5,000 men, including many skilled pilots. The United States lost the USS *Yorktown*, one of its three aircraft carriers. After this battle, the Japanese were forced to go on the defensive.

July 19, 1942—The Messerschmitt Me 262 flew for the first time, piloted by Fritz Wendel. The aircraft was the world's first operational jet fighter.

August 17, 1942—Eighth Air Force conducted its first heavy bomber raid in Europe. Twelve B-17s under the command of Col. Frank A. Armstrong, Jr., bombed railroad marshaling yards at Rouen in German-occupied France. The raid demonstrated the feasibility of daylight bombing.

October 3, 1942—Germany's liquid-fueled V-2, the world's first large operational ballistic missile, flew successfully for the first time.

December 1, 1942—Maj. Gen. Ira C. Eaker assumed command of Eighth Air Force in England, replacing Maj. Gen. Carl A. Spaatz (USMA 1914), who transferred to the Mediterranean theater.

January 5, 1943—Gen. Dwight D. Eisenhower (USMA 1915), commander of Operation Torch, activated Allied Air Force under Maj. Gen. Carl A. Spaatz (USMA 1914) in the Northwest African theater.

February 1, 1943—Navy crews in PBY-5 Catalina aircraft rescued Thirteenth Air Force commander Maj. Gen. Nathan F. Twining (USMA 1918) and 14 others near the New Hebrides Islands after they were forced to ditch their aircraft and spend six days in life rafts.

January 21, 1943—At the Casablanca Conference in Morocco, where U.S. and British leaders discussed war policy, Lt. Gen. Ira C. Eaker successfully presented his case for daytime bombing of Germany to Winston S. Churchill, prime minister of Great Britain.

March 19, 1943—Lt. Gen. H. H. Arnold (USMA 1907) is promoted to four-star rank, a first for the Army Air Forces.

August 1, 1943—Staging from Benghazi, 177 Ninth Air force B-24s drop 311 tons of bombs from low level on the oil refineries at Ploesti during Operation Tidal Wave. Forty-nine aircraft are lost and seven others land in Turkey. This is the first large-scale, minimum altitude attack by AAF heavy bombers on a strongly defended target. It is also the longest major bombing mission to date in terms of distance from base to target. More Air Force Medals of Honor are awarded for this mission than for any other in the service's history.

June 10, 1943—The Royal Air Force and the Army Air Forces launched the Combined Bomber Offensive against Germany. Eighth Air Force struck enemy industrial targets by day, while the Royal Air Force attacked enemy cities by night. The around-the-clock bombing was designed to cripple and then destroy the Germans' ability and will to continue the war.

October 14, 1943—Eighth Air Force conducts the second raid on the ball-bearing factories at Schweinfurt, Germany. As a result, the Germans will disperse their ball-bearing manufacturing, but the cost of the raid is high; 60 of the 291 B-17s launched do not return and 138 more are damaged.

December 5, 1943—Pilots of Ninth Air Force's 354th Fighter Group flew their new P-51s for the first time into combat, escorting Eighth Air Force B-17 bombers for a record distance of 490 miles to targets in Northern Germany. The fast and maneuverable aircraft, equipped with fuel tanks that allowed them to accompany the bombers all the way to the target, sharply reduced bomber losses to enemy fighters.

January 6, 1944—Lt. Gen. Carl A. Spaatz (USMA 1914), who had commanded U.S. air forces in the Mediterranean theater, assumed command of Eighth Air Force, replacing Lt. Gen. Ira C. Eaker. Spaatz had been Gen. Dwight D. Eisenhower's air commander in the Mediterranean. Eisenhower (USMA 1915) was moving to England to prepare for the invasion of France. At the same time, Eaker replaced Spaatz in the Mediterranean.

March 11, 1944—Essen, Germany, was the target for 4,738 tons of bombs dropped by 1,079 Eighth Air Force bombers—the highest tonnage of bombs dropped during World War II by the Army Air Forces on one target in a single mission.

June 5, 1944—More than 1,400 C-47s, C-53s, and gliders of Ninth Air Force dropped or landed three full airborne divisions in German-occupied France on the night before and during the Allied amphibious invasion of Normandy. The airborne troops endeavored to secure the land approaches to and from the beaches.

June 6, 1944—Allied forces based in the United Kingdom crossed the English Channel and invaded German-held Normandy in northern France to begin Operation Overlord, the largest amphibious attack in history. Previous Allied air attacks largely prevented interference by the Luftwaffe and cut German transportation arteries. On a day often called "D-Day," Eighth and Ninth Air Forces and the Royal Air Force supported the invasion with some 15,000 interdiction, close air support, and airlift sorties.

June 13, 1944—The Germans began launching V-1 jet-powered cruise missiles from France against England. Four of the first 11 hit London.

June 19, 1944—"The Marianas Turkey Shoot": in two days of fighting, the Japanese lose 476 aircraft. American losses are 130 planes.

June 22, 1944—The GI Bill is signed into law.

July 27, 1944—The executive committee of the NACA discusses robots and their possibilities for military and other uses.

August 14, 1944—Capt. Robin Olds (USMA 1943) records his first victory while flying with the 434th Fighter Squadron in the European Theatre of Operation (ETO). He would go on to tally 11 more kills by July 4, 1945. His next aerial victory would come on January 2, 1967, making him the only American ace to record victories in nonconsecutive wars.

September 8, 1944—The Germans launched V-2s—the world's first ballistic missiles— against Paris and London. Rocket scientist Wernher von Braun had developed the missile, almost impossible to intercept because of its speed, at a secret base at Peenemünde, Germany.

September 17, 1944—Operation Market Garden began when 1,546 Allied aircraft and 478 gliders carried airborne troops to the Netherlands in an effort to secure bridges on the way to cross the Rhine River at Arnhem, the Netherlands. (We note that the airborne effort was led by a Naval Academy graduate Lewis H. Brereton (USNA 1911.)

November 24, 1944—For the first time, B-29s bombed Tokyo. Previously unable to reach the Japanese capital from China, this time they took off from bases in the Mariana Islands. This was the first mission of XXI Bomber Command, under Brig. Gen. Haywood S. Hansell, Jr., and the first time Tokyo had been bombed since the Doolittle raid of April 18, 1942.

December 21, 1944—Gen. Henry H. Arnold (USMA 1907) became general of the Army. No other airman has ever held five-star rank.

January 20, 1945—Maj. Gen. Curtis E. LeMay succeeded Brig. Gen. Haywood S. Hansell, Jr., as commander of XXI Bomber Command in the Mariana Islands, taking charge of the nation's combat B-29s during a faltering strategic air campaign against Japan.

March 9, 1945—In a night air raid on Tokyo, more than 300 B-29 Superfortresses from bases in the Marianas dropped incendiary bombs that destroyed 16 square miles of the Japanese capital, about a fourth of the city. In terms of lives lost, this air raid was the most destructive in history. Undertaken by Maj. Gen. Curtis E. LeMay, commander of XXI Bomber Command, the attack reflected a shift in U.S. bombardment policy from high-altitude daylight attack on specific military targets to low-level area bombing at night. Fourteen B-29s were lost to flak, but none to interceptors.

March 18, 1945—Some 1,250 U.S. bombers escorted by 670 fighters dropped 3,000 tons of bombs on Berlin's transportation and industrial areas. In terms of numbers of bombers, this daylight attack was the largest of the war.

March 27, 1945—B-29 crews begin night mining missions around Japan, eventually establishing a complete blockade.

May 8, 1945—World War II ended in Europe (V-E Day).

June 22, 1945—Okinawa is declared captured by U.S forces. The price paid to capture this island— 16,000 men, 36 ships, and 800 aircraft—is a key consideration in the decision to use atomic bombs on Japan.

July 16, 1945—Maj. Gen. Curtis E. LeMay assumed command of Twentieth Air Force, which had been commanded directly by Army Air Forces Commander General Henry H. Arnold.

July 16, 1945—The world's first atomic bomb, having an explosive yield equal to 19 kilotons of TNT, successfully detonated at Trinity Site near Alamogordo, New Mexico.

August 6, 1945—In the first atomic bomb attack in history, Col. Paul W. Tibbets piloted a B-29 called *Enola Gay* from the island of Tinian in the Marianas to Hiroshima, Japan, destroying the city with a single bomb.

August 9, 1945—Three days after the destruction of Hiroshima, Maj. Charles W. Sweeney and his crew, flying a B-29 called *Bock's Car*, bombed Nagasaki in the second and last atomic bomb attack, which largely destroyed the city and killed at least 35,000 people.

August 14, 1945—Twentieth Air Force launched the final B-29 missions against Japan, mining waters around that country and bombing six cities with conventional weapons. By midnight, the Japanese had agreed to surrender, persuaded by a combination of the atomic bomb attacks, continued incendiary bombing, mining operations, and a Soviet declaration of war.

September 2, 1945—The Japanese officially surrendered to the Allied powers on board the USS *Missouri* in Tokyo Bay in a formal signing ceremony (V-J Day).

November 29, 1945—The Army Air Forces School, formerly the Army Air Forces School of Applied Tactics, moved from Orlando, Florida, to Maxwell Field, Alabama, and was assigned directly to the Army Air Forces as a major command. It later became the Air University.

December 3, 1945—The 412th Fighter Group received its first P-80 aircraft at March Field, California, becoming the first Army Air Forces fighter unit equipped with jet-propelled aircraft.

March 1, 1946—Gen. Carl A. Spaatz (USMA 1914) replaced General of the Army Henry H. Arnold (USMA 1907) as commanding general, Army Air Forces. Spaatz had been acting commander since February 9, while General Arnold prepared to retire.

March 21, 1946—Tactical Air Command (TAC) was activated, Continental Air Forces was redesignated Strategic Air Command (SAC), and Air Defense Command (ADC) was established.

April 16, 1946—At White Sands Proving Ground in New Mexico, the Army launched a German V-2 rocket in the United States for the first time.

July 1, 1946—An Army Air Forces crew in a B-29 called *Dave's Dream*, assigned to the 509th Composite Group, dropped an atomic bomb on 73 naval vessels off Bikini Atoll in the Pacific Ocean in a test known as Operation Crossroads. The explosion sank five ships and heavily damaged nine others.

July 26, 1947—President Harry S. Truman signed the National Security Act, which created a Department of the Air Force equal to the Department of the Army and the Department of the Navy; a National Military Establishment under the secretary of defense; and an Air National Guard as a reserve component of the Air Force.

September 18, 1947—W. Stuart Symington took his oath as the first secretary of the Air Force.

September 25, 1947—President Harry S. Truman named Gen. Carl A. Spaatz (USMA 1914) as the first USAF chief of staff.

October 14, 1947—Capt. Charles E. "Chuck" Yeager made the first faster-than-sound flight at Muroc Air Base, California, in a rocket-powered USAF research plane, the Bell XS-1, and won the Mackay Trophy for the most meritorious flight of the year.

April 26, 1948—Anticipating an executive order from President Harry S. Truman in July 1948, the Air Force became the first service to plan for racial integration.

April 30, 1948—Gen. Hoyt S. Vandenberg (USMA 1923) is designated to succeed Gen. Carl A. Spaatz (USMA 1914) as Air Force chief of staff.

June 1, 1948—The Air Force Air Transport Command and the Navy Air Transport Service merged into a new organization, the Military Air Transport Service (MATS) under the command of Maj. Gen. Laurence S. Kuter (USMA 1927).

June 12, 1948—Congress passed the Women's Armed Service Integration Act, establishing the Women in the Air Force program.

June 26, 1948—In response to a blockade instituted by the Soviet Union on June 24 of rail and road lines between the U.S., British, and French occupation zones of western Germany and their occupation sectors in western Berlin, the Allies launched the Berlin airlift. Called Operation Vittles by the United States and Operation Plane Fare by the British, the airlift delivered enough coal and food to sustain the city indefinitely and became the largest humanitarian airlift in history.

July 30, 1948—North American Aviation delivered to the Air Force its first operational jet bomber, the B-45A Tornado. Later it became the first USAF aircraft to carry a tactical nuclear bomb.

August 10, 1949—President Harry S. Truman signed the National Security Act amendments of 1949, revising the unification legislation of 1947 and converting the National Military Establishment into the Department of Defense.

September 30, 1949—The Berlin Airlift officially ended after 277,264 flights had delivered 2,343,301.5 tons of supplies—1,783,826 tons of which were carried by U.S. airplanes.

January 23, 1950—USAF establishes Air Research and Development Command (ARDC), which later will be redesignated Air Force Systems Command (AFSC).

March 15, 1950—The Joint Chiefs of Staff, in a statement of basic roles and missions give the Air Force formal and exclusive responsibility for strategic guided missiles.

June 25, 1950—North Korea attacks South Korea to begin the Korean War.

June 27, 1950—President Truman announces he has ordered the USAF to aid South Korea which has been invaded by North Korean communist forces.

June 28, 1950—The Far East Air Forces launched the first USAF air strikes of the Korean War, sending more than 20 B-26s of the 3d Bombardment Group to bomb the Munsan railroad yards near the 38th parallel and rail and road traffic between Seoul and the North Korean border. North Korean forces occupied Seoul, the South Korean capital, and nearby Kimpo Airfield.

July 6, 1950—The U.S. Air Force conducted the first strategic air attacks of the Korean War, sending nine B-29 Superfortresses to bomb the Rising Sun oil refinery at Wonsan and a chemical plant at Hungnam in North Korea.

August 10, 1950—The first two Air Force Reserve units were mobilized for Korean War service. By 1953, all 25 reserve flying wings had been mobilized.

August 16, 1950—In the largest deployment of air power in direct support of ground forces since the Normandy invasion of World War II, 98 B-29s dropped more than 800 tons of 500-pound bombs on a 27-square-mile area.

October 10, 1950—The first Air National Guard units were mobilized because of the Korean conflict. Eventually, 66 of the guard's combat flying units were mobilized, and some 45,000 air guardsmen—approximately 80 percent of the force—were called into federal service during the war.

October 20, 1950—In the first airborne operation of the Korean War, more than 100 C-119s and C-47s dropped some 4,000 troops of the Army's 187th Airborne Regimental Combat Team and more than 600 tons of materiel at Sukchon and Sunchon, 30 miles north of Pyongyang.

November 8, 1950—In history's first battle between jet aircraft, Lt. Russell J. Brown in an F-80 Shooting Star shot down a North Korean MiG-15. Seventy B-29 Superfortresses conducted the largest incendiary raid of the Korean War, dropping 580 tons of firebombs on Sinuiju, North Korea.

November 28, 1950—Combat Cargo Command C-119s and C-47s air-dropped and landed 1,580 tons of equipment and supplies, including eight bridge spans for the 1st Marine Division, which Communist Chinese forces had surrounded at the Chosin (Changjin) Reservoir area in northeastern North Korea. The C-47s also evacuated nearly 5,000 sick and wounded Marines from Hagaru-ri and Koto-ri.

March 15, 1951—A Boeing KC-97A Stratofreighter tanker successfully refueled a B-47 jet bomber in flight, demonstrating the bomber's long-range potential.

May 20, 1951—Capt. James Jabara, an F-86 Sabre pilot of the 334th Fighter-Interceptor Squadron, became the world's first jet ace, shooting down his fifth and sixth MiGs in the Korean War.

October 23, 1951—The first production B-47 Stratojet bomber entered service with the 306th Bombardment Wing. This aircraft became the workhorse for the Strategic Air Command through most of the 1950s.

February 1, 1952—The Air Force acquires its first general-purpose computer (a Univac I).

June 23, 1952—Air Force, Navy, and Marine Corps aircraft in coordinated attacks virtually destroyed the hydroelectric power plants of North Korea. The two-day operation, involving more than 1,200 sorties, was the largest single air effort since World War II.

November 1, 1952—The United States tests its first thermonuclear device at Eniwetok in the Marshall Islands. The device, codenamed Mike, has a yield of 10.4 million tons of TNT, 1,000 times more powerful than the bomb dropped on Hiroshima in World War II.

November 26, 1952—The Northrop B-62 Snark—a turbojet-powered, subsonic, long-range missile—flew for the first time.

March 16, 1953—Republic delivers the 4,000th F-84 Thunderjet to the Air Force. The F-84 has been in production since 1946 (with hundreds of variants produced, including those sold to other countries. USAF claims F-84s were responsible for 60 percent of the ground targets destroyed in the Korean War).

June 27, 1953—The Korean armistice goes into effect.

June 30, 1953—General Nathan F. Twining (USMA 1918) becomes Air Force chief of staff.

August 6, 1953—Operation Big Switch began. C-124, C-54, C-46, and C-47 transports airlifted more than 800 former prisoners of war from Korea to the United States by way of Japan after an armistice that ended the Korean War. The operation ended in October.

September 1, 1953—The Air Force announced the first in-flight refueling of jet powered aircraft by jet-powered aircraft after a KB-47 refueled a standard B-47 Stratojet.

September 1, 1953—The Sidewinder infrared-guided air-to-air missile made its first successful interception, sending an F-6F drone down in flames. The missile revolutionized aerial combat, offering pilots a method other than gunfire for shooting down enemy aircraft.

December 12, 1953—Maj. Charles E. Yeager pilots the rocket-powered Bell X-1A to a speed of Mach 2.435 (approximately 1,650 mph) over Edwards AFB.

March 1, 1954—The United States exploded the first (deliverable) hydrogen bomb in the Marshall Islands.

April 1, 1954—President Dwight D. Eisenhower (USMA 1915) signed into law a bill creating the U.S. Air Force Academy.

June 1, 1954—The Air Force directed its Air Research and Development Command to create the Western Development Division under Brig. Gen. Bernard A. Schriever to oversee acceleration of the Atlas intercontinental ballistic missile program.

June 24, 1954—Secretary of the Air Force Harold E. Talbott announced that the permanent location of the Air Force Academy would be a 15,000-acre tract of land six miles north of Colorado Springs, Colorado.

July 15, 1954—The Boeing 707, the first U.S. jet-powered airliner, made its first flight near Seattle, Washington, with Boeing pilot A. M. "Tex" Johnston at the controls. This aircraft revolutionized commercial aviation, replacing slower propeller-driven airliners, and became the prototype of the C-135 transport and KC-135 tanker, the latter designed to refuel the new B-47 and B-52 jet bombers.

July 26, 1954—Lt. Gen. Hubert R. Harmon (USMA 1915) was appointed the first superintendent of the Air Force Academy.

October 27, 1954—Benjamin O. Davis, Jr. (USMA 1936) became the first black general officer in the Air Force. He had served as commander of the 332d Fighter Group, the "Tuskegee Airmen"—the first fighter group that included black pilots.

April 6, 1955—The Air Force launched an air-to-air guided missile with an atomic warhead from a B-36 Peacemaker bomber to produce a nuclear explosion some six miles above Yucca Flat, Nevada—the highest known altitude of any nuclear blast.

June 29, 1955—The Boeing Aircraft Company delivered the first B-52 Stratofortress to enter USAF operational service to the 93d Bombardment Wing at Castle Air Force Base, California. The B-52 became—and continues to be— an important part of the Air Force's strategic bomber inventory.

July 11, 1955—The Air Force Academy admitted its first class, 306 cadets, at Lowry Air Force Base, Colorado—a temporary location until it could move to Colorado Springs.

May 21, 1956—An Air Force crew flying Boeing B-52B Stratofortress at 40,000 feet airdrops a live hydrogen bomb over Bikini Atoll in the Pacific. The bomb had a measured blast of 3.75 megatons.

September 7, 1956—Capt. Iven C. Kincheloe, Jr. (USAF), set the altitude record for manned flight at Edwards Air Force Base, California, piloting a Bell X-2 transonic, rocket-powered aircraft to a height of 126,200 feet. Captain Kincheloe received the Mackay Trophy for this flight. He later died in an F-104 accident.

September 27, 1956—Capt. Milburn Apt, USAF, reaches Mach 3.196 in the Bell X-2, becoming the first pilot to fly three times the speed of sound. Captain Apt is killed, however, when the aircraft tumbles out of control.

December 9, 1956—The 463d Troop Carrier Wing received the Air Force's first C-130 Hercules tactical-airlift aircraft. This four-engine turboprop airlifter had an unrefueled range of over 2,500 miles, could carry outsized cargo of almost 50,000 pounds or up to 92 troops, and could take off and land within about 3,600 feet. (The first flight of the C-130 was in August 23, 1954, and more than 40 variants of the aircraft have been produced and as of 2018 is still in service.)

June 11, 1957—The first U-2 high-altitude, long-range reconnaissance aircraft was delivered to the 4080th Strategic Reconnaissance Wing at Laughlin Air Force Base, Texas. The U-2 could fly 10-hour missions at exceptionally high altitudes at a top speed of 600 miles per hour.

June 28, 1957—The first KC-135 Stratotanker was delivered to Castle AFB, California. The jet tanker could cruise at the same speed as jet bombers while refueling, drastically reducing the time for in-flight refueling missions.

July 1, 1957—The first intercontinental ballistic missile wing, the 704th Strategic Missile Wing, activated at Cooke (later, Vandenberg) Air Force Base, California.

July 1, 1957—General Thomas D. White (USMA 1920) becomes Air Force chief of staff.

July 31, 1957—The distant early warning (DEW) line, a string of radar installations extending across the Canadian Arctic to warn of impending aircraft attacks, was declared fully operational.

August 1, 1957—The North American Air Defense Command, a joint United States–Canadian command with an air-defense mission, was informally established. An agreement ratified on May 12, 1958, formalized its existence.

August 15, 1957—Gen. Nathan F. Twining (USMA 1918) became the first USAF officer to serve as chairman of the Joint Chiefs of Staff.

October 4, 1957—The Soviet Union used an intercontinental ballistic missile booster to launch Sputnik I, the world's first artificial space satellite, into Earth orbit.

December 15, 1957—The 556th Strategic Missile Squadron, the first SM-62 *Snark* operational squadron, activated at Patrick Air Force Base, Florida. An air-breathing jet cruise missile equipped with two rockets for launch, the Snark was essentially a pilotless airplane with a warhead.

December 17, 1957—The Air Force first test-launched an Atlas intercontinental ballistic missile. Its reentry vehicle landed in the target area after a flight of some 500 miles.

January 1, 1958—The Air Force activated the 672d Strategic Missile Squadron, the first with Thor intermediate-range ballistic missiles, at Cooke (later, Vandenberg) Air Force Base, California.

January 31, 1958—Explorer I, the first U.S. satellite to go into orbit, was launched by the Army's Jupiter C rocket from Cape Canaveral, Florida.

June 17, 1958—Boeing and Martin are named prime contractors to develop competitive designs for the Air Force's X-20 Dyna-Soar boost-glide space vehicle. This project, although later canceled, is the first step toward the space shuttle.

October 1, 1958—Replacing the National Advisory Committee for Aeronautics (NACA), the National Aeronautics and Space Administration (NASA) was established to control nonmilitary U.S. scientific space projects.

December 18, 1958—The Air Force placed in orbit the first artificial communications satellite, a Project Score relay vehicle integral with the four-ton Atlas launcher. The next day, the satellite broadcast a taped recording, the first time a human voice had been heard from space.

February 6, 1959—The Air Force successfully launched the first Titan I intercontinental ballistic missile. With a range of 5,500 nautical miles, the two-stage liquid-fueled missile was to be deployed in underground silos and raised to the surface before launch.

February 12, 1959—Strategic Air Command retired its last B-36 Peacemaker, thus becoming an all-jet bomber force.

February 28, 1959—The Air Force successfully launched the Discoverer I satellite into polar orbit from Vandenberg Air Force Base, California. A polar orbit allows a satellite to fly over all surface points because of the Earth's rotation.

April 23, 1959—The GAM-77 (AGM-28) Hound Dog supersonic missile, designed to deliver a nuclear warhead over a distance of several hundred miles, was test-fired for the first time from a B-52 bomber at Eglin Air Force Base, Florida.

June 3, 1959—The Air Force Academy graduated its first class of 207 graduates.

June 8, 1959—Scott Crossfield piloted an experimental X-15 rocket airplane on its first flight, a nonpowered glide from a B-52.

September 9, 1959—A Strategic Air Command crew fired an Atlas intercontinental ballistic missile from Vandenberg Air Force Base, California—the first firing of the missile from the West Coast. By the end of the year, the Atlas had become the first U.S. long-range ballistic missile equipped with a nuclear warhead to be placed on alert status.

May 1, 1960—Francis Gary Powers, a Central Intelligence Agency U-2 pilot, was shot down over Sverdlovsk in the Soviet Union. Captured and put on trial for espionage, he was later exchanged for a Soviet agent captured by the United States.

August 1, 1960—The 43d Bombardment Wing at Carswell Air Force Base, Texas, accepted the first operational B-58 Hustler medium bomber. The first U.S. supersonic bomber, the delta-wing aircraft could fly at twice the speed of sound and could be refueled in flight.

August 19, 1960—Piloting a C-119, Capt. Harold F. Mitchell, USAF, retrieved the Discoverer XIV reentry capsule in midair, marking the first successful aerial recovery of a returning space capsule.

August 30, 1960—With six Atlas missiles ready to launch, the 564th Strategic Missile Squadron at Francis E. Warren Air Force Base, Wyoming, became the first fully operational intercontinental ballistic missile squadron.

February 1, 1961—The Minuteman intercontinental ballistic missile was launched for the first time at Cape Canaveral, Florida, in a major test. Under full guidance, it traveled 4,600 miles to its target area. The solid-fueled Minuteman could be stored more easily and fired more quickly than the liquid-fueled Atlas and Titan intercontinental ballistic missiles.

February 3, 1961—As part of a project called "Looking Glass," the Strategic Air Command began flying EC-135s to provide a 24-hour-a-day airborne command post for the president and secretary of defense in the event an enemy attack wiped out land-based command and control sites that controlled strategic bombers and intercontinental ballistic missiles. In 1998, the U.S. Navy fleet of E-6Bs replaced the EC-135C in performing this mission.

April 12, 1961—Cosmonaut Yuri Gagarin of the Union of Soviet Socialist Republics (USSR) became the first person to be launched into space and the first to orbit Earth.

May 5, 1961—By making a suborbital flight in Mercury capsule *Freedom 7*, Cmdr. Alan B. Shepard, Jr., United States Navy, became the first U.S. astronaut in space.

May 25, 1961—President John F. Kennedy, at a joint session of Congress, declares a national space objective: "I believe that this nation should commit itself to achieving the goal, before this decade is out, of landing a man on the moon and returning him safely to Earth."

June 30, 1961—Gen. Curtis E. LeMay becomes Air Force chief of staff.

July 21, 1961—Capt. Virgil I. Grissom became the second U.S. and the first USAF astronaut in space. He attained an altitude of 118 miles and a speed of 5,310 miles per hour in a 303-mile suborbital spaceflight.

November 15, 1961—The 2d Advanced Echelon, Thirteenth Air Force, activated in Saigon, Republic of Vietnam (South Vietnam), marking the official entry of the Air Force into the Vietnam War. In an operation called FARM GATE, a detachment of the 4400th Combat Crew Training Squadron began deployment to South Vietnam with special-operations aircraft.

February 20, 1962—Lt. Col. John H. Glenn, Jr., United States Marine Corps, became the first U.S. astronaut to orbit Earth. He flew for nearly five hours in Mercury capsule *Friendship 7*.

July 17, 1962—Maj. Robert M. White, USAF, piloted the X-15-1 hypersonic experimental aircraft to a world-record altitude of 58.7 miles, its initial design altitude. Maximum speed was 3,784 miles per hour.

October 14, 1962—An Air Force U-2 reconnaissance flight photographs nuclear-armed Soviet missiles in Cuba. Moscow subsequently agrees to remove the missiles under threat of U.S. invasion of Cuba.

October 27, 1962—A 4080th Strategic Wing U-2 reconnaissance aircraft piloted by Maj. Rudolf Anderson, Jr., was shot down over Cuba. Lost with his aircraft, Major Anderson was posthumously awarded the first Air Force Cross.

October 27, 1962—Strategic Air Command placed on alert the first 10 Minuteman I intercontinental ballistic missiles, emplaced in hardened silos and assigned to the 10th Strategic Missile Squadron at Malmstrom Air Force Base, Montana.

May 15, 1963—Astronaut Maj. L. Gordon Cooper, Jr., USAF, launched from Cape Canaveral, Florida, in Project Mercury capsule *Faith 7*. On May 16, after completing 22 orbits of Earth, he landed in the Pacific. Cooper was the last astronaut of Project Mercury and the first to orbit Earth for more than 24 hours.

April 21, 1964—The number of intercontinental ballistic missiles equaled the number of bombers on Strategic Air Command ground alert for the first time. Afterwards, the number of missiles surpassed the number of bombers in the nuclear-deterrent force.

September 21, 1964—At Palmdale, California, North American Aviation's B-70A Valkyrie flew for the first time, with company pilot Alvin White and Col. Joseph Cotton, USAF, at the controls. The huge delta-wing aircraft was a strategic bomber that could fly up to three times the speed of sound and at altitudes above 70,000 feet, but advances in enemy surface-to-air-missile technology prevented its production beyond the prototype stage.

December 15, 1964—Flying an FC-47, Capt. Jack Harvey and his crew conducted the first gunship mission in Vietnam. The FC-47, later called the AC-47, carried in its cargo bay a set of side-firing Gatling guns to strafe ground targets.

January 1, 1965—The Air Force's first SR-71 Blackbird unit, the 4200th Strategic Reconnaissance Wing, activated at Beale Air Force Base, California. The SR-71 could attain a speed of more than Mach 3 and altitudes beyond 70,000 feet, but it required special fuel and maintenance support.

February 8, 1965—The USAF performed its first retaliatory air strike in North Vietnam. A North American F-100 Super Sabre flew cover for attacking South Vietnamese fighter aircraft, suppressing ground fire in the target area.

March 18, 1965—Alexei Leonov of the Union of Soviet Socialist Republics became the first man to walk in space, performing the extravehicular activity (EVA) from the Voskhod 2.

April 20, 1965—Strategic Air Command shipped its last Atlas missile to storage facilities to be used as a launch vehicle in various research and development programs, thus completing the phase-out of the first generation of intercontinental ballistic missiles, all of which were liquid fueled.

April 23, 1965—The first operational Lockheed C-141 Starlifter aircraft was delivered to Travis Air Force Base, California. Capable of crossing any ocean nonstop at more than 500 miles per hour, the Starlifter could transport up to 70,000 pounds of payload, including 154 troops, 123 paratroopers, or a combination of troops and supplies.

June 3, 1965—Maj. James A. McDivitt, USAF, and Maj. Edward H. White, USAF, set a U.S. space endurance record of 97 hours, 30 seconds in 63 orbits around Earth. During this Gemini 4 mission, Major White became the first U.S. astronaut to "walk" in space.

June 18, 1965—Strategic Air Command B-52s flew for the first time in the Vietnam conflict when 28 Stratofortresses from Guam bombed Vietcong targets near Saigon. This was the first time B-52s had dropped bombs, although not nuclear weapons, in war.

June 30, 1965—At Francis E. Warren Air Force Base, Wyoming, the last of 800 Minuteman I missiles became operational when Strategic Air Command accepted the fifth Minuteman wing from Air Force Systems Command.

October 31, 1965—Strategic Air Command accepted its first 10 Minuteman II missiles, assigning them to the 447th Strategic Missile Squadron at Grand Forks Air Force Base, North Dakota. The Minuteman II was larger and more advanced than the Minuteman I, but it could be fired from the same silos.

November 1, 1965—Col. Jeanne M. Holm became director of Women of the Air Force.

January 1, 1966—Military Air Transport Service (MATS) was redesignated Military Airlift Command (MAC). At the same time, Eastern Air Transport Force and Western Air Transport Force were redesignated Twenty-First Air Force and Twenty-Second Air Force, respectively.

March 16, 1966—Astronauts Neil Armstrong and David Scott blasted into space atop a Titan II missile on the Gemini 8 mission. The two astronauts later performed the first docking maneuver in space, linking their capsule with an Agena target vehicle that had been launched by an Atlas booster.

March 31, 1966—Strategic Air Command phased out its last B-47 Stratojet. The first all-jet strategic bomber, it had entered active service in 1951, 15 years earlier.

April 12, 1966—B-52 bombers struck targets in North Vietnam for the first time, hitting a supply route in the Mu Gia Pass about 85 miles north of the border.

January 27, 1967—Three astronauts, Lt. Col. Virgil Grissom and Lt. Col. Edward H. White, USAF, and Lt. Cmdr. Robert B. Chaffee, USN, were trapped and killed in a flash fire in the Apollo 1 capsule while conducting a pre-flight rehearsal at Cape Kennedy, Florida.

February 29, 1968—Col. Jeanne M. Holm, director of Women in the Air Force, and Col. Helen O'Day, assigned to the Office of the Air Force Chief of Staff, became the first USAF women promoted to the permanent rank of colonel under the public law that removed restrictions on promoting women to higher ranks in all the armed services.

September 1, 1968—Serving as the on-scene commander during an attempted rescue of a downed American pilot, Lt. Col. William A. Jones III, USAF (USMA 1945) repeatedly flew his A1-H Skyraider aircraft over enemy gun emplacements, sustaining heavy damage and severe burns. For his heroic efforts, he received the Medal of Honor. He died the next year in an aircraft accident.

December 21, 1968—Apollo 8 becomes the first manned mission to use the Saturn V booster. Astronauts USAF Col. Frank Borman (USMA 1950), Navy Cmdr. James A. Lovell, and USAF Major William Anders become the first humans to orbit the moon.

July 20, 1969—Man sets foot on the moon for the first time. At 10:56 p.m. EDT, Apollo 11 astronaut Neil Armstrong puts his left foot on the lunar surface. He and lunar module pilot Col. Edwin "Buzz" Aldrin, Jr., USAF (USMA 1951) spend just under three hours walking on the moon. Command module pilot Lt. Col. Michael Collins USAF (USMA 1952) remains in orbit.

August 1, 1969—General John D. Ryan (USMA 1938) is appointed Air Force chief of staff.

October 1, 1969—*Air Force* magazine cover story "The Forgotten Americans of the Vietnam War" ignites national concern for the prisoners of war and the missing in action. It is reprinted in condensed form as the lead article in the November 1969 issue of *Reader's Digest*, is read in its entirety on the floor of Congress and is inserted into the *Congressional Record* on six different occasions. This article stirs the conscience of the nation and rallies millions to the cause of the POWs and MIAs. *Air Force* magazine publishes an MIA/POW Action Report from June 1970 until September 1974. (Frank Borman [USMA 1950] is assigned by President Nixon to visit 14 countries to gain support for release of the U.S. prisoners of war.)

May 5, 1970—The Air Force Reserve Officer Training Corps expanded to include women after test programs at Ohio State, Drake, East Carolina, and Auburn Universities proved successful.

June 6, 1970—Gen. Jack J. Catton, commander of Military Airlift Command, accepted delivery of the first C-5 Galaxy for operational use in the Air Force. At the time, the C-5 was the largest operational airplane in the world.

June 19, 1970—The first Minuteman III missile unit became operational at Minot Air Force Base, North Dakota. The Minuteman III could launch multiple independently targetable warheads (MIRVs).

July 16, 1971—Jeanne M. Holm, director of Women of the Air Force, was promoted to Brigadier General, becoming the first woman general in the Air Force.

August 21, 1970—Defense Secretary Melvin Laird announces the "Total Force" policy, leading to much greater reliance by the services on guard and reserve units.

July 26, 1971—Apollo 15 blasts off with an all Air Force crew: Col. David R. Scott (USMA 1954), Lt. Col. James B. Irwin (USNA 1951), and Maj. Alfred M. Worden (USMA 1955).

April 27, 1972—Four USAF fighter crews, releasing Paveway I laser-guided "smart" bombs, knocked down the Thanh Hoa bridge in North Vietnam. Previously, 871 conventional sorties had resulted in only superficial damage to the bridge.

May 10, 1972—F-4 Phantoms from the 8th Tactical Fighter Wing dropped precision-guided munitions on the Paul Doumer Bridge in Hanoi, North Vietnam, closing it to traffic.

June 11, 1972—B-52 Stratofortress aircraft used laser-guided bombs to destroy a major hydroelectric plant near Hanoi, North Vietnam.

July 27, 1972—One month ahead of schedule, company pilot Irv Burrows makes the first flight of the McDonnell Douglas F-15A Eagle air superiority fighter at Edwards AFB. The F-15 is the first USAF fighter to have a thrust-to-weight ratio greater than 1:1, which means it can accelerate going straight up.

September 9, 1972—Capt. Charles B. DeBellevue (WSO), flying with Capt. John A. Madden, Jr. (pilot) in a McDonnell Douglas F-4D, shoots down two MiG-19s near Hanoi. These were the fifth and sixth victories for Captain DeBellevue which made him the leading American ace of the war.

November 22, 1972—A B-52 was hit by a surface-to-air missile while on a mission over North Vietnam, becoming the first Stratofortress lost to enemy action. The crew members ejected over Thailand, where they were rescued.

December 7, 1972—Apollo 17, the final Apollo mission, was also the last manned space operation to land on the Moon.

December 18, 1972—President Richard M. Nixon directed the resumption of full-scale bombing and mining in North Vietnam—an operation known as Linebacker II. SSgt. Samuel O. Turner, USAF, became the first B-52 tail gunner to shoot down an enemy airplane.

January 27, 1973—In Paris, North Vietnam and the United States signed an "Agreement on Ending the War and Restoring Peace to Vietnam." The ceasefire was set to begin on January 29.

January 28, 1973—A B-52 Stratofortress crew performed the last Operation Arc Light sortie, bombing enemy targets in South Vietnam at 0628 hours local time. This operation had continued since 1965.

February 12, 1973—Military Airlift Command initiated Operation Homecoming, flying the first of 590 released American prisoners of war from Hanoi, North Vietnam, to Clark Air Base in the Philippines. The operation concluded on April 9.

July 1, 1973—Military conscription (the draft) in the United States ended, but the Selective Service continued to register young men of military age.

July 15, 1973—An A-7D Corsair II of the 354th Tactical Fighter Wing, based in Thailand, flew the last combat mission of the Southeast Asian War. All told, since February 2, 1962, the Air Force had flown 5.25 million sorties over South Vietnam, North Vietnam, Laos, and Cambodia, losing 2,251 aircraft—1,737 to hostile action and 514 for other operational reasons.

August 1, 1973—General George S. Brown (USMA 1941) becomes Air Force chief of staff.

October 14, 1973—During the "Yom Kippur War," USAF airlifters supporting Operation Nickel Grass flew 567 (C-141 and C-5) sorties from the United States, delivering 22,318 tons of war materiel to Israel. Regular and reserve units participated.

November 14, 1973—The first production McDonnell Douglas F-15A Eagle is delivered to the Air Force.

July 1, 1974—Gen. David C. Jones becomes Air Force chief of staff.

September 3, 1974—Strategic Air Command removed from alert its last Minuteman I intercontinental ballistic missile at the 90th Strategic Missile Wing, Warren Air Force Base, Wyoming, during conversion to Minuteman III missiles.

October 24, 1974—The Air Forces' Space and Missile Systems Organization carries out a midair launch of a Boeing LGM-30A Minuteman I from the hold of a Lockheed C-5A.

December 23, 1974—Company pilot Charles Bock, Jr., USAF Col. Emil Sturmthal, and flight test engineer Richard Abrams make the first flight of the Rockwell B-1A variable-geometry bomber from Palmdale, California.

January 26, 1975—The Force Modernization program, a nine-year effort to replace all Boeing LGM-30B Minuteman Is with either Minuteman IIs (LGM-30F) or Minuteman IIIs (LGM-30G), is completed as the last 10 LGM-30Gs are turned over to SAC at F. E. Warren AFB, Wyoming.

March 25, 1975—The United States organized an airlift to evacuate about 10,000 people a day from Da Nang, South Vietnam. Communist forces had completely cut land routes between this coastal provincial city and the rest of the country.

March 31, 1975—Completing the consolidation of all military airlift under a single manager, the Air Force transferred the tactical airlift resources of Pacific Air Forces, United States Air Forces in Europe, and Alaskan Air Command to Military Airlift Command. In December 1974, the Air Force had consolidated Tactical Air Command's airlift resources, including C-130s, with those of Military Airlift Command, which became the single airlift manager.

April 4, 1975—Operation Babylift, the aerial evacuation of orphans from Saigon, South Vietnam, began tragically as a C-5 Galaxy crashed in a rice field near the city. Miraculously, 175 of the 330 people on board survived the accident. The United States also began the fixed-wing aerial evacuation of Phnom Penh, Cambodia, which was surrounded by Khmer Rouge forces. By April 11, some 875 Cambodians had flown to Thailand aboard USAF C-130s.

April 29, 1975—Operation Frequent Wind began. Marine Corps, Navy, and USAF helicopters took part in this final evacuation of Saigon, South Vietnam, which concluded on April 30, when Saigon fell to enemy forces. The helicopters airlifted more than 6,000 evacuees from the South Vietnamese capital in two days. This major operation was the first to involve the flights of USAF helicopters from the deck of an aircraft carrier—the USS *Midway.*

July 15, 1975—Three U.S. astronauts and two Soviet cosmonauts rendezvous and dock their space vehicles in orbit during the Apollo-Soyuz mission.

September 1, 1975—Gen. Daniel "Chappie" James, Jr., USAF, became the first black four-star general.

November 29, 1975—The first annual Red Flag exercise began at Nellis Air Force Base, Nevada, ushering in a new era of highly realistic USAF air combat training for pilots and aircrews.

January 9, 1976—The first operational F-15 Eagle, a new air-superiority fighter aircraft, arrived at the 1st Tactical Fighter Wing, Langley Air Force Base, Virginia.

February 4, 1976—Using C-5s, C-141s, and C-130s, the Air Force airlifted 927 tons of relief equipment and supplies to Guatemala after a severe earthquake. The aircraft also transported 696 medical, engineering, and communications personnel.

March 22, 1976—The first A-10 Thunderbolt was delivered to Davis-Monthan Air Force Base, Arizona, for test and evaluation. The heavily armored jet attack aircraft, armed with a heavy Gatling gun in the nose and equipped with straight wings able to carry a variety of air-to-ground munitions, was designed for close air support missions.

June 28, 1976—Joan Olsen became the first woman cadet to enter the Air Force

Academy and the first woman to enter any of the three Department of Defense service academies.

September 29, 1976—The first of two groups of 10 women pilot candidates entered undergraduate pilot training at Williams Air Force Base, Arizona—the first time since World War II that women could train to become pilots of U.S. military aircraft.

January 8, 1977—The first YC-141B (stretched C-141 Starlifter) rolled out of the Lockheed-Georgia Marietta plant. Equipped with in-flight refueling capability, it was 23.3 feet longer than the original C-141A, enabling it to carry more troops and cargo.

March 23, 1977—Tactical Air Command's first E-3A Sentry aircraft arrived at Tinker Air Force Base, Oklahoma. The Sentry, the Air Force's first airborne warning and control system (AWACS) aircraft, carried a large rotating radar disk above its fuselage.

June 19, 1977—A C-5 Galaxy flew nonstop from Chicago to Moscow carrying a 40-ton superconducting magnet, the first time a C-5 had ever landed in the Soviet Union. The flight of 5,124 nautical miles required two aerial refuelings.

June 30, 1977—President James E. "Jimmy" Carter, Jr., announced cancellation of the B-1 Lancer bomber program after the production of four prototypes, citing the continuing reliability of B-52s and the development of cruise missiles.

August 12, 1977—Released at an altitude of 22,800 feet from the top of a specially modified Boeing 747, Enterprise—the first space shuttle—completed its first descent and landing.

October 12, 1977—The first class of USAF women navigators graduated, with three of the five assigned to Military Airlift Command aircrews.

February 9, 1978—From Cape Canaveral, Florida, an Atlas-Centaur booster hoisted into orbit the first Fleet Satellite Communications System satellite.

February 22, 1978—An Atlas booster launched the first Global Positioning System (GPS) satellite. A "constellation" of such satellites revolutionized navigation.

May 31, 1978—In Operation Zaire II, C-141s and C-5s airlifted Belgian and French troops from Zaire, replacing them with African peacekeeping troops. In 72 missions, they transported 1,225 passengers and 1,619 tons of cargo.

July 1, 1978—Gen. Lew Allen, Jr. (USMA 1946), becomes Air Force chief of staff.

November 30, 1978—The last Boeing LGM-30G Minuteman III ICBM is delivered to the Air Force at Hill AFB, Utah.

December 8, 1978—As a result of political tensions and disturbances in Iran, Military Airlift Command airlifted some 900 evacuees from Tehran to bases in the United States and Germany. The airlift included 11 C-141 and C-5 missions. Some 5,700 U.S. and third-country nationals left Iran on regularly scheduled Military Airlift Command flights until Iran's revolutionary government closed the airport in February 1979.

January 6, 1979—The 388th Tactical Fighter Wing at Hill Air Force Base, Utah, received the first General Dynamics F-16 delivered to the Air Force. The F-16, the newest multirole fighter, could perform strike as well as air superiority missions.

November 4, 1979—More than 3,000 Iranian militants stormed the U.S. embassy in Tehran, Iran, and took 66 U.S. citizens hostage. President James E. "Jimmy" Carter decided to exhaust diplomatic options before resorting to a military response.

December 27, 1979—The Soviet Union led a coup in Afghanistan that set up a new puppet regime, provoking a civil war and the entrance of thousands of Soviet troops, many of them by airlift, into the country.

May 18, 1980—Following the eruption of Mount Saint Helens in northwest Washington State, the Aerospace Rescue and Recovery Service, Military Airlift Command, and the 9th Strategic Reconnaissance Wing conducted humanitarian-relief efforts. During the operation, helicopter crews lifted 61 people to safety, while SR-71 airplanes conducted aerial photographic reconnaissance to assist rescue-and-recovery efforts.

May 28, 1980—The Air Force Academy graduates its first female cadets. Ninety-seven women are commissioned as second lieutenants. Lt. Kathleen Conley graduates eighth in her class. (Her father, a USNA 1950 graduate, became vice commander of ESD of the Air Force Systems Command as a major general. General Conley and the author flew together for many hours in the B-52G flight test program at Edwards AFB.)

January 11, 1981—The Boeing Company delivered the first USAF air-launched cruise missile (ALCM). Capable of delivering a nuclear weapon to a target 1,500 miles away, the new missiles contained a terrain contour matching system that allows extremely low-altitude flight to avoid detection by enemy radar.

March 17, 1981—McDonnell Douglas Aircraft Company delivered the first KC-10A Extender tanker/cargo aircraft to the Strategic Air Command. Substantially larger than the KC-135 tanker/cargo aircraft, the Extender not only could carry more fuel and cargo, but also could refuel more types of aircraft, including other KC-10s. (The author, as director of requirements, was heavily involved in the competition between the B-747 and KC-10A.)

April 12, 1981—The space shuttle orbiter *Columbia*, the world's first reusable manned space vehicle, makes its first flight with astronauts John Young and Navy Capt. Robert Crippen aboard.

May 2, 1981—An airborne laser destroyed an aerial target for the first time when the Airborne Laser Laboratory (ALL), a modified KC-135 aircraft armed with a carbon dioxide laser, shot down a drone over White Sands Missile Range, New Mexico. Two years later, the ALL successfully shot down five Sidewinder air-to-air missiles, proving its utility as an antimissile system.

June 18, 1981—The F-117 Nighthawk, the world's first stealth combat aircraft, flew for the first time.

October 2, 1981—Reversing former president James E. "Jimmy" Carter's decision to end the B-1 Lancer program, President Ronald W. Reagan announced that the Air Force would build and deploy 100 of these aircraft. President Reagan also announced that the M-X missile would be deployed initially in existing missile silos.

November 5, 1981—The first operational EF-111A defense-suppression aircraft was delivered. The EF-111A would eventually replace EB-66 and EB-57 aircraft to provide worldwide support of tactical air strike forces.

November 23, 1981—During the Bright Star '82 exercise, eight B-52 bombers assigned to the strategic-projection force established a record for the longest nonstop B-52 bombing mission. Flying 15,000 miles with three midair refuelings in 31 hours from air bases in North Dakota, the bombers delivered their conventional munitions on a simulated runway in Egypt.

June 9, 1982—Israeli pilots flying U.S.-made fighters achieved an unmatched 82–0 aerial victory ratio in combat against Syrian fighter pilots in Soviet-made MiGs over Lebanon's Bekaa Valley. They also destroyed 19 Syrian surface-to-air missile batteries and suffered no losses.

June 10, 1982—Strategic Air Command's first all-woman KC-135 crew, assigned to the 924th Air Refueling Squadron, Castle Air Force Base, California, performed a five-hour training mission that included a midair refueling of a B-52 Stratofortress aircraft.

July 1, 1982—Gen. Charles A. Gabriel (USMA 1950) becomes Air Force chief of staff.

September 1, 1982—Air Force Space Command (AFSC) is established.

September 21, 1982—A B-52 Stratofortress of the 416th Bombardment Wing, Griffiss Air Force Base, New York, conducted the first operational test of an air-launched cruise missile.

February 9, 1983—The first re-winged C-5A makes its first flight at Marietta, Georgia.

June 17, 1983—The Peacekeeper intercontinental ballistic missile, carrying multiple warheads, was launched for the first time at Vandenberg Air Force Base, California. The unarmed warheads landed in the Kwajalein target area in the Pacific Ocean.

June 18, 1983—Sally K. Ride became the first U.S. woman to journey into outer space. She was a *Challenger* crew member of the seventh space shuttle mission.

August 30, 1983—Lt. Col. Guion S. Bluford, USAF, became the first black astronaut to journey into space. He rode aboard *Challenger* on the eighth space shuttle mission.

October 23, 1983—After a terrorist bomb exploded at a Marine Corps barracks in Beirut, Lebanon, Military Airlift Command and Air Force Reserve cargo and aeromedical-evacuation aircraft transported 239 dead and 95 wounded Americans to the United States and Europe for burial and medical treatment.

October 24, 1983—In Operation Urgent Fury, American military forces raided the Caribbean island of Grenada to evacuate U.S. citizens, restore democracy, and eliminate a hostile Cuban/Soviet base. Military Airlift Command and Air Force Reserve C-5 Galaxy, C-141 Starlifter, and C-130 Hercules aircraft flew 496 missions to transport 11,389 passengers and 7,709 tons of cargo to Grenada. Strategic Air Command tankers and Tactical Air Command fighters, as well as Air National Guard EC-130Es, supported the operation, which accomplished its triple mission.

July 7, 1985—Strategic Air Command accepted its first operational B-1B Lancer, a long-range bomber with variable swept wings.

September 13, 1985—The first antisatellite intercept test took place when a weapon launched from an F-15 successfully destroyed a satellite orbiting at a speed of 17,500 miles per hour approximately 290 miles above the Earth.

January 28, 1986—The seven crew members of the space shuttle *Challenger* were killed in an explosion shortly after liftoff from the John F. Kennedy Space Center in Florida. The disaster delayed the U.S. manned space program for more than two years.

March 25, 1986—For the first time, an all-woman Minuteman missile crew served on alert duty; the crew was assigned to the 351st Strategic Missile Wing, Whiteman Air Force Base, Missouri.

July 1, 1986—General Larry D. Welch becomes Air Force chief of staff.

October 10, 1986—The Air Force placed the LGM-118A, also called the Peacekeeper or MX missile, on alert duty. Each of these new intercontinental ballistic missiles could deliver warheads to 10 different targets.

April 5, 1988—Eight C-5 Galaxies and 22 C-141 Starlifters of Military Airlift Command transported 1,300 security specialists from the United States to the Republic of Panama to counteract political instability that threatened the safety of several thousand U.S. citizens in the Canal Zone.

September 29, 1988—The launch of the space shuttle *Discovery* marked the resumption of the U.S. manned space program, delayed in the wake of the *Challenger* disaster of January 28, 1986.

November 10, 1988—The Air Force reveals the existence of the Lockheed F-117A Stealth fighter, operational since 1983.

November 22, 1988—Northrop and the Air Force roll out the B-2 Stealth aircraft.

April 17, 1989—Lockheed delivers the 50th and last C-5B Galaxy transport to the Air Force.

June 10, 1989—Capt. Jacquelyn S. Parker, USAF, became the first woman to graduate from the Air Force Test Pilot School at Edwards Air Force Base, California.

July 17, 1989—Northrop chief test pilot Bruce Hinds and Air Force Col. Richard Couch make the first flight of the Northrop B-2A advanced technology stealth bomber.

October 1, 1989—Air Force General Hansford T. Johnson, pinning on his fourth star and assuming command of U.S. Transportation Command and MAC, becomes the first Air Force Academy graduate to attain the rank of full general. He is a member of the Academy's first graduating class of 1959.

May 4, 1990—The AIM-120A advanced medium-range air-to-air missile passed its final flight test for use on U.S. fighters.

July 24, 1990—EC-135 Looking Glass flights ended after nearly 30 years. During the Cold War, they provided airborne nuclear command and control facilities.

August 2, 1990—Iraq invaded Kuwait and quickly occupied the entire country, provoking the Southwest Asia War (aka Gulf War).

August 7, 1990—The United States launched Operation Desert Shield to defend Saudi Arabia from a possible Iraqi invasion. Among the first deployments was a 15-hour, 8,000-mile flight of 24 F-15C Eagles from Langley Air Force Base, Virginia, to Dhahran, Saudi Arabia, with 12 inflight refuelings. The aircraft arrived on August 8.

September 8, 1990—Marcelite Jordan Harris became the first black woman to hold the grade of brigadier general in the Air Force.

October 30, 1990—General Merrill A. McPeak becomes Air Force chief of staff.

January 17, 1991—Operation Desert Storm, the liberation of Kuwait from Iraqi military occupation, opened with a massive barrage of air and cruise missile strikes against targets in Iraq and Kuwait.

February 24, 1991—After more than a month of air strikes that severely weakened Iraqi forces, the U.S.-led coalition launched a ground offensive from Saudi Arabia. C-130s had already airlifted elements of the Army XVIII Airborne Corps from eastern Saudi Arabia to Rafha, on the Saudi-Iraqi border. Flying more than 300 sorties a day in 10-minute intervals, the C-130s delivered 13,843 troops and 9,396 tons of cargo. This movement enabled coalition forces to encircle Iraq's Republican Guard in what Gen. Norman Schwarzkopf (USMA 1956), combatant commander of U.S. Central Command, described as the "Hail Mary maneuver." Within 100 hours, coalition ground forces, coupled with continued air attacks, totally overwhelmed the Iraqi ground troops. Between February 24 and 28, the Air Force flew 3,000 reconnaissance, close air support, and interdiction sorties.

February 28, 1991—Operation Desert Storm ended at 0800 hours with a coalition-declared cease-fire. During the war, coalition forces released approximately 16,000 precision-guided munitions against Iraqi forces and dropped some 210,000 unguided bombs. In 42 days of around-the-clock operations, USAF aircraft flew 59 percent of the nearly 110,000 combat sorties. U.S. aerial strength of approximately 1,990 aircraft comprised 75 percent of the total coalition air power. Extensive use of satellite technology during Desert Storm persuaded some USAF leaders subsequently to refer to the operation as the "first space war."

September 27, 1991—President George H. W. Bush ordered termination of Strategic Air Command's alert, initiated in October 1957, during which time crews stood ready around the clock to launch nuclear strikes. This event heralded the conclusion of the Cold War between the United States and the Soviet Union.

March 24, 1992—The United States joined 24 other nations in signing the Open Skies Treaty, which allowed any one of them to fly unarmed aerial reconnaissance missions over any other signatory nation. (We note that the concept of Open Skies had been a primary objective of President Eisenhower's during his term.)

June 1, 1992—The Air Force conducts a major reorganization. This reorganization coupled with the retirement of the last active duty general from the West Point classes of 1948–58 (General Donald Kutyna, USMA 1957) and the appointment of an Air Force Academy graduate (Gen. George L. Butler, USAFA 1961) as commander of the U.S. Strategic Command, marks the end of this timeline.

Chapter Notes

Preface

1. Theodore J. Crackel, *West Point: A Bicentennial History* (Lawrence, KS: University Press of Kansas, 2002), 9.
2. Clarence C. Elebash, *West Point and the Air Force: A Summary of the Collective Contributions of U.S. Military Academy Graduates to the U.S. Air Force After It Became a Separate Service*, Appendix D, January 2004 (revised and corrected April 22, 2005).
3. Crackel, 9.
4. Ibid.

Chapter 1

1. Bob Taylor, "Charles E. Taylor: The Man Aviation History Almost Forgot," *Air Line Pilot*, April 2000, 18.
2. Daniel L. Haulman, *One Hundred Years of Flight: USAF Chronology of Significant Air and Space Events, 1903–2002* (Maxwell Air Force Base, Montgomery, Alabama: Air Force History and Museums Program in Association with Air University Press, 2003), 4.
3. Carroll V. Glines, *From the Wright Brothers to the Astronauts: The Memoirs of Major General Benjamin D. Foulois* (New York: McGraw-Hill, 1968), 46.
4. Ibid., 44.
5. Ibid., 65.
6. Ibid., 141.
7. Ibid., 82.
8. 2010 West Point *Register of Graduates* (West Point: West Point Association of Graduates, 2010), 1–18.

9. "When General Halloran Met General Benny Foulois...," First Aero Squadron Foundation, February 8, 2016 at https://firstaerosquadron.com/2016/02/08/when-general-halloran-met-general-benny-foulois/, retrieved on October 16, 2018.
10. Glines, 296.
11. Arthur E. Kennelly, *Biographical Memoir of George Owen Squier 1865–1934*, National Academy of Sciences of the United States of America, Biographical Memoirs Volume XX, presented to the Academy at the Annual Meeting, 1938.
12. Stephen L. McFarland, *A Concise History of the U.S. Air Force* (Maxwell AFB, Montgomery, Alabama: Air Force History and Museums Program in Association with Air University Press, 1997).
13. When I was at West Point in 1950, I roomed with Bill Henn and Jim Skove in what was once Pershing's room and which today has become a museum!
14. Bill Yenne, *Hap Arnold: Inventing the Air Force* (Washington D.C.: Regnery History, 2013), 45.
15. Ibid., 46.
16. Ibid.
17. Yenne, 28.
18. C.V. Glines, "General Henry H. 'Hap' Arnold: Architect of America's Air Force," *Aviation History Magazine*, June 12, 2006.
19. Yenne, 77.
20. Glines, "General Henry H. 'Hap' Arnold."
21. https://www.rand.org/about/history/a-brief-history-of-rand.html, retrieved on October 16, 2018.

22. Yenne, 97.

23. Curtis E. LeMay and MacKinlay Kantor, *Mission with LeMay: My Story* (New York: Doubleday & Co., 1965), 387.

24. Walter J. Boyne, *The Influence of Air Power upon History* (Gretna, Louisiana: Pelican Publishing Company, Inc., 2003), 289.

25. John T. Correll, "1946: The Year After the War," *Air Force*, April 2016.

26. Elebash, *West Point and the Air Force.*

Chapter 2

1. In his book, *Reflections on Air Force Independence*, Herman S. Wolk emphasized that "it is difficult now to appreciate the absolutely essential role played by the AAF in World War II. The buildup of the air forces, from the smallest combat branch in the Army to the largest during the war, was unprecedented in American military history." (Herman S. Wolk, *Reflections on Air Force Independence* [Maxwell AFB, Montgomery, Alabama: Air Force History and Museums Program in Association with Air University Press, 2007], iii.)

2. Yenne, 47.

3. Herman S. Wolk, *Reflections on Air Force Independence* (Maxwell AFB, Montgomery, Alabama: Air Force History and Museums Program in Association with Air University Press, 2007), 7.

4. Richard P. Hallion, "The Great War in the Air," a presentation to the St. Louis Section, American Institute of Aeronautics and Astronautics, St. Louis, MO, November 15, 2018, slide 15.

5. Martin Van Creveld, *The Age of Air Power* (New York: PublicAffairs, 2011), 46.

6. Ibid.

7. Haulman, 2.

8. "Langley I (CV-1)," from Naval History and Heritage Command at https://www.history.navy.mil/research/histories/ship-histories/danfs/l/langley-i.html retrieved on April 4, 2019.

9. Walter J. Boyne, *Beyond the Wild Blue: A History of the U.S. Air Force, 1947–1997* (New York: St. Martin's Press, 1997), 350.

10. http://www.afhistory.af.mil/FAQs/Fact-Sheets/Article/459008/1935-the-general-headquarters-air-force/; retrieved February 22, 2018.

11. Ibid.

12. http://www.nationalmuseum.af.mil/Visit/Museum-Exhibits/Fact-Sheets/Display/Article/196932/general-headquarters-air-force/; retrieved February 22, 2018.

13. Arnold, like others, often received accelerated promotions during time of war and then later would be demoted at the conclusion of the conflict.

14. https://en.wikipedia.org/wiki/United_States_Army_Air_Corps; retrieved February 22, 2018.

15. Wolk, 13.

16. "Stewart Field [is Fifty!]," *West Point Assembly*, July 1992, 19. Reprinted from the October 1942 *Assembly.*

17. Ibid.

18. Ibid.

19. Phillip S. Meilinger, *Hoyt S. Vandenberg: The Life of a General* (Bloomington: Indiana University Press, 1989), 23.

20. Ibid.

21. Ibid., 40.

22. Herman S. Wolk, *Toward Independence: The Emergence of the U.S. Air Force, 1945–1947* (Maxwell AFB, Montgomery, Alabama: Air Force History and Museums Program in Association with Air University Press, 1996), 3.

23. Ibid., 4.

24. Ibid.

25. Ibid.

26. Ibid., 6.

27. Wolk, *Reflections on Air Force Independence*, 30.

28. Today, the Twentieth Air Force (20 AF) is part of the United States Air Force Global Strike Command (AFGSC), headquartered at Francis E. Warren Air Force Base, Wyoming. Its primary mission is ICBM operations. The co-author was assigned to Francis E. Warren when serving as an ICBM launch officer.

29. Wolk, *Reflections on Air Force Independence*, 7.

30. Ibid., iii.

31. 4-358 Memorandum for the Secretary of War, April 17, 1944, The Johns Hopkins University Press (http://marshall foundation.org/library/digital-archive/memorandum-for-the-secretary-of-war-63/) accessed on April 16, 2018.

32. Meilinger, 82.

33. 4-358 Memorandum for the Secretary of War, April 17, 1944.

34. Wolk, *Toward Independence*, 10.
35. Meilinger, 83.
36. Wolk, *Toward Independence*, 13.
37. Wolk, *Reflections on Air Force Independence*, 85.
38. Wolk, *Toward Independence*, 16.
39. Wolk, *Reflections on Air Force Independence*, 99.

Chapter 3

1. Joseph P. Buccolo, "Memories of West Point and Its Impact on the Class of 1950," 2005.
2. Lloyd R. "Dick" Leavitt, *Following the Flag* (Maxwell AFB, Montgomery, Alabama: Air University Press, 2010), 616–617.
3. Ibid., 616.
4. Dr. John H. Vanston, "Just Another Weapon," *American Heritage*, November 1996.
5. https://history.army.mil/html/moh/koreanwar.html#COURSEN retrieved on October 16, 2018.
6. Robert C. Mathis, *Korea: A Lieutenant's Story* (Bloomington, Indiana: Xlibris Corporation, 2006).
7. Buccolo, "Memories of the Class of 1950."
8. Leavitt, 58–60.
9. Earl H. Blaik and Tim Cohane, *You Have to Pay the Price* (New York: Holt, Rinehart & Winston, 1960), 35.
10. Ibid., 45.
11. Touchstone retired as Army's winningest lacrosse coach in 1957 after compiling a 214–73–4 record during a brilliant 29-year career that spanned four decades. He guided Army to a share of three national championships (1944, 1945, 1951), coached 42 first team All-Americans during his tenure at the helm of the Black Knights. From https://goarmywestpoint.com/news/2017/7/31/mens-lacrosse-touchstone-among-2017-imlca-hall-of-fame-class.aspx retrieved on June 25, 2018.
12. As Army's all-time coaching victories leader in both men's basketball and outdoor track and field, Leo Novak compiled an overall record of 326–115–1 (.739) during his quarter-century tenure at the Academy. In a combined 68 competitive seasons, spanning four sports, only three Novak-led Army squads suffered through a losing campaign. Novak guided men's basketball from 1927 to 1939 (crafting a record of 126–61), outdoor track from 1925 to 1949 (96–24) and cross country from 1928 to 1949 (93–28). In addition, he was the driving force behind the creation of Army's indoor track and field program, directing the team to an 11–2 mark during the initial eight years of its existence (1942–49). Under his tutelage, Army teams captured nine major indoor and outdoor track championships, including three IC4A titles and six Heptagonal crowns. In cross country, his teams won IC4A titles on three occasions. In addition, two cadets established world records while more than 50 athletes won Eastern and NCAA crowns. Retrieved from http://goarmywestpoint.com/hof.aspx?hof=33&path=&kiosk= on June 25, 2018.
13. Information Paper, "Korea Revisit Program," United States Military Academy, July 1, 1996.

Chapter 4

1. Herman S. Wolk, "When the Color Line Ended," *Air Force*, July 1998.
2. Daniel L. Haulman, *A Short History of the Tuskegee Airmen* (Maxwell AFB, Montgomery, Alabama: Air Force Historical Research Agency, 2015), 6. See also Stephen Sherman, *The Tuskegee Airmen: First Group of African-American Fighter Pilots in WW II*," June 29, 2011 from http://acepilots.com/usaaf_tusk.html, retrieved August 16, 2017.
3. Haulman, *A Short History of the Tuskegee Airmen*, 10.
4. Ibid., 7–12.
5. Ibid., 12.
6. "Benjamin O. Davis Jr." from Wikipedia, citing Holbert, Tim G.W. (Summer 2003). "A Tradition of Sacrifice: African-American Service in World War II". *World War II Chronicles*. World War II Veterans CommitteeIikiii Iiiii (XXI). Archived from the original on 2007-09-27. Retrieved on August 16, 2017.
7. Sherman L. Fleek, "What's in a Name? The Selection Process to Name the Davis Barracks," *West Point*, Fall 2017, 18.
8. Ibid., 20.
9. @ArmyChiefStaff. "The Army doesn't tolerate racism, extremism or hatred in our ranks. It's against our values and everything we've stood for since 1775." *Twitter*, 16 August 2017, 1:50 a.m.

10. Richard Cooper, "The All-Volunteer Force: Five Years Later," *International Security Program for Science and International Affairs*, Harvard University, Spring 1978, 101.

11. Theodore White, *America in Search of Itself* (New York: Harper & Row, 1982), 115.

12. Martha Lockwood, "Women's Legacy Parallels Air Force History," *Air Force News Service*, September 18, 2014.

13. Educational Outreach Staff, *Flying for Freedom: The Story of the Women Airforce Service Pilots*, a NMUSAF Teacher Resource Guide (Wright-Patterson AFB, OH: National Museum of the U.S. Air Force, 2018), 1–14, at: https://www.nationalmuseum.af.mil/Portals/7/documents/education/teacher_resource_flying_for_freedom.pdf, retrieved November 18, 2018.

14. Antonia Chayes, Office of Secretary of the Air Force, Supplemental to the AF Policy Letter for Commanders, No. 2-1980, *Women in the Military*, 1979.

15. Ibid.

16. Ibid.

17. Ibid.

18. Barbara Mahany, "Air Academy's Best: Just Call Her Sir," *Chicago Tribune*, May 29, 1986.

Chapter 5

1. Theodore von Kármán, "Toward New Horizons: A Report to General of the Army H.H. Arnold submitted on Behalf of the A.A.F. Scientific Advisory Group," December 15, 1945.

2. Working from the California Institute of Technology ("CalTech") in Los Angeles, Dr. Von Kármán and others later founded the Jet Propulsion Laboratory (JPL).

3. Fred Kaplan, *1959: The Year Everything Changed* (Hoboken: Wiley, 2009), 66. With great foresight, RAND's first report in 1946 was entitled *Preliminary Design of an Experimental World-Circling Spaceship*, a spaceship that later would become known as a satellite.

4. See RAND's website at https://www.rand.org/about/history.html to learn more about its history.

5. von Kármán, "Toward New Horizons."

6. Ibid.

7. Thomas A. Sturm, *The USAF Scientific Advisory Board: Its First Twenty Years—*

1944–1964 (Washington D.C.: Office of Air Force History, 1986), 10.

8. Yenne, 272.

9. Stephen B. Johnson, "Bernard Schriever and the Scientific Vision," *Air Power History Journal*, Spring 2002.

10. Louie Estrada, "Bernard Schriever Dies; General Led Missile Development," *Washington Post*, June 23, 2005.

11. Memoranda of August 11, 1976 from Edward Teller to Col. James L. Thompson, Jr., Executive Secretary USAF SAB.

12. Elebash, Appendix D-3.

13. As noted in its website (http://www.afit.edu/) AFIT has been identified under different names since 1919, as follows: 1919–1920: Air School of Application; 1920–1926: Air Service Engineering School; 1926–1941: Air Corps Engineering School; 1944–1945: Army Air Forces Engineering School; 1945–1947: Army Air Forces Institute of Technology; 1947–1948: Air Force Institute of Technology; 1948–1955: United States Air Force Institute of Technology; 1955–1956: Institute of Technology, USAF; 1956–1959: Air Force Institute of Technology; 1959–1962: Institute of Technology; 1962–Present: Air Force Institute of Technology.

14. The following members of the Class of 1950 received engineering degrees through AFIT: Frank Borman, Ted Crichton, Seymour Fishbein, Robert Grosclose, John Kulpa, Richard Lorette, Richard Nelson, Donald Novak, James Slay, Everett True, and James Wallace.

15. Letter to participants from Major General Frank J. Simokaitis, AFIT commandant, including Executive Overview of Current Technology, January 23, 1978. The author was a participant and graduate of this program.

16. Alex Abella, *Soldiers of Reason: The RAND Corporation and the Rise of the American Empire* (Orlando, Florida: Harcourt, 2008), 245.

17. Jacob Neufeld, *The F-15 Eagle, Origin and Development, 1962–1972* (Washington, D.C.: Office of Air Force History, 1974), v.

18. https://web.archive.org/web/20071114185331/http://www.wpafb.af.mil/asc/index.asp, retrieved July 2, 2017.

19. John T. Correll, "Opposing AWACS," *Air Force*, September 2015.

20. Dr. John T. McLucas, *Reflections of a*

Technocrat: Managing Defense, Air, and Space Programs During the Cold War" (Maxwell AFB, Montgomery, Alabama: Air University Press, 2006), 111.
21. Kaplan, 76.
22. Ibid., 78.
23. Production volume, years produced and unit costs sourced from Wikipedia entries for each aircraft. Note that unit costs varied widely based on variants of each aircraft model. Retrieved on July 25, 2018.
24. Richard P. Hallion, *Storm over Iraq: Air Power and the Gulf War* (Washington D.C.: Smithsonian Institution Press, 1992), 10.

Chapter 6

1. http://themedalofhonor.com/medal-of-honor-recipients/recipients/bong-richard-world-war-two, retrieved March 21, 2019.
2. An interesting anecdote about Major Bong is that when he left gunnery school he was assigned to a P-38 unit at Hamilton Field in Northern California. To celebrate one of his colleague's nuptials, Bong and two of his buddies flew a loop around the Golden Gate Bridge and then flew at low-level down Market Street in San Francisco! While this escapade earned him some disciplinary action from the commander, General George C. Kenney, the general stated: "If you didn't want to fly down Market Street I wouldn't have you in my Air Force." He was grounded and during this time his unit went to Europe. He later was assigned to a new unit going to the war in the Pacific.
3. Michelle Evans, *The X-15 Rocket Plane: Flying the First Wings into Space*, Forward by Joe Engle (Lincoln, Nebraska: University of Nebraska Press, 2013), xiv.
4. Ibid.
5. Phil Bardos, *Cold War Warriors* (Bloomington, Indiana: XLibris Corp., 2000), 244.

Chapter 7

1. Robin Olds, with Christina Olds and Ed Rasimus, *Fighter Pilot: The Memoirs of Legendary Ace Robin Olds* (New York: St. Martin's Griffin, 2010), 49.
2. https://coldwardecoded.blogspot.

com/2014/01/myasishchev-mischief-bison-and-bomber.html, retrieved April 8, 2019.
3. Richard Helms, director of CIA quoted in Ben R. Rich and Leo Janos, *Skunk Works: A Personal Memoir of My Years at Lockheed* (New York: Back Bay Books/Little Brown & Co.), 1994, 163–164.
4. Tom Huntington, "U-2," *Invention & Technology,* Winter 2007, Volume 22, Issue 3 by American Heritage retrieved from http://www.inventionandtech.com/content/u-2-0 on April 10, 2019.
5. https://www.sr-71.org/blackbird/sr-71/, retrieved May 29, 2018.

Chapter 8

1. Juno Beach Centre, "Ferrying Aircrafts Overseas" section of "Canada in the Second World War," retrieved March 3, 2019 at http://www.junobeach.org/canada-in-wwii/articles/ferrying-aircrafts-overseas/. We note that an entertaining mini-series, *Above and Beyond,* a 2007 Canadian Broadcasting Corporation movie, brings alive some of the dramatic events of the early days of the ferrying operation from Newfoundland to England.
2. Wesley Frank Craven and James Lea Cate, *The Army Air Forces in World War II, Volume 1: Plans and Early Operations, January 1939 to August 1942* (Washington, D.C.: Office of Air Force History, 1983), 313.
3. "Army Air Forces Aircraft: A Definitive Moment." Air Force Historical Support Division, January 11, 2011 at https://www.afhistory.af.mil/FAQs/Fact-Sheets/Article/459025/army-air-forces-aircraft-a-definitive-moment/, retrieved February 26, 2019.
4. Jack Kinyon, "Air Transport Command—Airlift during WWII," Air Mobility Command Museum at https://amcmuseum.org/history/air-transport-command-airlift-during-wwii/ retrieved on February 26, 2019.
5. For more information on flying the Hump, see John T. Correll's "Over the Hump to China," in the October 2009 issue of *Air Force,* 68–71.
6. Ibid.
7. Lt. General William H. Tunner, *Over the Hump,* Air Force History and Museums Program, reissued in 1998, 116.
8. C.V. Glines, "Flying the Hump," *Air Force,* March 1991.

9. Kinyon, "Air Transport Command."

10. Roger G. Miller, *To Save a City: the Berlin Airlift, 1948–1949*, Air Force History and Museums Program, 1998, 46.

11. Frank Ledwidge, *Aerial Warfare: The Battle for the Skies* (New York: Oxford University Press, 2018), 107.

12. *Aerospace Daily*, 1979.

13. Jack Kinyon, "Air Transport Command."

14. Roger D. Launius, "The Military Airlift Command: A Short History, 1941–1991," *Airlifter Quarterly*, Vol. 1, Num. 4, Spring 1991, 6.

15. Ibid., 7.

16. "Operation Homecoming for Vietnam POWs marks 40 years," February 12, 2013, from https://www.af.mil/News/Article-Display/Article/109716/operation-home coming-for-vietnam-pows-marks-40-years/, retrieved on April 2, 2019.

17. Military Airlift Command Office of History, *Anything, Anywhere, Anytime: An Illustrated History of the Military Airlift Command, 1941 to 1991*, 1991, 151.

18. Ibid.

19. Ibid., 154.

20. Allison Martin, "Legacy of Operation Babylift," *Adoption Today*, Volume 2, Number 4, March 2000 from https://www.adopt vietnam.org/adoption/babylift.htm retrieved on April 2, 2019.

21. "Betty Tisdale: Babylift Volunteer and Humanitarian," from https://www.adopt vietnam.org/adoption/babylift-tisdale.html retrieved on April 2, 2019.

22. Military Airlift Command Office of History, 154.

23. John T. Correll, "The Yom Kippur Airlift," *Air Force*, July 2016.

24. Walter J. Boyne, "Nickel Grass," air-force-magazine.com, December 1998 at https://www.nationalmuseum.af.mil/Portals/7/documents/education/teacher_resource_flying_for_freedom.pdf, retrieved March 5, 2019.

25. Correll, "The Yom Kippur Airlift."

26. Launius, 7.

27. Ibid.

28. Ibid., 8.

29. Military Airlift Command Office of History, 203.

30. Hallion, 119.

31. Military Airlift Command Office of History, 203.

Chapter 9

1. Robert L. Perry, *Origins of the USAF Space Program, 1945–1956* (History Office, Space and Missile Systems Center, 1997), 21.

2. Ibid., 37.

3. Harry G. Stine, *ICBM: The Making of the Weapon That Changed the World* (New York: Orion Books, 1991), 165–167.

4. Perry, 36.

5. Dwayne A. Day, *Invitation to Struggle: The History of Civilian-Military Relations in Space* at https://history.nasa.gov/SP-4407/vol2/v2chapter2-1.pdf, 243.

6. Stine, 189–190.

7. Mark Berhow, *U.S. Strategic and Defensive Missile Systems 1950–2004* (Great Britain: Osprey Publishing, Ltd., 2005), 39–43.

8. http://apps.westpointaog.org/Memorials/Article/13929/.

9. R. Cargill Hall and Jacob Neufeld, ed., *The U.S. Air Force in Space: 1945 to the Twenty-first Century* (Andrews AFB: Air Force Historical Foundation Symposium, September 21–22, 1995), 169.

10. Ibid.

11. Kenneth Gatland, *The Illustrated Encyclopedia of Space Technology* (London: Salamander Books Ltd., 1981), 60.

12. Hall and Neufeld, 170.

13. Berhow, 43–44.

14. Ibid., 44.

15. Despite the end of the Cold War, two features of the SIOP remain intact: it is perhaps the most secret document in our society and it is extraordinarily complex. Retired General George "Lee" Butler, former commander of Strategic Command, responsible for preparation of the SIOP at the end of the Cold War said: "It was all Alice-in-Wonderland stuff ... an almost unfathomable million lines of computer software code ... typically reduced by military briefers to between 60 and 100 slides ... presented in an hour or so to the handful of senior U.S. officials ... cleared to hear it." From William M. Arkin and Hans Kristensen, *The Post-Cold War SIOP and Nuclear Warfare Planning: A Glossary, Abbreviations, and Acronyms* (Washington D.C.: Natural Resources De-

fense Council, 1999), 1, at https://www.scribd.com/document/52181043/SIOP-Glossary-1999, retrieved December 22, 2018.

16. For a summary of the advantages and disadvantages of the different legs of the TRIAD, see "Pruning the Nuclear Triad? Pros and Cons of Submarines, Bombers, and Missiles," by Kingston Reif and Travis Sharp as updated by Usha Sahay from the Center for Arms Control and Proliferation, May 16, 2013 at https://armscontrolcenter.org/pruning-the-nuclear-triad-pros-and-cons-of-submarines-bombers-and-missiles/, retrieved December 22, 2018.

Chapter 10

1. ARPA was established in 1958 and later was renamed the Defense Advanced Research Projects Agency (DARPA). The Agency's primary research endeavors focused on space technology, ballistic missile defense, and solid propellants. For more information see https://www.darpa.mil/about-us/about-darpa.

2. Dr. Bruce Berkowitz, *The National Reconnaissance Office at 50 Years* (Washington D.C.: Center for the Study of National Reconnaissance, 2011), iii.

3. Hall and Neufeld, 33.

4. Ibid., 38.

5. Peter A. and Cathy W. Swan, *Birth of Air Force Satellite Reconnaissance: Facts, Recollections and Reflections*, SAFSP Alumni Association, 2015, 21.

6. In August 1960, President Eisenhower was presented with a spool of film from Corona 14, the first successful satellite photoreconnaissance mission, which had flown the week before. The satellite had captured images of airfields and other military installations in the Soviet Union. (See Dr. Bruce Berkowitz, *The National Reconnaissance Office at 50 Years* (Washington D.C.: Center for the Study of National Reconnaissance, 2011), 1.

7. Berkowitz, 12.

8. NRO fact sheet at: http://www.nro.gov/Portals/65/documents/about/nro/NRO_Fact_Sheet.pdf?ver=2018-04-09-143047-283.

9. https://en.wikipedia.org/wiki/Global_Positioning_System, retrieved July 30, 2018.

10. Hall and Neufeld, 172.

11. Keith J. Hamel, "West Point and America's Space Program," *West Point*, Fall 2016, 12.

12. The Mercury astronauts ("the "Mercury Seven") were M. Scott Carpenter, L. Gordon Cooper, Jr., John H. Glenn, Jr., Virgil I. "Gus" Grissom, Walter M. Schirra, Jr., Alan B. Shepard, Jr., and Donald K. "Deke" Slayton; from https://www.nasa.gov/mission_pages/mercury/missions/program-toc.html, retrieved July 19, 2018.

13. https://www.nasa.gov/mission_pages/mercury/missions/objectives.html, retrieved July 19, 2018.

14. https://www.nasa.gov/mission_pages/gemini/index.html, retrieved July 19, 2018.

15. Gene Kranz, *Failure Is Not an Option: Mission Control from Mercury to Apollo 13 and Beyond* (New York: Simon & Schuster, 2000), 202.

16. Apollo 204 Review Board Final Report at https://history.nasa.gov/Apollo204/find.html, retrieved July 26, 2018.

17. Kranz, 213.

18. David West Reynolds, *Apollo: The Epic Journey to the Moon, 1963–1972* (Minneapolis: Zenith Press, 2013), 86. "All up" test indicates testing all three stages in one launch rather than three consecutive launches.

19. Kranz, 45.

20. Reynolds, 99.

21. Kranz, 12.

22. Richard Benke, "Astronauts Look Back 30 Years after Historic Lunar Launch," Associated Press, December 21, 1998, from http://cgi.canoe.ca/SpaceArchive/981221_30.html, retrieved July 31, 2018.

23. Reynolds 105. Translunar injection is the maneuver made to propel a spacecraft on a trajectory toward the moon. It commences from a low circular parking orbit around the earth into an elliptical orbit that will intersect the craft with the moon's orbit. The TLI burn is precisely timed to target the moon as it orbits the earth. For more information on TLI maneuvers see: https://en.wikipedia.org/wiki/Trans-lunar_injection.

24. Ibid., 105.

25. Reynolds, 111.

26. Ibid., 323.

27. Brigadier General Earl S. Van Inwegen III, "The Air Force Develops an Operational Organization for Space," from *The U.S. Air Force in Space 1945 to the Twenty-first Century*, 135–137.

28. Van Inwegen, 139. As Van Inwegen noted: "on November 9, [1979] a watershed event occurred. An "untagged" test tape injected into operations at Cheyenne Mountain triggered a false alarm of a missile attack. It prompted a false alert that caused something of a national furor." Then, "On June 3, 1980, however, another missile attack false alert occurred in Cheyenne Mountain, this time caused by some bad chips in one of the computers. But this false alarm triggered numerous investigations and studies, some of which focused on the fact that ADCOM had been pulled apart. They generally found that insufficient emphasis had been placed on what was one of the most critical missions of the U.S. military space program, missile early warning and deterrence."

29. Ibid.

30. Ibid., 141.

31. As noted in Van Inwegen's paper on page 142: "There were a lot of concerns about that issue. Leaders of NASA, SAMSO, the NRO, and AF/RDS all expressed concern about placing non-engineers into operational positions. Above and beyond that, the name change was an issue. The complexity of space systems was an issue. The transfer of assets was an issue. Operational control was an issue. Resource management was an issue. The interface with the national space communities was an issue. The NORAD interface was an issue. The unified versus specified command was an issue. Advocacy was an issue. And wartime operations for space was an issue."

32. H. Norman Schwarzkopf with Peter Petre, *It Doesn't Take a Hero: The Autobiography of General H. Norman Schwarzkopf* (New York: Bantam Books, 1993), 582.

33. Dept. of Defense Report to Congress, "Conduct of the Persian Gulf War," Vol II, April 1992.

34. https://abcnews.go.com/Politics/trump-directs-creation-space-force-sixth-branch-military/story?id=55978674, retrieved August 17, 2018.

Chapter 11

1. Steven Simon, "Celebrating the Air Force Academy's 60th anniversary," April 4, 2014 from http://www.usafa.af.mil/News/ Features/Display/tabid/1527/Article/619 759.

2. Ibid.

3. Keith J. Hamel, "Flying Cadets, Flying Grads," *West Point*, Spring 2017, 71.

4. Phillip S. Meilinger, *Hubert R. Harmon—Airman, Officer, Father of the Air Force Academy* (Golden, Colorado: Fulcrum Group, 2009), 179, footnote 27 referencing Meilinger's *Hoyt S. Vandenberg: The Life of a General.*

5. Steven Simon, "Celebrating the Air Force Academy's 60th anniversary," April 4, 2014 from http://www.usafa.af.mil/News/ Features/Display/tabid/1527/Article/619759.

6. Meilinger, 180, citing, at footnote 32, the Planning Board Study.

7. Ibid. 182, citing the Planning Board study.

8. Ibid., 186.

9. Ibid., 204.

10. George V. Fagan, *The Air Force Academy: An Illustrated History* (Boulder, Colorado: Johnson Books, 1988), 56.

11. Ibid., 57.

12. Ibid., 58.

13. http://www.usafa.af.mil/AboutUs/ FactSheets/Display/tabid/1530/Article/ 618977/usafa-quick-facts.aspx.

14. https://www.usafa.af.mil/News/ News-Display/Article/2154760/vice-president-pence-to-attend-graduation-ceremony-for-nearly-1000-af-academy-c/, retrieved May 13, 2020.

15. "Oral History Interview with Lieutenant General Winfield W. Scott, USAF (Ret.)," sponsored by The Friends of the Air Force Academy Library and The Association of Graduates of the U.S. Air Force Academy, May 24, 2003, 2.

16. While General Eaker was a very distinguished senior officer, he was not a West Point graduate.

17. "Oral History Interview with Lieutenant General Winfield W. Scott," 86.

18. "Air Force Academy History," January 18, 2012. (http://www.usafa.af.mil/AboutUs/ FactSheets/Display/tabid/1530/Article/ 428274/airforceacademyhistory.aspx).

19. USAF archives at https://archive.is/ 8IDK saved from http://www.af.mil/index.asp.

20. Fagan, 63.

21. Meilinger, *Hubert R. Harmon*, 244–245.

22. Ibid., 258–259, footnote 40 citing M. Hamlin Cannon and Henry S. Fellerman, *Quest for an Air Force Academy,* 1974, 207; "AFA Official History," I, 409–11.

23. http://www.usafa.af.mil/News/Commentaries/Display/Article/646859/academy-stays-on-the-cutting-edge/, retrieved on May 22, 2017.

24. Paul T. Ringenbach, *Battling Tradition: Robert F. McDermott and Shaping the U.S. Air Force Academy* (Chicago: Imprint Publications, 2006), 19.

25. Ibid., 220.

26. Ibid., 239.

27. Fagan, 64–65, footnote 3 citing U.S. Air Force Academy Oral History Interview, No. 227, April 1979.

28. Ringenbach, 64.

29. Meilinger, *Hubert R. Harmon,* page 246, footnote 87, citing Meilinger's June 1979 interview with Brigadier General Robin Olds. Olds mentioned that there were numerous West Point athletes on the initial Air Force Academy staff, including Harmon, Stillman (football, lacrosse and boxing), Zimmerman (lettering in three sports), Whitlow (lettering in football, basketball and baseball), Merritt (football), Robert R. Gideon (polo), Benjamin B. Cassiday (track), Louis T. Seith (football), Henry L. Hogan (track), Thomas J. Hanley (golf), and William C. McGlothlin (boxing).

30. Meilinger, *Hubert R. Harmon,* 247, footnote 88.

31. USAF archives at https://archive.is/81DK saved from http://www.af.mil/index.asp.

32. Meilinger, *Hubert R. Harmon,* 218, footnote 77, citing the U.S. Congress, House hearings before the Armed Services Committee, *To Provide for the Establishment of a United States Air Force Academy,* 83rd Congress, 1st session (Washington DC; GPO, 1954), 14–15.

33. Ibid., 261, footnote 47 citing "AFA Official History," I, 585–86.

34. Buccolo, "Memories of West Point and its Impact on the Class of 1950."

35. Letter, Frank Zagorski to Charles F. G. Kuyk, Jr., February 2, 1995.

36. Fagan, 64.

37. https://www.usafa.edu/character/honor/, retrieved March 31, 2017.

38. "Oral history interview with Lieutenant General Winfield W. Scott," 22.

39. Ibid., 27.

40. Christina Olds and Ed Rasimus, *Fighter Pilot: The Memoirs of Legendary Ace Robin Olds* (New York: St. Martin's Griffin, 2010), 360.

41. Ibid., 28.

42. Fagan, 184.

43. Olds and Rasimus, 355.

44. Ibid., 356.

45. https://en.wikipedia.org/wiki/List_of_United_States_Air_Force_Academy_alumni, retrieved May 22, 2017.

46. https://www.academyadmissions.com/about-the-academy/about-us/awards-and-accolades/, retrieved May 22, 2017.

47. Sullenberger described the events of U.S. Airways Flight 1549 in his 2009 book, co-authored with Jeffrey Zaslow, *Sully: My Search for What Really Matters,* on which the 2016 film, *Sully* was based.

Chapter 12

1. Peggy Anderson, *Great Quotes from Great Leaders* (Naperville, Illinois: Simple Truths, LLC, 2017), 14, 17.

2. Richard H. Kohn and Joseph P. Harahan, *USAF Warrior Studies* (Washington D.C.: Office of Air Force History, 1986), 47.

3. Anderson, 65.

4. Olds and Rasimus, 6.

5. Edgar Puryear, *American Generalship: Character Is Everything: the Art of Command* (Novato, California: Presidio Press, Inc., 2002), 167–175.

6. Ibid., 171.

7. Wayne Biddle, "General Killed in Nevada Crash Flew Soviet Jet," *New York Times,* May 3, 1984.

8. Van Inwegen, 139–140.

Epilogue

1. Presentation by Donald R. Baucom (USAFA 1962), "The Formative Years: Technology and America's Cold War Strategy," presented at the conference, "U.S. Air Force in Space 1945 to the Twenty-first Century," Andrews AFB, Maryland, September 21–22, 1995, 60.

2. Hallion, 252.

3. Ibid., 1.

Bibliography

Abella, Alex. *Soldiers of Reason—The RAND Corporation and the Rise of the American Empire*. Orlando, Florida: Harcourt, 2008.

"Air Leadership—USAF Warrior Studies." Proceedings of a Conference at Bolling AFB, April 13–14, 1984 sponsored by the Air Force Historical Foundation.

Ambrose, Stephen E. *Americans at War*. Jackson: University Press of Mississippi, 1997.

_____. *Duty, Honor, Country—A History of West Point*. Baltimore: The John Hopkins University Press, 1966.

Arkin, William M. and Hans Kristensen. *The Post-Cold War SIOP and Nuclear Warfare Planning: A Glossary, Abbreviations, and Acronyms*. Washington, D.C.: Natural Resources Defense Council, 1999.

"Army Air Forces Aircraft: A Definitive Moment." Air Force Historical Support Division, January 11, 2011.

Atkinson, Rick. *The Long Grey Line—The American Journey of West Point's Class of 1966*. New York: Picador, 1989.

Barbree, Jay. *Neil Armstrong: A Life of Flight*. New York: St. Martin's Press, 2014.

Bardos, Phil. *Cold War Warriors: The Story of the Achievements and Leadership of the Men of the West Point Class of 1950*. Bloomington, Indiana: Xlibris, 2000.

Berhow, Mark. *U.S. Strategic and Defensive Missile Systems 1950–2004*. New York: Osprey Publishing, Ltd., 2005.

Berkowitz, Bruce, *The National Reconnaissance Office at 50 Years,* Washington, D.C.: Center for the Study of National Reconnaissance, 2011.

Blaik, Earl H., and Tim Cohane. *You Have to Pay the Price*. New York: Holt, Rinehart & Winston, 1960.

Borman, Frank, with Robert J. Serling. *Countdown*. New York: Silver Arrow Books, 1988.

Bowen, Robert Sidney. *They Flew to Fame*. Racine, Wisconsin: Whitman Publishing Company, 1963.

Boyne, Walter J. *Beyond the Wild Blue*. New York: St. Martin's Press, 1997.

_____. *The Influence of Airpower upon History*. Gretna, Louisiana: Pelican Publishing, 2003.

Bradley, James. *Flyboys: A True Story of Courage*. Boston: Little, Brown, 2003.

Brodie, Bernard. *Strategy in the Missile Age*. Princeton: Princeton University Press, 1959.

Broughton, Jack (USAF Colonel, ret.). *Thud Ridge*. Philadelphia: J.B. Lippincott, 1969.

Buccolo, Joseph P. "Memories of West Point and its Impact on the Class of 1950."

Caldicott, Helen. *The New Nuclear Danger*. New York: The New Press, 2002.

Chayes, Antonia. Office of Secretary of the Air Force, Supplemental to the AF Policy Letter for Commanders, No. 2-1980, Women in the Military, 1979.

Collins, Michael. *Carrying the Fire: An Astronaut's Journey*. New York: Farrar, Straus and Giroux, 1974.

_____. *Mission to Mars*. New York: Grove Weidenfeld, 1990.

Cooper, Richard. "The All-Volunteer Force: Five Years Later," International Security Program for Science and International Affairs, Harvard University, Spring 1978.

Coram, Robert. *Boyd: The Fighter Pilot Who Changed the Art of War.* Boston: Little, Brown, 2002.

Correll, John T. *The First 60 Years—The Air Force, 1947–2007.* Arlington: Air Force Association, 2006.

_____. "Opposing AWACS." *Air Force,* September 2015.

_____. "Over the Hump to China." *Air Force,* October 2009.

_____. "The Yom Kippur Airlift," *Air Force,* July 2016.

Crackel, Theodore J. *West Point: A Bicentennial History.* Lawrence, Kansas: University Press of Kansas, 2002.

Crane, Conrad C. *American Airpower Strategy in Korea 1950 to 1953.* Lawrence, Kansas: University Press of Kansas, 2000.

Craven, Wesley Frank, and James Lea Cate. *The Army Air Forces in World War II, Volume 1: Plans and Early Operations, January 1939 to August 1942.* Washington, D.C.: Office of Air Force History, 1983.

Davis, Richard G. *The 31 Initiatives—A Study in Air Force–Army Cooperation.* Washington, D.C.: Office of Air Force History, 1987.

Day, Dwayne A. *Invitation to Struggle: The History of Civilian Military Relations in Space,* NASA. https://history.nasa.gov/SP-4407/vol2/v2chapter2-1.pdf.

Demers, Daniel J. "Pioneer Airman's Tragic Destiny," *Aviation History,* July 2012.

Drewes, Robert W. *The Air Force and the Great Engine War.* Honolulu: University Press of the Pacific, 2005.

Duggins, Pat. *Trailblazing Mars: NASA's Next Giant Leap.* Gainesville: University Press of Florida, 2010.

Educational Outreach Staff. *Flying for Freedom: The Story of the Women Airforce Service Pilots.* NMUSAF Teacher Resource Guide. Wright-Patterson AFB, Ohio: National Museum of the U.S. Air Force, 2018.

Elebash, Clarence C. *West Point and the Air Force—A Summary of the Collective Contributions of U.S. Military Academy Graduates to the U.S. Air Force After It Became a Separate Service."* Appendix D. Pensacola, Florida: N.p., 2004 (revised and corrected April 22, 2005).

Ellis, General Richard H. "SAC Looks at the '80s." Kelly AFB, TX: Air Force Service Information and News Center, 1980.

Estrada, Louie. "Bernard Schriever Dies: General Led Missile Development," *Washington Post,* June 23, 2005.

Evans, Michelle. *The X-15 Rocket Plane: Flying the First Wings into Space.* Lincoln, Nebraska: University of Nebraska Press, 2013.

Fagan, George V. *The Air Force Academy: An Illustrated History.* Boulder, Colorado: Johnson Books, 1988.

Farquhar, John T. *A Need to Know: The Role of Air Force Reconnaissance in War Planning, 1945–1953.* Maxwell Air Force Base, Montgomery, Alabama: Air University Press, 2004.

Ferguson, Niall. *The War of the World: Twentieth-Century Conflict and the Descent of the West.* New York: The Penguin Press, 2006.

Fleek, Sherman L. "What's in a Name—The Selection Process to Name the Davis Barracks." *West Point,* Fall 2017.

Foulois, Maj. General Benjamin D., with Colonel C.V. Glines, USAF (ret.). *From the Wright Brothers to the Astronauts—The Memoirs of Major General Benjamin D. Foulois.* New York: McGraw-Hill, 1968.

Gaston, Colonel James C., USAF (ret.). "Interview with Lt. General Winfield W. Scott, Jr., USAF (Retired)." The Friends of the Air Force Academy Library and the Association of Graduates of the US Air Force Academy, 2002.

Gatland, Kenneth. *The Illustrated Encyclopedia of Space Technology.* New York: Harmony Books, 1981.

Glines, Carroll V. *The Compact History of the United States Air Force: The Story of the American Airman and the Force in which He Serves.* New York: Hawthorn Books, 1963.

_____. *The Doolittle Raid—America's Daring First Strike Against Japan.* New York: Orion Books, 1988.

_____. "Flying the Hump," *Air Force,* March 1991.

Glines, Carroll V., Harry M. Zubkoff, and F. Clifton Berry. *Flights: American Aerospace Beginning to Future.* Montgomery, Alabama: Community Communications, 2004.

Graham, Colonel Richard H., USAF (Ret.). *SR-71 Revealed: The Inside Story.* Osceola, Wisconsin: MBI Publishing Co., 1996.

Hall, R. Cargill, and Jacob Neufeld, ed. *The U.S. Air Force in Space: 1945 to the Twenty-first Century.* Andrews AFB: Air Force Historical Foundation Symposium, September 21–22, 1995.

Hallion, Richard P. *Storm over Iraq: Air Power and the Gulf War.* Washington, D.C.: Smithsonian Institution Press, 1992.

_____. *Test Pilots—The Frontiersman of Flight.* Garden City, New York: Doubleday, 1981.

Hamelin, Joseph P. *To Fly and Fight: Memoirs of a Triple Ace.* New York: St. Martin's Press, 1990.

Hampton, Dan. *The Hunter Killers: The Extraordinary Story of the First Wild Weasels.* New York: Ascalon, 2015.

Hansen, James R. *First Man: The Life of Neil A. Armstrong.* New York: Simon & Schuster, 2005.

Haulman, Daniel L. *One Hundred Years of Flight: USAF Chronology of Significant Air and Space Events, 1903–2002.* Maxwell AFB, Montgomery, Alabama: Air Force History and Museums Program in Association with Air University Press, 2003.

_____. *A Short History of the Tuskegee Airmen.* Maxwell AFB, Montgomery, Alabama: Air Force Historical Research Agency, 2015.

Hearn, Chester G. *Air Force: An Illustrated History.* Minneapolis: Zenith Press, 2015.

Heit, Elliot E. *One of Eight.* Victoria, British Columbia: Trafford Publishing, 2006.

Jervis, Robert. *The Meaning of the Nuclear Revolution: Statecraft and the Prospect of Armageddon.* Ithaca, New York: Cornell University Press, 1989.

Johnson, Stephen B. "Bernard Schriever and the Scientific Vision." *Air Power History Journal,* Spring, 2002.

Jones, Ray. *Memoir: Dynamite, Check Six.* Bloomington, Indiana: AuthorHouse, 2013.

Kaplan, Fred. *1959: The Year Everything Changed.* Hoboken, New Jersey: Wiley, 2009.

Kinyon, Jack. "Air Transport Command—Airlift during WWII." Air Mobility Command Museum.

Kranz, Gene. *Failure Is Not an Option: Mission Control from Mercury to Apollo 13 and Beyond.* New York: Simon & Schuster, 2000.

Krylov, Leonid, and Tepsurkaev, Yuriy. *The Last War of the Superfortresses: MIG-15 vs. B-29 over Korea.* West Midlands, England: Helion, 2016.

Kurson, Robert. *Rocket Men—The Daring Odyssey of Apollo 8 and the Astronauts Who Made Man's First Journey to the Moon.* New York: Random House, 2018.

Launius, Roger D. "The Military Airlift Command: A Short History, 1941–1991." *Airlifter Quarterly,* Vol. 1, Num. 4, Spring 1991.

Leavitt, Lloyd R. *Following the Flag.* Maxwell AFB, Montgomery, Alabama: Air University Press, 2010.

Ledwidge, Frank. *Aerial Warfare: The Battle for the Skies.* New York: Oxford University Press, 2018.

LeMay, General Curtis E., with MacKinlay Kantor. *Mission with LeMay.* Garden City, New York: Doubleday, 1965.

Mahany, Barbara, "Air Academy's Best: Just Call Her Sir." *Chicago Tribune,* May 29, 1986.

Marrett, George J. *Cheating Death: Combat Air Rescues in Vietnam and Laos.* Washington, D.C.: Smithsonian Books, 2003.

_____. *Contrails over the Mojave: The Golden Age of Jet Flight Testing at Edwards AFB.* Annapolis, Maryland: Naval Institute Press, 2008.

Mathis, Lt. General Robert C. *Tactical Air Command 1980.* Kelly AFB, Texas: Air Force Service Information and News Center, 1980.

Mathis, Robert C. *Korea: A Lieutenant's Story.* Bloomington, Indiana: Xlibris Corporation, 2006.

McCarthy, James P. (editor in chief). *The Air Force.* Fairfield, Connecticut: Hugh Lauter Levin Associates, 2002.

McCullough, David. *The Wright Brothers.* New York: Simon & Schuster, 2015.

McGill, Lt. Col. USAF (Ret.) Earl J. *Jet Age Man: SAC-B-47 and B-52 Operations in the Early Cold War.* West Midlands, England: Helion, 2012.

McLucas, Dr. John L., with Kenneth J. Alnwick, and Lawrence R. Benson. *Reflections of a Technocrat: Managing Defense, Air, and Space Programs during the Cold War.* Maxwell AFB, Montgomery, Alabama: Air University Press, 2006.

Meilinger, Phillip S. *Hoyt S. Vandenberg: The Life of a General.* Bloomington, Indiana: Indiana University Press, 1989.

_____. *Hubert R. Harmon*. Golden, Colorado: Fulcrum Group, 2009.

Mellberg, William F. *Moon Missions: Mankind's First Voyages to Another World*. Plymouth, Michigan: Plymouth Press, Ltd., 1997.

Military Airlift Command Office of History. *Anything, Anywhere, Anytime—An Illustrated History of the Military Airlift Command, 1941 to 1991*, 1991.

Miller, Roger G. "To Save a City: the Berlin Airlift, 1948–1949." Air Force History and Museums Program, 1998.

Momyer, General William W., USAF (Ret.). *Airpower in Three Wars (World War II, Korea, Vietnam)*. Washington, D.C.: Office of Air Force History, 1986.

Neal, Valerie, Cathleen S. Lewis, and Frank H. Winter. *Space Flight: A Smithsonian Guide*. Boston: Ligature, Inc., 1995.

Neufeld, Jacob, *The F-15 Eagle, Origin and Development, 1962-1972*. Office of Air Force History, 1974.

Olds, Robin, with Christina Olds and Ed Rasimus. *Fighter Pilot: The Memoirs of Legendary Ace Robin Olds*. New York: St. Martin's Griffin, 2010.

"Oral History Interview with Lieutenant General Winfield W. Scott, USAF (Ret.)," sponsored by The Friends of the Air Force Academy Library and The Association of Graduates of the U.S. Air Force Academy, May 24, 2003.

Overy, Richard. *Why the Allies Won*. New York: W. W. Norton & Co., 1995.

Pape, Robert A. *Bombing to Win: Airpower and Coercion in War*. Ithaca, New York: Cornell University Press, 1996.

Perry, Robert L. *Origins of the USAF Space Program, 1945-1956*. History Office, Space and Missile Systems Center, 1997.

Puryear, Edgar, Jr. *American Generalship: Character Is Everything: the Art of Command*. Novato, California: Presidio Press, Inc., 2002.

Quanbeck, Alton H., and Archie L. Wood. *Modernizing the Strategic Bomber Force: Why and How*. Washington, D.C.: The Brookings Institution, 1976.

Reynolds, David West. *Apollo: The Epic Journey to the Moon, 1963-1972*. Minneapolis: Zenith Press, 2013.

Rich, Ben R., and Leo Janos. *Skunk Works*. New York: Little, Brown & Co., 1994.

Ringenbach, Paul T. *Battling Tradition: Robert McDermott and Shaping the U.S. Air Force Academy*. Chicago: Imprint Publications, 2006.

Schwarzkopf, H. Norman, with Peter Petre. *It Doesn't Take a Hero: The Autobiography of General H. Norman Schwarzkopf*. New York: Bantam Books, 1993.

Shiner, Linda M. (ed.). *Spy Planes: Pilots and Drones Flying the World's Most Dangerous Missions*. Washington, D.C.: Air & Space Smithsonian, 2016.

Stine, G. Harry. *ICBM—The Making of the Weapon that Changed the World*. New York: Orion Books, 1991.

Sturm, Thomas A. *The USAF Scientific Advisory Board: Its First Twenty Years 1944-1964*. Washington, D.C.: Office of Air Force History, USAF, 1986.

Suskind, Ron. *The Way of the World: A Story of Truth and Hope in an Age of Extremism*. New York: HarperCollins, 2008.

Swan, Peter A., and Cathy W. Swan. *Birth of Air Force Satellite Reconnaissance: Facts, Recollections and Reflections*. SAFSP Alumni Association. Lulu.com, 2015.

Swan, Peter A., Cathy W. Swan, and Rick Larned, eds. *Birth of Air Force Satellite Reconnaissance: Facts, Recollections and Reflections*. SAFSP Alumni Association. Lulu.com, 2015.

Tunner, William H. *Over the Hump*. Air Force History and Museums Program, reissued in 1998.

Ulsamer, Edgar. "A Solid Case for MX." *Air Force*, April 1980.

USAF Test Pilot School: 1944-1979. Prepared by the USAF Test Pilot School at its 35th Anniversary reunion. American Yearbook Company.

Van Creveld, Martin. *The Age of Airpower*. New York: Public Affairs, 2011.

Vanston, Dr. John H. "Just Another Weapon." *American Heritage*, November 1996.

von Kármán, Theodore. "Toward New Horizons—A Report to General of the Army H. H. Arnold submitted on Behalf of the A.A.F. Scientific Advisory Group." December 15, 1945.

Walker, Bryce. *Fighting Jets*. Chicago: Time-Life Books, 1983.

Werrell, Kenneth P. *Sabres over MIG Alley: The F-86 and the Battle for Air Superiority in Korea*. Annapolis, Maryland: Naval Institute Press, 2005.

White, Rowland. *Into the Black: The Extraordinary Untold Story of the First Flight of the Space Shuttle Columbia and the Astronauts who Flew Her*. Great Britain: Bantam Press, 2016.

White, Theodore. *America in Search of Itself*. New York: Harper & Row, 1982.

Wiest, Andrew (ed.). *Rolling Thunder in a Gentle Land: The Vietnam War Revisited*. Oxford, England: Osprey Publishing, 2006.

Wilcox, Robert K. *Wings of Fury: From Vietnam to the Gulf War—The Astonishing True Stories of America's Elite Fighter Pilots*. New York: Pocket Books, 1996.

Wolk, Herman S. *Planning and Organizing the Postwar Air Force, 1943–1947*. Washington, D.C.: Office of Air Force History, 1984.

_____. *Reflections on Air Force Independence*. Air Force History and Museum Programs, 2007.

_____. *Toward Independence: The Emergence of the U.S. Air Force, 1945–1947*. Air Force History and Museum Programs, 1996.

Wood, Archie L. "Modernizing the Strategic Bomber Force without Really Trying—A Case Against the B-1" and response. Reprinted from *International Security*, Fall 1976, Vol. 1, No. 2.

Yenne, Bill. *Hap Arnold: Inventing the Air Force*. Washington, D.C.: Regnery History, 2013.

Index

Page numbers in **_bold italic_** refer to illustrations.

271